# 5 Days in January

## - About dad, me and a bastard called Lewy

By Robert B. Landeck

# Table of Content

Introduction
Prologue
Part I - Dad, Mum & Me
Chapter 1 - Growing up Landeck-style
Chapter 2 - From Denmark to India
Chapter 3 - Barbecues, Booze & Orangutans
Chapter 4 - Growing Pains
Chapter 5 - That which does not kill us...
Part II - The Rollercoaster
Chapter 1 - TIA
Chapter 2 - Shadows
Chapter 3 - Lewy Tips His Hat
Chapter 4 - The D-word
Chapter 5 - Scrambled Words
Chapter 6 - Hope Always Floats
Chapter 7 - Home is not a Place
Chapter 8 - Paranoia
Chapter 9 - Another Step on Lewy's Ladder
Chapter 10 - Beginnings and Endings
Chapter 11 - Waking Sleep
Chapter 12 - Lewy Ping Pong
Chapter 13 - Dusk
Part III - 5 Days in January
Day 1
Day 2
Day 3
Day 4
Midnight
The last Day
Epilogue

\- 5 Days in January -
ISBN 978-0-473-40688-2
Author Robert B. Landeck
Publication Date: 08/2017

"I'm never gonna hold you like I did
Or say I love you to the kids
You're never gonna see it in my eyes
It's not gonna hurt me when you cry
I'm never gonna know what you go through
All the things I say or do
All the hurt and all the pain
One thing selfishly remains
I'm not gonna miss you"

-    Glen Campbell

For you, dad.

# Introduction

"One is never afraid of the unknown; one is afraid of the known coming to an end."

— Jiddu Krishnamurti

If you are reading this you have no doubt picked up this book either because you know someone with dementia, you are someone working in the field of dementia care or you yourself are suffering from its onset. I therefore hope that you may find something useful in it, whatever your reason for reading it. The truth is though, that from the beginning it was never meant to be more than a simple account. The account of dad's and my story, of our relationship, which of course began long before Lewy Body dementia, or "bastard Lewy", as I like to call it, took a hold and started picking apart him, us and pretty much life as we knew it.

This book covers our, dad's and my, our journey together and I understand some may not be terribly interested in what is essentially a son and dad story. Nevertheless, I needed to tell it as a whole, as without it, this book would be but the story of a man with Lewy Body dementia. Dad was so much more than that, as was, and still is, our relationship, which was marked as much by love as it was by discord in the course of our lives. It was perhaps the latter, which ultimately allowed us to become closer than we ever had, only for Lewy to come and rob us of our precious accomplishment.

Initially therefore I wanted to create a lasting memory of dad and me and how we got to that fateful day in January. Not because I felt the urge to share intimate and sometimes very personal family stuff with the rest of the world, but simply for fear that one day these precious memories too might be gone.

However, as I started writing down our story I also eventually saw that it provided a unique opportunity to zoom out and take a big picture view of events, thoughts, behaviors, and actions taken around

6

dad's illness from onset to end stage. I have learned a lot as a result, not least that the old adage of "hindsight is perfect" is truer than ever when it comes to the dementia journey with a person you love.

Dementia's malice lies in both its arbitrariness and how it chooses to make itself known. I say "choose", because there are times when its moves seem almost orchestrated, deliberately malevolent. In the beginning, it loves cameos, fleeting guest appearances, easily dismissed as quirks of character. Then later, it takes on the leading role. And in between it "plays" its part as it wants to, making sure to occasionally release the person from its clutches just long enough to realize what is happening; long enough to despair in the knowledge that their mind is no longer theirs. Its cruelty is always meticulous.

Moreover, while we all tend to react with shock to its displays, our individual coping mechanisms are as different and varied as people themselves are. Some means of coping may seem irrational, almost delusional. Others may appear cold and apathetic. Coping under stress can bring out the best, the worst, and anything in between.

That is also why I chose not to write some kind of "guide" or "how to" book. Thanks to its shiftiness, Lewy Body is different for everybody and such effort would thus simply miss the mark.

Yes, there are commonalities, milestones and symptomatic stuff, which, like landmarks in the wilderness, stand out across individual patient histories, but you do not need someone like me to point them out to you. You will know them when you see them.

Much like me at the onset of dad's illness, or should I say the first time when someone pointed their finger at Lewy as the likely culprit, you will constantly and I'm sorry to say, futilely find yourself searching for answers; answers that will never come or come too late and if they do, only with hindsight.

One of the greatest knowledge gaps we faced as a family was what actually happens in the later stages. Yes, there are many blogs, dissertations, books even that cover the symptoms and chronology, but we found they all fell short of providing insights into that last and most painful chapter, the one thing that sadly could have helped us prepare ourselves for what was to come. Not completely prepare, of course. I do not think that is ever possible. But it would have helped nonetheless, as both doctors and nurses remained tightlipped throughout and never gave more than an inkling to be read between the lines, when all we wanted were some hard truths.

I would be remiss in my mission though, if I did not at least name a few lessons I, or dare I say we took away from Lewy's assault on dad and our lives. I apologize if perhaps these are not terribly revelatory to you or might not apply. But then again they may be and may do. And who knows, there may be other things you might pick up from our story. Bits and pieces that prove useful to you, amongst the debris of the crash site Lewy left behind for us.

The first one sounds quite simple, yet given the complexity of the lives most of us live today, is also one of the hardest: "Just go and be with them. Be there for them."

For 3 ½ years I tried to balance overseas contracts, running a company, working in conflict and natural disaster zones, maintaining a livelihood and last, but by no means least keeping our marriage healthy against the need to be with dad, to spend time, help back home and give him the love he deserved. Did I succeed? Who knows...?

The second is even harder and requires a family that is built on love and acceptance without judgement: "Everyone deals with things the best way they can. It may not be your way. It may seem irreverent, misplaced, obsessive, or downright offensive sometimes, but remember: they are just trying to cope. There is no monopoly on, no one-stop solution for dealing with the situation."

The third is probably the hardest, as it is human nature not to want to stare at the abyss. But once we give it a try, the occasional glimpse can actually be therapeutic: "Don't judge how things are going on a day by day basis. Keep an eye on the road ahead. If you make your own or your family's happiness subject to Lewy's whim, he will drag you down with him. Rejoice in the things your loved one is still able to do, but stay realistic about what the next stage will look like. In short, expect the worst each day. That way you may grieve, but will never be disappointed.

The last one has been repeated many times over. It is so old that it may sound like a tired cliché. But the funny thing about clichés is after all, that many are essentially true, just as it is with this one: "Love those close to you with all your heart. Forgive them. Hold their hand occasionally and always, always tell them "I love you." Because in the end, when all else has fallen away and the darkness comes, love is the only thing that can prevail."

Lastly, apologies if my writing style ends up clunky and sometimes perhaps not as eloquent as it should be. I am neither a professional writer, nor is English my first language. Thus, I kindly ask for your indulgence in the hope that *what* I have to say outweighs whatever mistakes may have crept into the narrative.

I wrote this book for you and if this, dad's story, can provide just an iota of value as a companion on your journey, then he, too, would agree that what happened to him at least did not happen in vain.

# Prologue

*"Here we are, trapped in the amber of the moment. There is no why."*

– Kurt Vonnegut Jr.

The numbness takes hold. Nobody can see it coming, but I can feel it creeping across my mind, dragging its dull grey mass over every sense like a low-pressure front over a plain.

I should be going to the gym. Haven't gone in a few days. First, there was an energy born from anger, from the bursting feeling in my head, in my heart. But that momentum is gone.

In its place, a reel of images flickers through my head in a never-ending loop. Sleep used to be a savior. It has left town. What *are* left are empty ceilings at night, along with echoes of those last moments like an eerie soundtrack. Isn't it strange that we never really recognize defining moments for what they are until they have passed: These brief instances of profound and all-encompassing impact, which indelibly change what is, a watershed from where all things past fall away, giving rise to what ultimately will be?

It took my father 5 days to die. 120 hours, each of which we died with him by his bedside, breathing each labored breath, looking into his dry, glazed and motionless eyes that betrayed the battle that was raging within him. 7200 minutes of looking for a sign, any sign, praying for relief, for release, for mercy; 432,000 seconds of riding that rollercoaster between despair and pathetic apathy in the face of the inevitable.

Lewy Body took my father's mind, dismantling it with cold precision. In a death of a thousand cuts it took away any and all his abilities, some slowly, others suddenly, until even swallowing became impossible and even massaging his throat could no longer prevent him from drowning in his own phlegm.

Nobody and nothing prepares you for this.

10

## Part I - Dad, Mum & Me

## Chapter 1 - Growing up Landeck-style

I have learned in the process of what happened that it is all too easy to confuse a person's symptoms for who that person really is. It is easy to overlook that this broken vessel of a body, this malfunctioning mind, are but a product of the workings of this illness and to forget the personality, a character shaped by the collective experiences of a lifetime, and the spirit that still reside within the person. These make them not just who they but all of us really are below all the visible layers of confusion and decrepitude. This is part of the reason why I wanted to tell dad's and my, our family's story: So as not to let what dad became in the course of his illness be confused with who he really was. Dad was always still there. I simply refuse to believe otherwise.

Throughout history, father and son relationships have been fraught with all manner of difficulties. Ours was no different, at least initially:

Growing up was fun, mostly. Of course, our life has its problems, but looking back now and comparing it to what is going on in the world today, those problems were miniscule, every day stuff, no real dramas.

My parents met when they were in their teens, rowing for the same club in Frankfurt, Germany. Their relationship came into being against a backdrop of hardship and was fraught with challenges. Not surprising, given they had suffered as children through World War 2 and its aftermath. Even today my mother still recalls the hunger they endured, following extensive food shortages and how her biggest delight at age 5 had been a piece of bread with sugar sprinkled on it; something she had never had before. How they had gathered up potato peels from wherever they could get them, to make soup that could feed the family. As a single mum of three, my grandmother struggled and consequently they moved a lot: From their hometown of Luebeck to Austria, then back to Luebeck and finally to Frankfurt. My mother still recalls these relocations and how other kids ridiculed her for her Northern German accent; the feeling of homelessness despite having a home.

When my grandmother met mum's stepdad, they moved to Frankfurt and things stabilized. And while their journey through war-torn Germany as such came to an end, the draconian upbringing imparted on her and her siblings by their step dad, created yet another kind of suffering. There were verbal abuse, excessive restrictions, and ultra-conservative family rituals. There were beatings.

PTSD didn't have a name yet and much of what happened mum now balances against her step dad's, my grandfather's, fervent dedication to his wife and adopted children; at times to the point of self-starvation when he had once again sent all the money he earned to them for their own subsistence. But it was clearly a pressure cooker of 3rd Reich experiences, World War 2, economic hardship and a world that must have felt alien to my grandparents who had literally lived much their adult lives in pre-war Germany.

My father and his family had gone through similar turmoil before they reached Frankfurt, the place where he would later meet my mother. Born in former Prussia, a mere 3 months before the onset of the war dad got to spend less than 5 years in the farmland surrounds that had sustained generations of our ancestors before him. Fearing the brutality and scorched earth tactics of the approaching Russians rapidly pushing back the German frontlines towards Berlin, my grandparents decided it was time to abandon their home and spent weeks on the road traveling with my infant dad and his brother.

Dad's parents never really spoke about the war or the hardship they went through after, but there were anecdotes, small stories relayed here and there over the years by my father that told of the difficulties they, too, had faced.

He would talk about the food shortages and how people had resorted to slaughtering and eating horses in the street. For many though, even horsemeat was out of reach. During the direst times my grandmother would cook what she called "roof rabbit", my father used to tell me with a wink, a word that sounded a lot better than cat, which is what it was.

I am positive that the war had left its scars and that much of the experience kept bubbling away under the surface and although – much like with my mother's parents - it was likewise rarely mentioned at my dad's parents place, there were glimpses of it here and there, when memories floated to the surface.

I remember feeling bewildered when as a 6 or 7 year old I watched my granddad as he sat in his favorite chair by the window of their two bedroom apartment under the roof of a 6 story block and cried as he recalled an air raid on a train he was traveling on.

Granddad was not in the army, but the Reichsbahn – the German Railways - which was also their landlord.

He told me how they had dived to the floor of the car they were in as bullets began piercing it from top to bottom; and how the colleague who had dived on top of him, in the chaos had his foot shot off. My grandfather was usually a calm and kind man, at least towards me; almost introvert at times you could say.

I say "towards me" as anecdotally, long after his death my mother revealed to me just how different a person he was towards my grandmother. He had been a painter by trade and as many tradespeople was no stranger to a drop or two, often getting drunk with his pals and allegedly visiting houses of ill-repute, while my grandmother tried to hold things together with the little they earned. I don't think he was a violent man, but something sure ate away at him, even as a kid I could see that. And now here he was, his red face contorted and the tears flowing as he was fighting against the memory of the war that had suddenly overcome him and reduced him to something I had not seen before.

There were other times though especially during sports competitions, when his hatred shone through for the pain and suffering inflicted on him and his family. I will never forget how agitated he would become during soccer matches between England and Germany for example. He would kick the leg of the coffee table and swear at the screen, his face depicting the summary agony of his past experiences. The things he would yell most certainly went beyond a passion for the national team. Enough said.

For me as a kid growing up in Germany's 1970 economic wonderland, this was both perplexing and at the same terrifying. I often wondered what had happened to my family during these years that nobody openly spoke about, but seeing the results of whatever it was, the thought of asking outright was simply out of the question. It was clearly a taboo, best to be left alone and instead covered with the soothing bliss the new-found good life of the economic boom of the 50's and 60's provided.

Of course, later in high school, the details of Nazi Germany's horrific history were covered in detail, but even this knowledge never reached deep enough to help me understand my own family's past. Now, I am not saying there was anything untoward there and I have since been able to establish that neither mum's, nor dad's parents were affiliated with "the party" during that time, but when you see an old photo of your grand uncle wearing a Wehrmacht helmet, it certainly makes you think.

And so it was finally after much displacement, relocation and travel around Germany, fate would have it that my parents met.

It is hard to imagine today how this new generation of Germans would have felt about their own future in light of their then recent past. Although the war left its indelible marks, both mentally and physically, I believe it was also a time of renewed hope and of opportunity as Germans, following the end of the war did what they are stereotypically known to do best: organize themselves and systematically rebuild.

By the time my parents had hit their teens in the 1950s, the rubble many cities had been reduced to, was but a distant memory and in its stead emerged the new Germany, a nation determined not to repeat the mistakes of the past and instead focused on reinventing itself. And reinvent itself it did.

As the 1950's gave way to the 1960's, the economy boomed and with it came job opportunities to the point where the German workforce, somewhat decimated by the war, could no longer keep up with the growth. Italian workers and laborers from all over Europe were brought in to fill the gap and in the process became an inseparable part of the country's cultural fabric.

Italy as a holiday destination was virtually fetishized; Italian music was the rave, as was cheap Chianti and motor scooters. Rock 'n Roll, the rebellious new trend from the US blurted from vinyl records at parties and instilled a sense of ultimate breaking away from the past for this new generation.

I often look at old photos of my parents from that time; both of them young, vibrant, and beautiful; moments of happiness, of streamers and old-fashioned champagne glasses, captured in black and white. People in silly costumes, student fraternity parties (the kind where people still wore uniforms and daggers, not the American, beer-guzzling aberration that has largely replaced it today) and picnics with white linen, wine and cold cuts. My parents had been through a lot and this was their time. Their time to change things and make a life for themselves and for the family they aspired to have.

My dad ended up becoming an engineer, and a very good one at that. Whatever he touched, thanks to his dedication and attention to detail, he succeeded in. In fact, throughout his professional life he received awards, along with recognition from all manner of official bodies, held honorary positions and was highly respected within the industry and by his peers. Yet, he never spoke about it, never even once showed false pride or even arrogance. People like to use the word 'humble' in these situations and as a result, it has become somewhat of a cliché. But that's exactly what he was: humble, thorough and utterly dedicated.

I look at my parents meeting as something of a miracle; perhaps one that occurred more frequently in a time when the term 'individualism' was still confined to dictionaries and instead concepts such as servitude, sacrifice and "forever" were still firmly associated with marriage. But a miracle nonetheless.

15

My mother has told me many times how important my dad was to her even prior to their engagement and ultimately wedding. He was there for her through some pretty dark times; dark enough not be elaborated on here.

Then on 26 May 1967, I arrived. A game changer no doubt for both mum and dad, but by all accounts a planned and very welcome one. Many a parents would have taken it as an opportunity to solidify their base, to settle down and stay in place. But dad was never one to let his reach be limited by his grasp. He had a vision for mum, himself and now me and that vision required money. Well, perhaps his motives were not quite as selfless as this may sound, but be that as it may, 6 months after I was born dad took on a contract in India. I can only imagine what would have gone through mum's mind when he came home with the news! Dad had an uncanny talent to keep the big stuff quiet until the last moment and it would not have been the first time that he casually, over dinner, mentioned major changes that where afoot with him already having unilaterally decided and known for months. A year before, dad had gotten his first taste of travel when his company sent him to work on a project in Cleethorpes, England; undoubtedly a credit to dad's skills and diligence. After all, he was still relatively junior. Uttar Pradesh in the 1960s however was a far cry from Northeast Lincolnshire and would be no cake walk, no matter what 'package' would have been provided. Although he was a stickler for details, these types of things never really concerned dad all that much, or at least not yet. Mum, ever dutiful and me too young to care or have a say, packed bags and traveled along.

Naturally, my memory of India is non-existent, but based on anecdotes and the many picture slides that still exist from our time living in Uttar Pradesh it would have been a rather "adventurous" time. We were accommodated in some kind of a townhouse. Expat compounds the way we may know them today, did not exist. I think dad even took rickshaws to work, instead of today's 4WD vehicles, often complete with local drivers. Mum and I got around mainly on foot, her pushing me around in my pram. Apparently, my bright blond hair was a favorite with the locals and mum spent much time trying to keep me away from the many people wanting to touch it. I was of course blissfully unaware, but underneath the seemingly affectionate gestures towards me, was also a violent undercurrent of resistance against foreign economic involvement, if not xenophobia and mum has told me of occasions where we had virtually been under siege by mobs with less than amicable intentions.

Meanwhile dad went about his usual business days: Leave in the morning, come back in the afternoon. I think he enjoyed working with his Indian counterparts, who proved highly skilled and every bit as diligent as he was. On weekends, sightseeing trips were on the cards. One of my favorite picture slides from that time is of mum and I in front of the Taj Mahal, which would have been one hell of a story to tell back then, when international air travel was far from the routine it has become since.

I know that thanks to my needs as an infant mum struggled throughout our time in India. Making somewhat hygienic baby food was a daily challenge, formula was hard to come by, the area was prone to unrest and dad was at work during day, unable to assist with whatever other challenges mum encountered. But as on so many other occasions in their lives, I guess dad's sense of adventure was matched by mum's resourcefulness and positive outlook born from the confidence that her 'Norbert" would be by her side. As long as he had the future sorted, she could cope with the now. They were a team in the truest sense. They had rowed at the same club on Frankfurt's Main River. And even now in their life together it was just like rowing: One looks ahead and steers, while the others face they opposite way and give their all, completely trusting the one that is determining both pace and direction.

I do not think mum or dad ever consciously realized, but rowing ultimately became their life's motto.

My father was a very active person. He always had been, at times to excess, as my mother often lamented when my dad spent yet another entire Sunday playing tennis, riding his mountain bike with friends or working to the point of exhaustion on his pride and joy, their immaculately landscaped garden. He was also a meticulous planner,

17

his attention to detail permeating everything he; at times to the point of borderline OCD. I recall when wanting to build even simple things like a shelf or a coffee table, working with my dad would inevitably result in project planning otherwise only reserved for the space program. Pencils were sharpened, blueprints drawn to scale, measurements made once, twice, sometimes three times, angles worked out, and the level given a thorough workout in the process. I suspect my lackadaisical approach to home improvement often drove him crazy and am sure my devil may care attitude towards precision made him question my genes more than once. However, my father was also a patient man and I do not recall him ever losing his cool beyond a simple "Ach, Robert", spoken more in frustration than in anger. In fact, "Ach, Robert" at least throughout the ill-fated attempts at DIY during my youth, became somewhat of a mantra. Even today, whenever I need to put up a poster, hammer together a shelf or whatever is the order of the DIY day, I still look at the usually less than perfect result and I can hear "Ach, Robert" somewhere from the corner of my mind. Dad worked precise and by fractions of a millimeter. I did things in broad strokes. Good enough was my motto, precision was his.

It was that quiet and persistent determination to achieve the perfect balance of that little bubble on the level, whatever the project, that made him who he was and allowed him to succeed in life. Dad was very much a product of the culture instilled in him during the 1950s and 60s. Job, Home, Family were core, non-negotiable achievables and their realization rested on the man of the house. Yet, he never played the patriarch's role or felt the need to assert either his position or himself. He just kept at it. Quietly and diligently, stubbornly even perhaps; something that during his illness much later in his life would be a recurring theme, quite possibly becoming as much as a hindrance and a blessing in the process. But it worked nonetheless. Mum, much a product of the same era herself yielded, willingly and voluntarily. In a world where opportunities still fell almost exclusively to men, realization of goals in a marriage relied, no, were contingent upon drawing the line along social norms. Sounds strange from today's perspective, but I know neither my mum nor dad, much like most of their peers, never gave this a second thought. He worked.

18

Worked hard. She did everything she human possibly could to support him, and then me once I arrived. Each morning my dad's shirts and suits were pressed, there was breakfast on the table and mum would kiss him good-bye as he left the house for work, before repeating the process before I went to school. In the evening, he would come home, often late and visibly exhausted. He would drop into his two seater in the living room corner, undo his tie, and put his feet up on the low coffee table. His eyes always had dark rings around them. He was mostly quiet in the evenings. Strange that one forgets so many things from one's childhood and yet often remembers the smallest details. I still recall the sense of excitement in the evening when it got to the time that dad would come home. Especially in winter, when it would get dark early and us kids couldn't stay out that long, I would often kneel on the a seat under the kitchen window, which looked out over the front yard and driveway of our family home. "Let's give dad half an hour to himself" mum would whisper to me in the kitchen when dad finally opened the door and hung up his suit jacket after particularly stressful days at work. I never could understand how dad could possibly not reciprocate my excitement, but usually obeyed with quiet, albeit short-lived discontent and bided my time. Then I would jump up onto his lap or find my favorite spot in the settee corner, comforted by his arm around me. I sometimes wish back to this gift of a child's mind's fleetingness, where forgetting misery and instead conjuring up excitement is as easy as breathing. His greeting never echoed my exuberance and yet his eyes, his warmth, his calm acknowledgement, and that spot in his arm spoke deeper than any words ever could. We would spend hours together like this, until inevitably it was time for me to go to bed. The evening news, sports, political analysis and documentaries, they all became interesting, not because of what they were, but because of where I *was*. Meanwhile mum would fix our favorites: simple one-plate meals. The dinner table was for weekends, the couch was for weekdays. The couch was my favorite. Fried potatoes with egg, pasta with tomato sauce. apple and raisin pancakes: I loved them all and so did dad. We would consume catering-sized pan-loads of the stuff. I recall dad occasionally drinking a glass of wine, but not often. Weekdays weren't drinking days.

On weekends, it was different, starting Friday nights. Dad would go upstairs and don neat track pants and a polo shirt. School was out for the week and I was allowed to stay up longer. Sometimes we would go out for dinner with mum and dad's friends; sometimes with colleagues. Just like the old joke about what happens when you put three Germans together, social life in Germany much revolved around clubs. There were clubs for everything. And mum and dad belonged to their share of them. The German bowling club, the 10-pin bowling club, the hiking club, the tennis club, the card club. For me mum's and dad's club life meant copious amounts of Schnitzel and playing tag with their friends' and colleagues' kids. Simple country-style restaurants with trees, gardens and often active farming operations; treasure coves bearing all manner of secrets to be discovered in the twilight of late summer evenings, running around with bellies full of crumbed chops while our parents stayed inside, dank wine and Schnapps and had lively discussions about this and that; their laughter reassuringly echoing beyond the stained glass windows through the rustling leaves of big oak trees and into the cool evening air now usually blanketing the adjacent wheat fields and forests with a light mist.

Dad loved being club president. Not overtly. He never boasted or even acknowledged the fact that he seemed to be elected to the post within the shortest amount of time once he joined a club. He simply enjoyed the trust that people placed in him and it was engrained in his DNA that to disappoint would not only be unacceptable, but border on sacrilege. He liked to serve quietly, yet with the same diligence afforded to his work, home improvement or any other aspect of his carefully planned out life.

He never talked about what he achieved. He never praised himself or shunned those that did not succeed. Quite the opposite: He counted friendship above everything and acted accordingly. Only later mum told me that sometimes one or the other friend had come to him for help; sometimes for advice, other times for money. Although one might have mistaken dad for a rationalist on account of his rarely, if ever speaking about his religious convictions, his deeply fervent devotion to Catholicism and the concept of loving one's neighbor never allowed him to deny anybody. He always gave freely and without the expectation of return.

It was this quiet about dad, which also made him mysterious, not only when I was a kid, but also throughout most of my teenage and adult years. I remember the joy I felt when he would laugh out heartily, so heartily that sometimes we would both end up in stitches; his face red and cramped, tears rolling down it, as he would nearly double over on the couch, gasping for air while I was rolling on the floor in all-consuming fits of laughter that were as delightful as ultimately physically painful. He retained that infectious laugh until August 2013, that fateful day Lewy Body sucker-punched our souls.

Mum would usually follow suit to some extent, but then reverted to looking at her "two men" in contented delight, before refocusing her efforts on resupplying us with calories, usually for a perfect ending to the evening. It was dad who always owned the gift of laughter in our family.

During winter, with temperatures dropping to well below 0 degrees Celsius, casting a thick layer of ice and snow over anything that didn't move, that laughter was confined to the indoors and to evenings spent around tables in living rooms made comfortable by oil-fueled central heating. We actually had our own oil tank buried in the front yard, neatly disguised by rose bushes and various native flora whipped into perfection by dad's unwavering green thumbs. Except for a large metal lid I was explicitly disallowed to stand upon – as not to damage its slightly domed shape – and a ventilation pipe there was little to give away the fact that we sat on our own virtual gas station. Nothing uncommon for Germany, but in retrospect and looking upon where I have spent my life since, a luxury not to be taken for granted. Each year prior to the onset of winter a fuel truck would arrive with men in stained overalls smelling of diesel, for the annual ritual of refueling the large tank. Each year the men would carefully study the fuel counter as it ticked away with each liter of heating oil, nodding at each other and shaking their heads as if evaluating a scientific experiment. The bill at the end of the procedure was inevitably the subject around the dinner table and beyond. What was refilled in December this year was compared to what was used the previous year, which in turn depended on the weather. It was no surprise then that usually much theorizing and forecasting would follow in various settings: The card club, the tennis club, the 10-pin bowling club, the German bowling club...annual oil tank refills were always a ubiquitous subject of debate.

The tank not only constituted a mystery in my young mind, but it also fed my nemesis: the burner and central heating system in the bowels of our home's cellar; a giant device in which the incinerated fuel would heat water which would circulate throughout the arterial piping system covering every room in our house, keeping it at a comfortable warmth and at times beyond, even if proverbial hell froze over: Central heating, of course, but for a kid, nothing short of mesmerizing and terrifyingly mysterious. I was what some may call a spoiled kid, with access to all manner of educational materials, books and records from dinosaurs to the constellations of deep space, and yet many of the things most baffling to my little mind were left unexplained; presumably too "everyday" to warrant the effort by either mum or dad. Thus the giant central heating unit and what motivated it to spring into action, let alone the infernal sound it made when it did were left shrouded in mystery and conjured up all manner of figments of my imagination.

Our cellar was like every other German cellar. Not like what the Americans call "basement", which merely resides below the floorboards of the rooms above, but instead a cavernous affair, buried under a solid cover of concrete and often extending beyond the physical boundary of the structure above. Not only that, but because of its nature – perhaps in part as a homage to the coal cellars and bomb shelters of yesteryear or simply a natural result of stringent German construction standards, it was solid. Solid in the sense of complete separation from the world above, the only connection to the latter provided by a spiral stairway to the underworld below, its cavernous interior completely belied by the simple wooden door under the stairs leading to the first floor.

The original German family home featured an internal garage and as such, the cellar was not just a functional space but also provided access by car. Dad in his ingenuity though soon saw an opportunity for expansion and banished the garage from the house and into a separate building, adding to what even mum considered his "kingdom" but inadvertently also expanding what to me represented an underground realm of childhood fears. Expansion in this case was also a sign of additional disposable income, as a result of which dad soon established a small "wine cellar" just around the corner from the bottom steps on the way to the former garage, which had become a multi-purpose room.

The wine cellar was also where the other drinks were stored. Before the advent of throwaway plastic bottles, all drinks, not just beer and wine, were sold in glass bottles; between 12 and 20 bottles per plastic crate, to be exact. People – well, those who could afford it – would buy several crates of whatever they needed or wanted at a time. And the cellar was where it was all stored.

It was therefore only natural for my mother to occasionally ask me, as soon as I was old enough, to go and get a new bottle of this or that from the cellar. From. The. Cellar. Yikes! It is hard to describe the trepidation and horror that would overcome me as soon as my mum would utter the request. The cellar was the embodiment of my nightmares, the manifestation of every fear, past, present, and future. It was a gaping hole that surely one day would swallow me up in its clutches of horror, making me its eternal prisoner unable to return to the world above. It was where everything unholy dwelled; or so my little mind told me.

I would always carefully open the wooden door (it was worse when the simple skeleton key had to be turned as every click of the lock felt like I was ringing the dinner bell for the evil forces below), before quickly reaching into the dark – careful not to overstep the door's boundary – to where I knew the switch was that would turn on the lights down the stairs. My mind going through the mission, timing

23

every move and envisioning my unscathed return, I would take a deep breath, only too aware of my heart by now beating through my chest and a thin film of sweat coating my palms. One. Two. Three. Go.

Dashing down the stairs, careful to avoid slipping on the brown tiles, towards the much darker bottom below, time would stand still as tunnel vision took over. Quickly, around the corner, one hand already outstretched to retrieve the bottle of whatever I was to get. If I was lucky the crates were not stacked, if unlucky I would have to unstack them. Careful, not too much noise! I could hear my breathing. Panicked glances over my shoulder only revealed the fact that I was a million miles away from 'topside'. I was sure the darkness of the wine cellar hid prying eyes of creatures yet unseen. The rest of the bottles would rattle as I grabbed one, surely giving away my position. And then, without a fault it would happen: The central heating would kick in. Like an asthmatic dragon's breath followed by an almighty "Whooomph" it came to life, filling the entire space with the hellish noise of pressurized burners. I am not sure if childhood stress contributes to heart conditions later in life, but I swear in those moments I came close to a heart attack. Propelled by fear to a speed that could rival modern rockets any day of the week I would run, no leap, no virtually fly up those stairs back to the light. Glancing manically over my shoulder I would make the final push, barely touching the ground as I passed the light switch that would instantly return darkness to this infernal place, and slammed the door shut in a last ditch effort to keep at bay the monsters that were surely but a hair's breadth away from dragging me back into the blackness.

Then, having caught my breath and praising the powers above for letting me live to fight another day, I would ever so casually wander into the kitchen and place the bottle on the counter. As. If. Nothing. Ever. Happened. No. Big. Deal.

At least there would be no more visits to the cellar that day. Not unless someone was unusually thirsty.

Of course the fact that in the summer months, when it stayed light outside until late at night – a fact that was hard to fathom at the best of time, given my bedtime was 7pm – I would often secretly stay awake and stealthily make my way down the large wooden staircase from my bedroom on the first floor, to take a sneak peek through the usually slightly open living room door. The fifth or sixth step from the bottom was usually the best position, allowing a direct line of sight to the TV, while at the same time not only concealing me from mum and dad's view, but also providing plausible deniability. In the event of discovery, as technically still being on the stairs I would always be able to fake a nightmare or pretend to be in search of a glass of water or similar. You see, this wasn't just a sleepless kid trying to catch a glimpse at late night TV. These were missions carefully planned and forged in bed during the long evening daylight hours and sometimes even rehearsed during the day. I knew which stair was 'creaky' or which would sound hollow if treaded upon too heavily. I also knew which angle to view from between the broad spokes of the dark wood banister. I remember one time, mum even walked right past me on her way to the kitchen, prompting a commando style crawl back up to the bedroom on my part.

There was a downside to these nighttime excursions though. Programs screening at that time were obviously not designed for kids, in fact quite the opposite. And so I got more than I bargained for more than once. Let's just say a late night viewing of an Alfred Hitchcock murder mystery, complete with corpse, to a 7 year old while sitting alone in the dark on a large wooden staircase goes above and beyond your everyday movie experience and didn't help matters when it came to beverage retrieval missions in the cellar.

Dad loved watching late night TV and often, as mum would have him know in no uncertain terms, found it next to impossible to find his way into bed. I guess for a man who had a lot on his shoulders, this was the only time that truly belonged to him; where he could switch off unencumbered by whatever had kept him pressurized during the day. Whenever I sit and watch TV late at night (which is far too often these days) I think back in kinship with what he must have felt; feet up, head rested on one arm, often with a glass of wine

25

in front of him and maybe a bowl of peanuts, letting the screen's flicker wash over him until his eyes could stay open no longer. Quiet times. Good times.

Dad was often tired by the time I got to see him. Not because he was weak, but because he did nothing in half measures. Whatever he put his mind to, he pursued to the point of physical and mental exhaustion. As a kid I never understood this drive, no, this almost obsessive compulsion to go all out. In fact, later as a teenager I would consciously rebel against it, as I could often see what it did not just to dad, but also mum and their relationship.

If he planned to do the garden on the weekend, he would be in the garden; all day, without stopping, let alone perhaps for a glass of lemonade brought to him mum. Even once the sun started setting and dinner was on the table, mum would often struggle to tear him away from his landscaping. "Norbert…..Nooooorbert!!! Ach, now come in already. Dinner is getting coooold!" was mum's battle cry shouted into the twilight most of these nights.

Then came summer and with it, tennis season. I hated it. Don't get me wrong, summer was a great time for us kids. We would race our bikes back from school to literally jump into our swimming trunks faster than our mothers could say "sunscreen", which in those days was actually still quite uncommon; potential sunburn was somewhere between an afterthought before and a badge of honor when it happened.

Afternoons were longer, so much longer than in wintertime, when a wet icy blanket of grey, dark nothingness would decent on our village as early as four thirty in the afternoon. The general rule was that you had to be home when the streetlights came on; a rule that became more difficult to enforce in summer since, well, they just didn't until very late in the evening. In summer, you could hear a chorus of mothers up and down the neighborhood, calling their kids to wash up for dinner instead. Ball games on hot asphalt stopped and everyone scattered. Compliance somehow came natural for most of us.

Yet, the same rules never applied to dad for some reason, who went straight from work to the tennis club up the road. There he would play tennis, hang out with other dads and local business people. Prior to the advent of golf, tennis was considered a, if not *the* elitist sport and belonging to "The Club" as it was casually referred to, was part of elevated social standing. I do not think my dad ever really saw it that way. He was not someone who would posture or openly revel in wealth. He had worked for it too hard not to value what it stood for: a better life for his family. And throughout his life he never forgot where he had come from, and what it had taken – first his parents and then himself - to get there. Perhaps that is why he was liked so much by those around him. He lacked the pretentiousness that often accompanies "new money" and was never afraid to round up the troops, roll up his sleeves, and work for the good of a worthy cause, whatever it was. Of course he also enjoyed the fruits of his labor. Anybody would have! But it was genuine enjoyment that even increased when he was able to share it with others. I firmly believe that in another life my father would have made a great humanitarian.

For me dad's life in "The Club" simply translated into seeing him less, and a feeling of loss many an evening, when mum would with a sigh would speculate on the fact that he had probably gotten "stuck" again at the club, where an after-tennis round of drinks was often followed by another as match losers shouted rounds to winners, winners shouted rounds because they had won and others not even having played shouted rounds since they subsequently felt obligated. It was never a piss-up during the week, but enough to keep "men of status" with a fondness for the good life busy for hours. They all had endured hardship growing up during and after the war and few had been born with a proverbial silver spoon in their mouth. Yes, the economic boom during their teens and twenties had provided ample opportunities, but even those had required hard-nosed dedication and long hours to get where they had arrived now. I guess that is a good word to describe it: there was a shared sense of "arrival" among them.

For me, arrival during working days in summer months usually meant dad poking his head in the door of my bedroom while I was almost asleep, if I was lucky.

That is also, why summer *weekends* were my favorites. Between barbecues with the bowling club, which largely consisted of neighbors that lived next door or at least within a stone's throw, visits to family or seasonal festivities at "the club", it meant dad was, if not always immediately accessible, at least *there* with us and in sight. And I was there with him along with other kids, usually, meaning there was plenty to do, play and discover. And since the adults would be in a wine and beer infused jovial mood, treats and exceptions to rules in place for us otherwise were only ever a "can I please" away.

I remember the feeling of bliss when towards the end of the evening, with feet burning from running around playing catch with the other kids on the hot asphalt outside, I would drape myself over my mother's lap and close my eyes, half-tired, half curious about the adult conversation still in progress. My mother would prop me up in her arms to make me comfortable, often spreading a sweater or jacket over my little legs to keep me warm, creating the most comfortable blanket the world has ever known, almost perfectly still and only shifting occasionally when the weight of my body became uncomfortable for her. I would lie there, pretending to be asleep, letting the voices, the laughter, clinking of glasses and occasional heated discussions wash over me like a soothing wave, the scent of the now cooler fresh air from the fields and forests mixed with the odor of wine, beer and the odd cigar sending me into a dreamlike state of bliss.

Dad's laughter was always infectious and heartfelt and at least to me, always stood out from the rest. He liked to laugh at his own jokes; not because he thought himself some kind of comedian, but he genuinely thought they were funny. He would literally crack himself up that way at times.

When there were no festivities or tournaments at the club, mum and dad would have people over for barbecue parties. Summer Saturdays were barbecue days all around and late afternoons mouth-watering

28

smoke created by meat sizzling over charcoal would waft through virtually empty streets, accompanied by laughter and conversations of the parties that were in progress at homes all over the village.

Despite their casual appearance, pulling off these feats of perfect hosting normally required a rather laborious build-up of preparatory steps, usually since morning:

The sidewalk in front of the house had to be swept, the garden brought into tip top shape, lawns mowed to golf course green conditions, leaves picked up from the yard, the car washed, the veranda swept, furniture arranged, drinks bought, salads made, meat bought and marinated, desserts prepared, ice cubes frozen, the BBQ cleaned and primed, ready for ignition, music selected, table cloths ironed, napkins folded, glasses polished….the list went on and on.

With dad quite particular about who could use his lawn mower - namely only himself - and what other chores required some hidden set of elevated skills I had not yet and probably would never master, I was usually relegated to the rather inglorious duty of sweeping the sidewalk: 80 meters of paved and guttered walkway lined by several enormous birch trees - the kind of tree, which would relentlessly shed either leaves or seeds throughout the year and across all seasons, except perhaps in the deep of winter. Consequently it was not only one of the more laborious jobs in the array of chores, but given that it neither involved operating a machine (which by virtue of the fact would have made it somewhat "cool"), nor had any value in terms of kids' street cred, nor any recognizable value or lasting effect given the birch trees' incessant shedding of plant matter, to me also one of the more demeaning.

Our house was located in the center of our small town, right across its only real intersection, the one and only school bus stop and a poster and public announcement column on a small grassy island used predominantly by lazy dog owners as a destination of choice for their dog's to do their 'business'. I mention the concrete column for event posters and public announcements only as it is central to an anecdote, which tells of the probably only outburst of rage dad ever had to my knowledge:

Somehow – and it is still a mystery why, since such things were not part of our usual repertoire of meals – dad one day had attempted to cook an octopus. He had tenderized the thing with a mallet. It refused to yield. He had boiled it. It was still tough. He had boiled it again, for hours. It. Stayed. Tough. In the end and infuriated by the critters refusal to turn into something edible, dad had yelled, "I have had it. If it doesn't cook through I am going to nail it to the column!" Of course, the octopus took up the challenge and despite more time in the pot remained rubbery. Let's just say mum still laughs today when she talks about the incident and the expression of bewilderment on the face of the man who, walking his dog around the advertising column the next morning, found an octopus in the grass.

But back to the chore of sweeping: Our house was in very public view, making having to sweep its sidewalk so much more uncool. Barefoot kids in shorts and tank tops would zoom past me on their chopper bicycles, laughing and racing each other through the largely empty streets of our 500-strong village. Occasionally they would stop and look for a while as I did my best to pretend I did not exist as I tried to scrub clean the seemingly endless pavers with that giant broom. Spotless was the standard and nothing less would do, not even along the gutter; a standard I not only struggled with then, but the strict enforcement of which still affects my behavior today. Funny how small things early in life can have a profound impact later. The way my father approached the sidewalk outside our house was one of those. Sweeping up leaves was not easy. Our house sat on a corner and across from a fork in the singular main road that ran into the forest and dead ends in all other directions. As such any air movement, from slight summer breeze to the rather brisk gusts in autumn was certain to involve our sidewalk one way or another. Usually if you swept from right towards the left, the next gust of wind would come exactly from the opposite direction. If you swept towards the right, it reversed. A mysterious pattern which added to my frustrations as it would routinely mean re-gathering leaves from areas swept clean only a moment ago; a *Sisyphean* task if ever there was one, even on calm days. Dad in some superhuman fashion could complete it perfectly in 45 minutes. I could do a half-assed job in maybe 2 hours.

First, sweep the leaves and pick up by hand any that would stubbornly resist the hard bristles of the oversized broom. After that revisit the same area and re-sweep to gather leftover dust and sand. Then sweep the gutter, repeating the previous steps, all the while piling leaves and dirt into neat little heaps along the way, before collecting them in a bucket using a smaller broom and dustpan. Then for the final touch revisiting the former location of each little pile and sweep up any remaining dust or dirt in the same fashion.

For dad, that was his standard. For the sidewalk. And for his life. For me it was a contest of the will as much as it was my personal Nemesis.

Suffice to say that week by week I was given the task and most weeks I did not live up to dad's expectations. What made it worse was that sometimes, when my less than enthusiastic efforts had led to a particularly abysmal result, he would redo the entire job himself. I still remember the deep feeling of uselessness that would overcome me and the anger at him having to repeat what I considered an exercise in futility and public shaming each week in the first place.

I don't think dad ever saw it that way or recognized what it was doing to me. Dad had his standards. And he never questioned them. Since I was obviously unable to graduate beyond this task, the lawnmower or any other chores of marginally more interest to a boy my age stayed permanently out of reach.

Consequently, any DIY or other improvement projects I ever undertook later in life, I would make sure were completed without my dad's knowledge. Today I can laugh about our different approaches and even dad I think eventually resigned himself to the fact that as for such projects undertaken by myself, 'good enough' was the highest achievable standard. In fact, I now believe that he appreciated that I even tried, although I don't recall him ever saying so. Fair enough, too, I would say, given he was an engineer through and through and anything constructed with less than a small arsenal of tools and an exact level ultimately could not and would not pass muster.

But he did appreciate my efforts somewhat at least: I remember on one occasion, while mum and dad had gone on one of their weekend trips with the bowling club, or some other group of friends, I decided I would build a small door to cover the entrance to a small cave-like basement area under our house's large veranda. Dad, much in contravention of his own standards, for years had hung a large piece of vinyl cut from a fertilizer bag to cover what I am sure even he considered an unsightly hole leftover from the construction period of the property, its small cavernous interior now used as storage for various gardening bits and pieces.

Perhaps due to my desire to do something other than sweep the sidewalk or to just make him happy – I can't remember which – I built a fully functioning little wooden door, complete with anchored hinges. It was crooked and tilted to one side, but it worked and by all accounts looked better than the vinyl anyway. I also know it was definitely not up to spec as far as dad was concerned. It did not take a genius to figure that one out.

But here's the thing: For as long as it hung, dad never touched it. He didn't try to straighten it, never attempted to tighten its rattling hinges, paint it or change it in any other way. He left it as is and in fact used it every weekend when storing his various gardening tools.

It think that is what I ultimately and despite him perhaps making me feel a little useless at other times, came to respect about dad: He may not have been the man to express his emotions openly back then, but when I tried to do something right, he would acknowledge it the best way he could.

Sadly, it took many years for both of us, some rough patches, and a lot of growing up on my part to realize this. But that is a different story.

Once all the Saturday chores were complete, the house sparkling clean from top to bottom and everything laid out just right for the guests' arrival, there would always be this moment of unity, of

"Team Landeck" reveling in its success. In these few minutes just before the first early birds would show, mum and dad would take an "aperitif" or a cold drink and we would all stand or sit together in perfect peace. Everything was ready. Time to entertain.

And entertain, my parents did:

So and so liked a particular brand of beer, and you could be sure a crate of it would be chilling in the cool cellar. Another one preferred to have Campari and Orange Juice. A bottle would already be on the table. Someone liked to drink a "Spritzer" in summer. Sparkling mineral water was placed in a chilly bin next to the table. And so it went on and on until mum was sure every known whim of their friends and other guests had been catered for.

As a rule, neither drink nor food could run out. It was unwritten law, considered somewhere between epic fail and sacrilege not to be able to offer more at any given point. And thus amounts were copious and events long, often lasting until the wee hours of the morning. Between sizzling pork belly slices and homemade potato salad and the "midnight soup" – usually a big pot full of rich brown chili con carne style stew – served late at night in an effort to help soak the copious amounts of alcohol consumed in the form of beer and Schnapps, all manner of things made their way to the table in a never-ending procession. Most guests would leave after midnight, full to bursting and in varying states of inebriation. Mission accomplished. Sometimes I would watch mum and dad from my banister vantage point on the stairs, as they gathered dirty dishes and collected glassware, laboring in the kitchen and on the veranda in the early hours of the morning to restore the house to its former and hard-earned state of perfection. Most times, even the absence of a curfew on weekends could not prevent me from succumbing to sleep as adult conversations inevitably turned to subjects less interesting to a child, the novelty of the evening thinned and my eyelids grew heavy. On rare occasion though I managed to stay up and sit with mum and dad in the living room at the end of a long evening, while they breathed sighs of relief, rubbed their feet and enjoyed a peaceful nightcap while they digested the evening in quiet conversation.

Dad was always on the go, it seemed. He always strived to improve things. Some might have labeled him a perfectionist, but the term would not have done him justice. He liked doing things with great accuracy and enjoyed a job well done; never boastful, never gloating, just quiet enjoyment. Whether sitting on the town council, as president of the local tennis club, as chief executive of the company or at home in the garden, I cannot remember a time dad didn't strive to improve something, create something new or simply make things more efficient. It was not until much later in life, actually, until he became ill, that I can recall a memory of dad that didn't involve some sort of activity. Sure, in the evenings, he would put his feet up and enjoy a glass of wine, but outside of that his life was filled with, no his life *was* activity.

There was but one exception to the above and that was Sports on TV. Dad loved sports, on and off the screen and live broadcasts of tennis, formula 1 or international soccer tournaments could turn weekends otherwise filled with all manner of projects into virtual TV marathons. Much like in all that he did, dad there, too, showed an unrivalled tenacity, an unparalleled endurance and spent many a night glued to the screen until well after midnight.

I never really followed the TV sports schedules. I did not need to: unusually rushed gardening on a Saturday morning was always a surefire sign that a broadcast would air in the afternoon.

As a kid, I always felt that I lost dad to many of his projects, hobbies and activities. I always saw him *do* things, but our interests somehow diverged. In retrospect, I wonder whether he would have liked me to show more of an interest or aptitude in the things he did and if he was disappointed that I didn't share his enthusiasm. I guess as a kid one lacks the insights one is granted much later in life, often for the better I am sure. But not making more of an effort is one of those regrets I now carry with me.

It seemed hard to etch out "me time" with dad that didn't revolve around something that needed to be done or was part of his busy schedule. This made the occasions when dad and I spent together doing things away from the routines all the more special.

## Chapter 2 - From Denmark to India

There was one glowing exception to dad's sometimes-frantic schedule each year: our summer holidays.

For years each summer, throughout my early childhood and into my teens mum and dad, together with my "adopted" uncle and aunt, would rent a beach house in Denmark, where we spent the best part of the 6-week long school break. No work, no projects, no gardening, except that what was necessary to maintain the property. The small beach community consisted almost entirely of summer homes their Danish owners would rent out to Germans and a handful of other Scandinavians. And each year the same families from different parts of Germany, Sweden and other parts of Europe would arrive in their station wagons packed to the brim with anything and everything a family could need for the holidays and they would occupy the same houses, along the same gravel street, within easy reach of the little town's "Promenade" and the beach and Baltic sea beyond it.

There, every day seemed like a festival, a celebration, a never-ending succession of laughter, good food and copious amounts of Fuglsang beer, charcoal BBQ and Aquavit. The sunny days were spent at the beach, the cloudy ones trawling the nearby towns for souvenirs, pottery, art, and clothing. Visits to the German library were among my favorites, as were trips with dad to buy fresh fish at the wharf where a small fleet of trawlers supplied the locals with their daily catch of flounder, cod, and other seafood.

Time slowed down each year in Denmark. Not only did dad relax, but it was also the one time during the year were I got to feel part of "the men". Whatever dad did during these holidays, I was always included. And with this inclusion came the feeling of actually being *with* dad in a real sense; something that I felt was often lacking from our daily lives back home. Even helping dad and my uncle with clipping the enormous hedges surrounding the summerhouses, raking the mowed the lawn and other tasks I would ordinarily have balked at, became effortless and even enjoyable in the knowledge that I was part of the "team".

Each morning, provided I was able to get up early enough, dad, my uncle and I would head for the beach for dad's early morning swim in the often freezing Baltic waters. Each year the first of these walks were excruciating, as our feet had been softened by wearing shoes all through winter and spring and as a result had to get reacquainted with the sharp rocks of the gravel path. We would jump, hiss, and squirm, trying to leap between areas not covered by stones and for the first few days, there was always a collective sigh of relief when we reached the tarmac of the main road. By the end of the summer, the soles of our feet would harden and we would comfortably make the journey without as much as a flinch. Shoes were for wimps by then.

When it came to swimming in freezing water, dad was intrepid. He took pride in being the first and often only swimmer in the morning, even when temperatures dipped to a point that discouraged most from even wetting their toes. I cherished spending time with dad and my uncle in this way and unlike in other settings felt, for lack of a better way of describing it, that in those moments I was able to be the son he wanted me to be; that I was able to live up to that elusive image, which for all I know only existed in my own head. Seeing dad smile at me meant the world. It always did.

One of our summer neighbors was Hans, a homicide detective from Hamburg and apart from his uncanny ability to regale everyone, at times ad nauseam, with stories from his casefiles; his other annual "contribution" was fishing trips with dad and me in his small fiberglass dinghy. The tiny boat, when not in use would remain on the beach, turned-over, for the remainder of the year, but every summer he would bring with him a puny outboard motor and, having patched up any small cracks the boat had sustained during winter, go out into the bay to fish for flounder and cod. Dad and I accompanied him on many occasions, the growling propeller churning the cold waters as the shallow boat, low in the water from the weight of 2 ½ men, would chug through the chilly waters . Often we would dig the beach during low tide for sand worms, to be used as bait. A task I was not exactly fond of, but which became a fun activity in dad's company. The long, slimy, finger-thick, bearded worms had to be dug out carefully as not to rupture their fragile

36

bodies filled with yellow ooze, which would inevitably drip all over your fingers once they were placed on a hook. My favorite spot was at the back of the boat, right next to the motor. There, I could lean over, watch it churn the water and look through to the bottom of the ocean floor at less than 3 meters depth, changing colors as it passed below, the deep blacks of beds of algae and the greens giving way to beige-colored large sandy patches in between. A sandy bottom was best for flounder, and we often circled for a while until we found what Hans deemed the right spot. At times the small anchor was dropped, other times we would tie up to a pole normally used by sailing boats or other vessels too big to be landed on shore. There, we would sit quietly in the tiny light green boat, each one of us holding a weighted line with two hooks, a worm on each. For hours, few words were said with only the sound of the waves lapping against the hull, the occasional seagull and the wind through the fishing lines the only soundscape. We would sit still and silent, the only movement interrupting the gentle sway of the boat the occasional yank on the line each time someone felt a fish nibbling on the hooked worm in the deep below. Sometimes we caught fish, other times we did not. But we often stayed until last light regardless, usually freezing by then as the disappearance of the summer sun turned the mild ocean breeze into a rather chilly affair that would have us shiver in our yellow raincoats all the way home. But it was always worth it, regardless of a catch or lack thereof. With much of my time during the year spent almost exclusively with mum, being one of the "men" was something special and I will never forget how proud dad was the that year I caught a cod so big I had trouble holding it up for the photo that followed.

Maybe these experiences are why I have always felt so at home near the ocean. Who knows. But why else would a kid from landlocked central Germany develop such a fondness for the sea?

Preparations for our summer holidays in Denmark were as much of a ritual as most of the events during the stay. There was much shopping to be done and things to be packed. We would hit the road around 2am for the 8 or 9-hour drive north and mum would plan everything with a meticulousness ordinarily reserved only for the military. There were sandwiches, hot coffee, and all manner of snacks and of course surprises! Mum would secretly buy books or children's magazines, which she would give to me once I woke from my sleep, nestled in thick blankets on the back seat of our station wagon, usually waking up somewhere just South of Hamburg. Sleeping on the back seat with dad driving through the night was one of my favorite things to do. Even today, I still wish that I could once again experience that indescribable feeling of warmth and absolute security these drives brought with them, as I hugged the down duvets my mum would use to transform the back seat of our Volkswagen Passat into the most comfortable bed imaginable.

There was one particular event on the annual itinerary of summer holiday traditions, which everyone, without exception looked forward to: the dinner at Lunding Kro.

Lunding Kro, a small rural hotel and restaurant was located a short drive from our coastal village. Surrounded by farmland its understated exterior did not look much different from any other historic buildings in the area and completely belied the feast that awaited our reunited group of holidaymakers once a year. Even today, having traveled around the world and having spent more time at hotel buffets than I care to remember, the annual feast at Lunding Kro still stands out as one of the greatest dining experiences of my life.

With most of our summer spent barefoot and in shorts, this was the one time everyone dressed up in their (comfortable) best and the evening was always highly anticipated by all. The adults would fast throughout the day; in the belief, their stomachs could thus better withstand the culinary onslaught that was to be unleashed that evening. This was the big one of the summer. No festivity came close. Lasting from around 6pm until late in the evening, course after course was served to our group of 20-odd people until even the most gluttonous could take no more. A short break of speeches and aquavit followed each course, allowing things to settle before the next arrived. Danish pickled herrings in a variety of sauces always led the charge, accompanied by thinly sliced dark rye bread lathered with salted butter. Soon followed other cold dishes before the hot courses began. From crumbed flounder with remoulade, Danish Frikadeller with sweet red cabbage, roasted chicken and of Stegt Flaesk with caramel potatoes and stewed kale, there was always a succession of countless hot courses, ultimately and inevitably leading to desserts, cheeses and more drinks. By the end of the 5 to 6 hour meal, most of us were barely able to stand, let alone walk and back home many a trouser button were popped open to allow strained waistlines a little extra freedom. It was a meal that was talked about throughout the year. There was a warmth to the evening that somehow no other event could replicate; a knowledge of forthcoming delight and the contentment that comes with enjoying the good things in life in the company of reunited dear friends and family, perhaps only otherwise experienced at Christmas, was what made this evening so special, each and every year. With one exception.

No matter how busy he was and how much his work, community and social engagements took out of him throughout the year, during our summer holidays dad always managed to leave it all behind and spend time away from the pressures the effects of which, by the time the holidays came round, were usually visible even physically. In a time when there was no internet, personal computers, laptops or mobile phones it was generally accepted that in all but the gravest of circumstances employees were considered off duty and they would not be contacted. After all, most holiday destinations had very few landline connections or fax machines and unless the staff member would be able to resolve the prevailing issue over the phone there and then and without access to files or records, there was little point in contacting them at all in the first place. This was the case for many years, but as dad climbed the ranks in the company, the frivolous spending of its disingenuous owners resulted in one crisis after another. What had been a thriving business, more and more edged to the brink of disaster. By that time, dad had worked his way up, from apprentice technical illustrator to fully fledged engineer, department head and finally senior manager and authorized signatory; the latter putting him on a direct collision course with the company's owners, whose affinity towards racehorses and other lavish lifestyle pursuits over the years had begun to undo the hard work dad and his co-manager had done; the stellar rise of the company among its competition a direct result of their skill and dedication. I recall dad's ashen face when he came home after particularly hard days, when once again mismanagement of finances meant that lay-offs were looming and client contracts hung in the balance. Dad and his close friend and colleague Horst managed to avert these downturns, but not without an emotional toll, each and every time the firm was again at tipping point.

It was thus during one of our 'sacred' summer holidays that dad received a telegram, saying he was needed back at work urgently. This was the only time I can remember where mum and dad got into a proper argument during our vacations. I am sure they had their disagreements just like any other couple, but those were usually aired in private. This was in the open and the disappointment my mother voiced somehow told me that she, too, had been making sacrifices for the benefit of the company for a long time. No matter the profligate imbeciles that owned it behind the scenes, Dad *was* the company and by that virtue, mum as well.

Of course as a kid, I had no idea about company management, finances, employment, let alone what a job actually was; all I knew was that dad was happy when he was at home on weekends and tired to the point of exhaustion when he came back from the place he went to in the morning. And yet, his demeanor and the snippets of conversation I was able to grasp here and there, were enough for me to understand even at such a young age that the people who owned this *place* could simply not be good people; not if they played a part in turning my father into the drained husk of a person that came home each weeknight.

And so, after much heated debate, with mum leaving no doubt in everyone's mind that breaking the holiday was an affront not accepted (or forgiven) lightly, dad undertook the long drive back home; by himself, to fix yet another one of multiple mounting issues. He was back a few days later, but I sensed that something else had been broken. The sanctity of our summer tradition that had stood firm above all pressures and commitments had been compromised. The times had changed. They would reach him, no matter what.

These days, schools have "take-your-kid-to-work" days, fathers come into classrooms and describe what they do, and many workplaces make it a policy to encourage family interaction in order to improve work/life balance, overall employee satisfaction, and ultimately retention. Back then the workplace was the workplace, the company was the company, and the family was the family. Seldom did the two mix. And as a result my knowledge or even interaction with dad's work and colleagues was mostly restricted to private outings, but only very rarely included company events.

In fact, I only recall two such official occasions from my childhood: one where dad showed me his drawings and scaled models of industrial plants on the top floor of their multi-story office block and a staff BBQ in the parking lot, complete with tent, bar and traditional German fare from the spit roast. In usual fashion, dad was always in amongst it, helping prepare and serve both colleagues and subordinates in true team spirit. I think that is what amazed me most about dad: his humility and eagerness to participate for the benefit of others, irrespective of rank or background. He was just as comfortable in a corporate box, conversing with superstars of German soccer, as he was serving roasted meats to employees at a company party.

No wonder then that when asked in 2nd or 3rd grade what "my father did for a living", my answer – not knowing any better – was "roast pork"; much to the amusement of both fellow classmates and my mother, when she later explained what I had meant to the somewhat puzzled teacher.

Dad, like many of his generation were part of a dying breed, all but eradicated by modernization and a new business world that values youth over experience, profit over principles and image over substance. It was not unusual, no, the norm in fact, to spend one's entire career with a singular employer; to rise through the ranks, so to speak, and that way become an integral part of the company. You entered in the basement and if you proved yourself, you got to the top. It was not just a way of working life, it was a mentality, an attitude, a life philosophy. Entrepreneurship meant little more than initiative and having good ideas for the benefit of the company. The career path from study to management was long and hard. Overnight CEO's and startups were viewed with suspicion. Tradition reigned supreme. In a business world that subsequently yielded to globalization, where the theme of individualism replaced social ideas as a guiding principle and where corporate memories focus but on recent successes over track record and reliability, dad's generation sadly was the last to follow this path.

It wasn't until much later that I fully understood not just the severity of the company owner's mismanagement and reckless disregard for their employees, but also the complete lack of scruples, let alone the faintest degree of sympathy for those who again and again rescued their cash cow from certain bankruptcy. For his retirement dad, after more than 40 years of diligent, dutiful service to his employer, having saved their hide more times than anyone would care to remember, received a thank you, a handshake and in what can only be described as an almost satirical homage to an age old cliché, a gold watch.

But the indignation of this travesty as it turned out wasn't enough. Dad had invested in a company pension scheme for decades, but when it came to payout, the bosses' sudden refusal to release the funds was what I today believe probably constituted the first of several shocks that would ultimately put dad on the road to decline several years later. Today science suggests that continued emotional stress or stress events of great magnitude can trigger or at least worsen not just Lewy Body Dementia, but other degenerative illnesses like Parkinson's, among others. This was money he had worked hard for and earned. It represented part of his life's work; it formed an integral part of his meticulously planned retirement finances. Mum and dad were about to emigrate to New Zealand, joining me there to make a new start, to enjoy their retirement in a country they had loved since our first North to South trip in 1983. It was the one thing he could hold on to, the one thing that somehow made all he had gone through worthwhile in the end. And the bastards refused to pay.

I was not there when it happened, but mum has certain ways, certain words to describe when things aren't well. She never exaggerates the bad stuff, quite the opposite. I have learned over the years that when she says "not good", it means the worst. And facing retirement without the pension fund dad had contributed to so fervently was one of those, if not the mother of "not good" moments. I don't remember what exactly happened in the course of dad's fight for his entitlement. My dad was the most peace-loving man you could ever know. In fact, I cannot ever recall him, prior to his illness raising a hand or getting into an altercation, not even a verbal one. He knew how to stand his ground and fight in other ways, but he never descended into displays of physical anger or violence. In this case, too, I believe he managed to get the upper hand without force in the end: for years he had been privy to the company's book keeping and tried to deal with the owners' mismanagement as best as he could. And that knowledge, that information now gave him a degree of leverage. I don't believe threats were necessary; more like *gentle reminders* of what he had witnessed in his role as authorized company officer. Suffice to say the company paid what was owed, but not without the whole affair taking yet another considerable toll on dad.

Loss would become a common theme during retirement, despite dad's lifelong efforts to secure his family's financial future to the best of his not inconsiderable ability. The pension fund incident was thus but a prelude to a series of not only unfortunate but detrimental events which I have no doubt in aggregate eventually accelerated progression of his illness.

But of course his career also had its perks. These enabled us to do things, which under normal circumstances and perhaps unless one grew up in diplomatic circles, would have been impossible for an average family to achieve. International trips were one of them and I firmly believe that dad's overseas contracts planted in me very early a certain "travel bug" which would be nurtured throughout my formative years.

So while other baby photos were taken in the front yards of German houses or during family outings in the Odenwald or Black Forest,

43

mine are in a stroller in front of the Taj Mahal. Shortly after I was born, dad took up a contract in India and mum and I went with him. Not a big deal by today's standards perhaps, but in retrospect, as already mentioned elsewhere, in 1967 this was nothing short of exceptional. I am positive today that his time in India added fuel to his desire for adventure, which he maintained as much as he could until his illness took it from him.

## Chapter 3 - Barbecues, Booze & Orangutans

It was not long after India before dad eyed other overseas contracts which initially led him all over Europe. But it wasn't until 1980 that he undertook the one contract which would change his and our lives forever. It would provide such a rich and deep experience that it ended up becoming part of our DNA to the point where subsequently its mention even in the darkest days of memory loss during the later stages of his illness, could still send a flicker of joyful recollection across his otherwise distant and expressionless face.

His company had secured an order for piping design and construction of a fertilizer plant in Indonesia. A small patch of land had been cleared near the East coast of Borneo and plans existed to industrialize and ultimately populate the region. Big oil and gas firms already had stakes in parts of the area and logging had begun further inland. It was 1980 and environmental impact was a foreign concept. There was of course one small hitch in dad's plans to go to one of the most remote parts of Indonesia: he had known for months, yet had failed to mention it to mum! So one night at dinner a mere few weeks before his scheduled departure, I can't remember whether it was with friends or just us, dad casually and factually dropped the bomb. I did not witness the fallout that followed, but let's just say mum's descriptions of dad pulling a fast one aren't flattering, even today. I think it may have actually been one of very few times, if not the only time, where dad pushed their marriage to the verge of collapse; and it took a lot for things to get that way!

In the end though and in hindsight, even my mother agrees that the package dad negotiated made up for this "little blunder": He was offered two years, with generous pay and benefits, including regular free travel to and from site for mum and me. And so after his first few months on the job, getting acquainted with the environment and "setting up shop", mum and I were on our way to Bontang, East Borneo. Communication beforehand was only possible by airmail, Telex, or a satellite phone call on but the rarest of occasions. Even then connections in the 80's were far from what they are today and resembled a ping pong game of echoes, whereby you would have to take turns at speaking, lest conversations would get completely garbled and ultimately the line clogged. There was no internet, no search engines or photos to look at. There were only a few letters dad had written in the evenings and sent via airmail, with short descriptions of his surrounds and life in what would become known as "the camp".

I remember the excitement and magic of air travel back then. The giant Garuda Air Boeing 747, one of the old Jumbo Jets, decked out in what would today be considered lavish furnishings, colorful interior, wide seats and plush carpets took us from Frankfurt via, Rome, Abu Dhabi and Bangkok to Jakarta. There we would overnight before taking the next plane to Balikpapan and ultimately another flight to a landing strip near the site. In a time when the home video cassette recorder for most was still an unattainable novelty and thus watching new release movies limited to actual visits to the cinema, watching films on an airplane at 10,000m was simply mind-blowing. The ceiling mounted, clunky video projector cast its pulsating red, green and blue beams of light across the front rows onto a slightly curved screen covering the wall just aft of the galley, magically combining the colors into a watchable, yet slightly blurry image. Entertainment was always announced as if it were a real theatre presentation, including synopsis, who starred etc. etc.

Sound was another matter altogether and unlike today's headphones which feature wire plugs and connections, the headsets consisted of hollow rubber tubing, which when plugged into the onboard system, would receive and relay the sound from tiny speakers built somewhere into the seat panel. Not the most comfortable, but back then the embodiment of technological progress in in-flight entertainment. To top it all off, food was served in copious amounts, using real crockery and cutlery as well as glassware. I can remember trips where both mum and I disembarked utterly stuffed from all the food and snacks that had been offered. After all, the flight made 3 stops along the way and each time catering stocks were replenished, while the passengers got to stretch their legs window shopping inside the airport. No long-haul flights or constant security checks; even our hand luggage could remain onboard during intermittent stops! The good old days of air travel.

Eventually these trips would become somewhat of a routine for mum and me as we repeated them every two to three months, but they never ceased to excite and I was always immensely looking forward to them; though never again more than I had to that first trip in spring of 1980. Mum had spoken with the school principal and he had agreed that I could take some materials with me instead of attending class, as long as I was there to sit exams and my grades would not suffer. My excitement at what no doubt would be prolonged vacations knew no bounds!

For the first trip, dad met us in Jakarta and the moment we arrived at the airport I somehow knew that this trip, unlike our annual summer holidays in Denmark, would be unlike any other our family had undertaken before. I still recall the hot and humid night air as the hotel shuttle took us from arrivals to the 5 star hotel reserved by the company. With the window down, I let the smells of city invade my nostrils. There was a sweet smell of tropical plants, wafts of open sewerage and fried spices. And all the while the darkened, sparsely lit suburbs with their low-lying corrugated iron shacks interspersed by businesses and new developments, rushed past in an avalanche of new sights and sounds. The hotel, in typical 5-Star Southeast Asian fashion, was decked out in marble and teak, its lobby pleasantly cool after the long ride, with a scent of orchids completing the luxurious ambience together with soothing piano tunes emanating from the ground floor cocktail bar. This was unlike any other place I had ever visited or seen; a sentiment that would become the theme for much of what would follow during the next almost 3 years. The rest of our overnight stay in Jakarta is a bit of a blur as the impressions were many and the fog of jetlag slowly took over. We took in our 5-star rooms, ate as the only remaining guests at the hotel's high end restaurant, where we were eventually fare-welled with small chocolate dipped balls of ice cream, brought to the table in the most dramatic fashion: Sparklers on a giant bowl of dry ice, glowing as it bellowed clouds of mist in the low lights which had been dimmed specifically for the spectacle. I was in wonderland.

The next morning I was jolted into consciousness from what I am sure was either a sensory or chocolate overload induced sleep. The room's heavy blackout curtains ensured a disorienting darkness. What sounded like long screams and yells blasted through the tall windows from the outside, instantly snapping me out of my slumber. My mother still recalls the look of complete bewilderment on my face as she flicked on the lights. She, too, had jumped out of bed as soon as the screaming had started. I sat upright, my face pale and confused and all I managed to utter was: "Something is wrong mum, someone is being murdered!" As my senses slowly settled, I was able to distinguish a melody in the yelling and screaming, a singsong of sorts, very different from the sounds of the foul play I had suspected. As it turned out, our rooms were in rather close proximity to a neighboring mosque, where from its minaret the muezzin called for prayer. Nowadays a sight and sound certainly much more common than in 1980, this was my first encounter with the early morning Muslim prayer, a story that even today my mother never fails to retell during strolls down memory lane.

Dad looked different and unlike I had ever seen him before. His usual attire back home was suit and tie, polished shoes and a briefcase in keeping with his job as a white collar professional. Here he wore Khaki pants, a short-sleeved sand colored shirt, and hiking boots. Even his beard was longer and he certainly had lost weight. It was hard to tell whether this was because of conditions on site or due to yet another one of his Yo-yo diet fads; the latter usually much-lamented by my mother as they would leave him looking like a POW after a few weeks of starving himself to achieve whatever body weight he had set for himself.

Either way, he had about him an aura of adventure and his excitement was palpable as our family of three embarked on the next leg of our trip to Bontang Baru. The flight from Jakarta to Balikpapan, as we would find out later, was always somewhat of a gamble. Yes, one could book tickets and even have them issued at the local travel agent. But this by no means would guarantee a seat on the plane, especially for "wealthy" westerners. Dad thus always carried a bottle of whiskey or a carton of cigarettes to give to the check-in counter staff, who often expected bribes in return for boarding passes. As soon as we entered the airport, the wall of people

48

and noise, along with the heavy, sweet smell of cloves emanating from hundreds of Kretek cigarettes threatened to send our senses in a spin. Dad walked ahead with confidence, weaving through the crowd and we did our best to keep up. Before long, a carton of cigarettes was casually placed by the counter and disappeared silently behind it as our boarding passes were issued. This ritual would be repeated on either side of the trip multiple times and I can only imagine how coveted these positions of relative power were in an environment rife with poverty.

The planes would get smaller with each leg of the trip, and by the time we landed in Bontang Baru, we had stepped down from the twin-engine jet from Jakarta to Balikpapan, to a single prop for the remaining couple of hours. Just a few sets of double seats lined with canvas and a drop door at the back, we bounced along the dirt runway, the tiny plane's engine sputtering as we came to a stop next to a small single story building. Since takeoff, we had seen nothing but thick, impenetrable jungle with less than a handful of logging roads randomly cutting through the lush green blanket below us. Several Land Rovers and Toyota Landcruisers stood at the ready as the 8 or so passengers – the maximum number the plane accommodated - disembarked and made their way across the dry and dusty forecourt of the small reception building. Dad had been given a Land Rover to share with two of his German colleagues. I got excited by the mere sight of it. After all the only times I had seen one before was in documentaries about the "Camel Trophy" (sponsored by the cigarette brand – something unthinkable by today's standards) or wildlife films on television. It constituted the essence of adventure; a long time before adventure became mainstream and suburbia got flooded with 4-wheel drives, which would never see anything but city council-maintained tarmac. And so we climbed into the big dusty white Rover, our luggage along with the supplies that had accompanied us during this last leg from Balikpapan as the nearest trading post and outcrop of, for lack of a better word, civilization, filling up the rest of the vehicle and part of its roof rack. Dad was driving and the enjoyment of doing so in this environment was written plainly across his face. He had never really been obsessed with cars like other dad's I knew, who constantly

49

pursued the latest models or tried to upgrade on a regular basis. Back home he had been issued with a company vehicle for several years now. Long gone were the days of our two tiny Dutch DAF 66 saloons, dad had bought when we had moved into our first family home. His love for Formula 1 racing and driving fast, often too fast for mum's liking, on the Autobahn, yet this somehow never translated into a passion for owning motor vehicles. Perhaps dad was too pragmatic for this, as he seldom "splashed" out on new things, unless they would ultimately benefit our entire family. But this, much like the company provided BMW's during his executive days, was a different story and dad truly enjoyed being at the helm of something not many were able to afford, let alone drive in such a remote and exotic location. He was usually quite reserved, and seldom allowed himself to let his inner child shine through. But here he did and it showed.

The vehicle's hard suspension did little to mitigate the state of the dirt road, which snaked through valleys and across hills for another hour, all the while passing through lush rain forest, swamps, and clusters of low-lying thatched-roof farmers' huts made from bamboo matting. Small naked children played in the shade of banana trees and chicken scattered hurriedly to cover as passing vehicles kicked up clouds of fine dirt, bathing everything behind us in an eerie fog of orange dust. Occasionally dad would suddenly slow and almost come to a halt as other roads intersecting ours appeared out of nowhere among the thick foliage. These were different to the one we were one. Looking as if they had been churned, scarred by a hundred heavy machines, with deep trenches of caked dirt bearing tire marks along their edge, they disappeared quickly into the thick of the forest on either side. "These are dangerous", dad explained as he brought the land Rover to a stop near the intersection, and stuck his head out the window. "Logging roads", he continued, "they are heavy trucks carrying huge trees from the hills further inland". He wound the window back up, restarted the engine, and quickly crossed the intersection. "Most of them don't have breaks or at least don't or can't use them once they start going downhill. They don't stop until they reach the coast down there", he pointed in the vague direction of the ocean, somewhere behind the green wall of the jungle around us. "We have had some horrific accidents here, so best to be careful."

The raised single dirt road that led in and out of the area was notorious for accidents. It regularly had a habit of luring drivers into a false sense of security, but its dips and curvature could easily cause vehicles to lose control, roll, and slam into one of its deep ditches or adjacent swamps. Its condition was even worse during the rainy season, when repeated heavy rainfall turned its claylike surface into a virtual Slip-N-Slide and the normally loose dirt got churned into such a sticky mess that it would cake clumps of soil onto people's footwear, turning it into platforms shoes within minutes. My father's friend and co-worker, a Canadian and former fire fighter in charge of site safety, was more than once called out to and had the grisly job of documenting instances where dump trucks, carrying site construction workers in their open-box bed, had lost traction on the slippery surface - usually on a downhill slope - and had subsequently skidded and rolled, trapping anyone not thrown from the truck under its chassis. One time one of his sons showed me scene photographs of the carnage caused by one of these accidents and despite it being over 40 years ago, I can still clearly remember the mangled bodies, crushed limbs and other horrific injuries.

The camp we finally arrived at, was a neat array of simple, but by local standards luxurious wooden two bedroom family homes, interspersed with containers fitted out to accommodate single and short-term expat employees. Dad's company was working as a sub-contractor under American supervision and in true American style, everything the expat workers needed was catered for in the barbed wire fenced, 5-acre compound that had been wrestled from the jungle next to the site earmarked for construction of the fertilizer plant. Although less than 1 km from the coast, we were now almost 400km from the nearest town. As such, the camp had been designed to be virtually self-sufficient: there was a small commissary, stocked with all the essentials and even some non-essentials catering to the international crew. There was a swimming pool, a multi-purpose hall with a bar and even a diner-style restaurant across from the large community building, where a projector was installed and movies screened on a nightly basis for the camp residents. Outside the camp and apart from a small nearby farmers' village, was nothing but jungle. We kids were usually instructed to stay inside the camp. East Kalimantan, like other parts of Indonesia, at the time was not necessarily a place friendly disposed towards development projects carried out by foreign companies on behalf of the government and it was rumored that Communist rebels were active; something the armed guards at the camp served as a constant reminder of. Apart from the occasional brief excursion into one of the nearby small banana plantations or along one of the few paths into the forest accessible by foot, life took place inside the wire-mesh fence of the compound.

Apart of course from this new world to be discovered and new friends to be made among the multitude of expat kids, there was another major difference here to our life back home: Dad worked less than a kilometer away from our little house and although the routine of going to work in the morning didn't change, due to the proximity of his work and the communal nature of the place I saw more of him than ever before. Dad didn't have to leave for work during hours of darkness as he often had to do back in Germany, he came home for lunch and was back shortly after the day was done, with daylight to spare. On weekends, since our house's "garden" was little more than some tall grass and a banana tree and there were no sports broadcasts on account of there being no TV, dad and us would spend time together attending one of the many often themed parties that were routinely held either in the community hall or at one of his colleagues' houses and which would feature all manner of goodies, imported for the occasion. At the same time, seeing more of dad didn't necessarily translate into more quality time; quality time I had often been missing in the years prior, as dad's work took him if not all over Europe, then at least away from home longer than probably even he deemed tolerable. Dad always loved the company of his colleagues and friends, and many of the people around him became both over the years. This was no different here in the camp, where in his usual industrious manner, dad had quickly rallied up the troops and contributed to, if not created a blossoming scene of social events to break up the monotony of camp life. As idyllic as the descriptions

52

may sound, life in this enclave in the middle of nowhere was not for everyone and the project would see several colleagues almost lose their mind in the process, as the isolation, the lack of communication with family back home, the harsh environment and working conditions took their toll on anyone but those able to stay focused or maintain a high level of resilience by some other means.

I am certain dad also had times where he struggled. His job involved the piping design and construction for the plant, a complex, and difficult job at the best of times, often made even more complicated by the mix of contractor personnel, setbacks during testing and the ever-looming deadlines, which undoubtedly came with penalties for the company. It was no surprise then, that most packages included an R&R clause which allowed staff to leave and rest up somewhere in the region on a regular basis. Both mum and dad relished life in this small community, which despite its artificial nature, managed to gel well and quickly produced a hardy group of like-minded internationals. Between the Germans, the Americans, the Canadians, the French, the British, Austrians, the Irish and even the Indonesians, there was enough talent and often mischief to go around to make life in the camp, at least during evenings and on weekends far from mundane. Themed butter crème cakes, lavishly decorated by an Austrian chef in charge of the site canteen were all the rave and there rarely ever was an event where one wasn't produced to complement the ubiquitous array of tropical fruit usually served for desert. People created costumes from all manner of materials, sports contests were held utilizing whatever was available within the limited facilities and barbecues featuring wild boar caught on behalf by local farmers were the highlight of many a party. And dad, ever the organizer would always be in the middle of it, managing logistics, setting up tables, procuring things, allocating jobs and getting stuck right in. Life in the camp allowed his true self to rise to the surface and unfold unencumbered by the drag and confines of his office work back home. His life was about unwaveringly putting all his energy into creating something where before there was little or nothing. And this was the perfect environment for it.

Now 12, going on 13, I roamed around the camp with a bunch of American and Canadian kids. Initially unable to speak a word of English, in the company of my new friends and completely immersed in the language I acquired it within less than 3 months. Our days were spent swimming in the pool, playing mini golf, watching movies, eating burgers and noodle soups at the snack bar, poking around bushes and drains in search of wildlife and generally getting up to mischief as teenagers do. The paradoxical thing about the situation was, that although I felt closer to dad on account of sharing this experience with him, during this first year I seemed to do so from the sidelines much as before, as most of his spare time was spent socializing with colleagues and friends. I felt that I was ready to be part of his world and yet I didn't seem to be able to access it. I don't know if at the time I was consciously aware of this sentiment, but with the benefit of retrospective I believe that is how I saw and felt about things.

While some of this would change later on when his contract went into its second year, the feeling of distance somehow remained and was of course most pronounced during the long periods in between visits to the camp, during which communication with dad was highly limited. I know in my heart that his feelings were quite the opposite: that he loved me beyond words and did so even during my rebellious years that would soon follow. Displays of emotion however did not come easy to his generation and it took dad many years and I am assuming much gentle nurture by my mother to express his feelings more openly.

That said, life on the sidelines was pretty darn good and spending time, at the very least in dad's vicinity was as good as things had ever been. This was especially true during R&R time, which we would spend traveling in the region; Singapore, among other places. With the added disposable income and the company paying for travel and accommodation, dad spared no expense in making the time as special as possible for our family. From mountains of ice cream on Orchard Road to home-cooked Indian dinners at colleagues' homes, seafood restaurants and shopping sprees, it was a case of "anything goes". At times, I was allowed to bring along one of my camp buddies and, having been given ample pocket money even let loose ourselves on what was known to be one of the safest cities in the world.

But before I go on, I think some clarification is needed on the "life on the sidelines" statement earlier.

I guess you could say that dad, in a nutshell, was a genuine, community spirited provider. And a gentle one at that. He received joy from three things: creating joy for others, his family, and his own achievements. And he did so unpretentiously and ever-giving. I thought I should mention this at this juncture as not to do so may otherwise run the risk of letting other comments in this book seem unkind, unwarranted or spitefully made by a spoilt and ungrateful offspring (which by the way I think I was and sadly, as my wife reminds me at times, probably still am).

I should therefore make the point that throughout my childhood and formative years, dad was indeed there for all key moments; something I am sure was not easy to do in the context of his busy life. He proudly placed a red go-cart under the tree for my third Christmas and was utterly distraught when I unable to experience the excitement he had hoped for that evening as I suffered from one of my many high fevers. He held the seat of my bicycle, pushing me forward as he taught me to ride. He held me against the waves of the Baltic Sea, teaching me to swim, just like he propped me up and time and time again, supported me, came to my aid without so much as a frown, when his wayward son was yet again up against one rope or another. He did so the way he knew best, as a provider; never asking, never questioning. Apart from coming from a generation where being metro-sexual would surely have been termed a weakness of character if not mental illness, based on what my mother related to me much later, he also suffered from the emotionally dysfunctional home he grew up in. Between my grandfather's affinity towards booze and by all accounts extra marital activities (although this is not how I remember my grandfather at all), the after effects of their escape during World War 2 and my grandmother's stoic exterior which betrayed the hard life she had lived, displays of affection were a luxury, if not dismissed as misplaced quirks of character. Consequently and in the absence of the warmth and tenderness we would today like to think a prerequisite for balanced upbringing, dad grew up between the chairs, so to speak and it is only for my mother's loving persistence that he made the prior to their marriage unheard-of transformation from traditional father figure to a modern, emotionally conversant man; a transformation which took dad most of my childhood and teenage years and I suspect only fully came to being when his retirement at the age of 59 brought with it the relief, the peace of mind that he had done everything he could and successfully so, to look after his family to the point he himself had set for himself; almost as if he could now allow himself the emotional freedom he had denied himself on his mission to secure his family's financial future.

Dad's contract in Indonesia was a defining moment in that sense. It was almost like dad had been waiting for me to get to an age where he could finally share with me the things he loved. An age where I would understand him and his world and where I could interact with him, if not as an equal then at least as someone or something close to it. Until then my insights into dad's life had been limited to what I witnessed when he came from work in the evenings, the snippets of conversation between him and mum and perhaps observing him during one of the many parties and summer BBQ's at home. Additionally his frequent international trips served little to alleviate my lack of understanding.

But here in East Kalimantan it was different. On one side his work and social life in this small camp community were inseparably intertwined, which meant I got to learn a lot more about what dad did and what his work entailed. On the other side, and perhaps more importantly though, I was now 13 and rapidly maturing into young adulthood, which made all the difference to dad: One late afternoon when I arrived back at our little house from spending the day with my camp pals a small party was already in full swing and a number of men, sweating and full of grime from starting a charcoal pit fire, were busy in the yard scraping the bristles off a wild boar which was to be that night's dinner. In the kitchen, a group of tiny-figured Indonesian maids were cooking up a storm, rolling up and frying hundreds of finger-sized Lumpia and pounding chili and garlic in preparation for Udang Goreng. All manner of coolers, plastic tubs and other containers were filled to the brim with cans of beer floating in iced water. Cooking, much like drinking was always a communal event and everyone contributed what he or she could. If you couldn't cook, you brought booze. Everyone always chipped in. As I returned from my afternoon beers were already flowing freely and the 30 people or so were clearly in a good mood. In the midst of people chatting, carrying trays back and forth between the pit fire and the kitchen, people setting up the big table in the living room and people just having a good time was dad, wearing his Khakis and sand colored work shirt, as always engrossed in conversation, joking and laughing and completely in his element. It is still today one of those images that is vividly etched into my memory. He immediately saw me as I entered and waved me over to him across the crowded room. He put his arm around my shoulder and patted me on the back with a look of love and pride. "There you are son", he smiled. "You want a beer?" This was the first time my dad had ever publically offered me an alcoholic beverage, and my mother who was standing nearby was quick to voice her perturbation: "Norbert, the boy is too young. He will get drunk!"

Dad turned around to mum, shrugged his shoulders, and smiled. "Then let him get drunk. He's almost a grownup". I am sure he had already had a couple of drinks himself by that time and was clearly in party mode. I had seen him like this many times before, but he had never included me in this way, as his equal. Mum was not happy, but I think she too could sense that this was a unique and important moment for both of us and so she let it happen without further comment. If only she hadn't! Feeling suitably empowered by my dad's acknowledgment and permission I was out to prove that I had indeed entered the realm of adulthood by drinking beer like the other men. One or two were no problem, as my camp pals and I, sitting on the mini putt after dark, had secretly begun practicing with whatever alcohol someone was able to scrounge from their parents' drink cabinet. But by the third my head began to spin and I certainly noticed the effects. Much of what followed is still a blur, but I believe I made it to number six, apparently much to dad's amusement and once again mum's dismay. All I can remember is being on all fours in the grass of the front yard of our little house just next to the little pineapple my dad had planted a few days prior, hanging my head over the 3 foot deep concrete drainage ditch that ran the length of the street in an effort to relieve myself of the excess alcohol along with my stomach contents, while dad held the back of my collar to keep me from toppling over. The front yard chundering session was quickly followed by a cold shower, during which I allegedly broke out into all manner of singsong, before collapsing onto my bed in a drunken stupor.

Until today I don't know why dad had allowed me, no, even encouraged me to drink that night. I have heard that some fathers make their sons smoke whole packets of cigarettes in an effort to ensure they will never touch smokes again once they've been sick once. But that wasn't dad's style. The only explanation I have is that he truly relished me entering into adulthood and that this was his way and the first occasion to test how far I had come.

Indonesia was a magical time for our family and despite the work stresses; dad loved the work and camp life. When mum and I intermittently went back to Germany, he more or less lived a single life, in the company of many other singles and I am sure their "gang" got up to all manner of untold mischief then. Of course, not much was said about what happened during our absence, but occasionally an anecdote, usually a hilarious or adventurous story would slip. I know dad, in part on account of his deep beliefs but probably more so because of his love for mum never forgot he was married, but was always up for a trip with his colleagues who often ventured out to one of the fishing villages built on stilts out into the swamp of the intertidal zone, to savor local food and "entertainment", the latter consisting of a few ramshackle bars cum whorehouses which had sprung up as a result of the recent influx of industry. The rickety boardwalks held up by uneven wooden stilts more than 6feet above the swamp would here and there give way under the weight of a well-fed Westerner and the stories of so-and-so ending up hip-high in the mix of mud and effluence below always ensured a laugh at one of the ubiquitous booze-ups. I was never allowed to go there, of course, but the other kids and I would listen with red-hot ears every time one of the older teenagers had been allowed to accompany his dad to this for us younger ones very mysterious location. One of those was my Canadian friend Greg, whose father was a hardy firefighter turned professional safety contractor, a little rough around the edges, but the kind of guy you could utterly rely on and whom anyone would be proud to have in their corner when the paw paw hit the fan. Greg

58

was a few years older and so his dad would occasionally take him on one of his drinking excursions to explore the local "flora and fauna". According to Greg, his dad had even paid for a hooker to celebrate his son's 16th birthday. A great story, which of course none of us quite believed until Greg, having accompanied mum and I back to Germany for the fun of it was diagnosed with an STD; much to mum's and his parents' embarrassment. I don't think his dad took him along much after that and I can only imagine the kind of explanation he might have come up with towards his wife.

I know someone reading this might accuse me of being naive and say, yeah right, I am sure your father was no saint. And I am sure he wasn't; after all, who is? But the one thing I *am* sure about is that dad would have never done such a thing to mum. It was not in his nature to entertain tendencies like this and as much as he liked hanging out in the company of his colleagues and pals, he loved us more and always knew where to draw the line.

During the week, I would study before hanging out with the other kids who usually got dropped back to camp in the afternoon from an American school, which had been established by an Oil and gas company in the small town we had first landed in; or I would play with the young orphaned Orangutan we had "freed" from its tiny cage at the back of one of the Indonesian workers' residences and which had taken up residence in the tree right outside our house. In the morning dad would go outside and call "Leila", as we had named her, and she would climb down and jump straight into his arms. She was too wild to let loose inside the house, but at least for a few hours each morning she would join me in bed, stretch out wearing the white nappies we slapped on her every time she came inside and slept for a couple more hours. The rest of the day, I would spend either playing with her on our veranda or carry her with me to the commissary and other places I would usually hang out. She hung onto me like a baby and was one of the most kind and placid animals I have ever known. Understandably though, we couldn't keep her for long and eventually we had to move her from the camp to a nearby farm where an orphaned male also had taken up residence and was cared for by the farmer. A sad farewell, but she needed the company of her own kind. I had always had a fondness for wildlife and there was no shortage of animals and critters in and around the camp. At some stage our neighbor, a guy from Malaysia even had a big walk-in sized cage built for a young Gibbon he had rescued and I spent days and days sitting in the cage, wearing a thick jacket and garden gloves, with the monkey biting me until I slowly gained the traumatized animal's trust.

From then on, we would sit opposite each other or it on top of my head "delousing me" and exchange Gibbon sounds. Those were unforgettable experiences.

Our absolute favorite times though were weekend trips, which provided a rare opportunity to leave the camp and seek true adventures. We would often take one of the company's aluminium hull boats and head for one of the tiny islands or sandbanks and go snorkeling in the unspoiled coral reefs, while the boatmen built fires for our afternoon barbecue. Even water skis were available here and there and these outings were much looked forward to by all. We would stay until sunset and the image of dangling my feet in the water off the back of the boat, with the orange glow of the sinking sun among tropical storm clouds casting fiery reflections across the darkening waters are something that still endure today.

One weekend dad had something special planned for us. He gathered up a handful of his closest colleagues, along with an additional Land Rover and a Landcruiser, and we all made for the jungle, using an abandoned logging road to get deep into the forest until we reached a broken log bridge high over a river that had carved out a series of natural rock pools below during the centuries it had snaked its way through the forest.

There, next to the overgrown log bridge we made camp, parking the vehicles in a U-shape, and covering them with a tarp. This is where we stayed the weekend, cooking lentil stew over an open fire, with the clear starry sky above us and the noises of the jungle all around. We sat and swam in the rock pools, flung ourselves from long vines and explored the forest, pretty much everyone becoming a kid again in the process. It was an experience you simply couldn't book with a travel agent. It was something straight out of the pages of National Geographic magazine and we relished each moment of it. At night, we would open one of the many coconuts with a machete and top its sweet liquid up with Bacardi each time someone had a sip until it practically turned into a Bacardi nut. Silly stories and jokes were told and before long, everyone fell silent as they drifted off to sleep out in the open. I slept on the roof of the Land Rover, saturated with insect spray against the myriad of mosquitos and staring into the night sky for hours until the sound of the cicadas and forest noises of the night carried me off to sleep. This is where dad was truly in his element: constructing, setting up, and again creating things where there was nothing before. He had the spirit of adventure always and this was everything he had ever wanted.

And so almost three years went by. Mum and I traveling back and forth between Germany and Indonesia and dad working in the camp. At the end of the contract dad even took us on a North to South road trip through New Zealand, which would eventually, much later become my country of citizenship and my parents' home.

At that time dad and mum had actually made plans for us to move to Australia and pretty much all arrangements had been concluded, including our papers and a new job. But mere weeks before departure dad's bosses finally realized that without dad the company was looking down the barrel and they promoted him, and made him an offer he couldn't refuse. Who knows how our story would have continued, had we really made the move. As it were, dad took the offer and with it the long struggle and stress that came with trying to keep the company afloat despite the owners' continued negligence. I think ultimately they simply exploited dad's sense of duty to the company and his colleagues and subordinates for whose livelihoods he had long felt responsible.

## Chapter 4 - Growing Pains

It was hard getting re-accustomed to life at home. Apart from the photo albums, the souvenirs and mementos from various trips around Indonesia and the rest of Southeast Asia, including those from an upriver journey by my mum and several of her female camp companions all by themselves to the Dayak tribe in central Borneo, little seemed to have changed about out life back in Germany. Dad quickly followed his old routines of gardening, home improvements, tennis, hiking and of course work. The latter especially seemed to take up more and more of his time as the struggle to keep the company's finances in the black while being sucked dry by its owners became fiercer.

I don't know if dad found it hard to readjust. All I know is that he dived headlong into DIY projects, single-handedly converting the attic of our 2-story house into a giant loft room for me. I had until then occupied a room next to mum and dad's bedroom and dad had decided that I needed and deserved more space. He poured a lot of money, sweat and hours into the project, which as was the case with everything he did came out picture perfect and would serve me well into late teens. It was his way of showing that he cared and I am today ashamed to admit that back then I never saw it as that, nor really appreciated it. You see, time spent with dad on things that we both liked or loved was the most important thing to me and I thus did not truly understand the magnitude of his gesture, as his *time* was the one thing that again was mostly spent on other stuff. That is not to say he and mum didn't try to bring me in on things. They truly made every effort. But as it so often happens with fathers and sons, my interests lay elsewhere and all the tennis lessons and garden work in the world could not spark even the slightest bit of enthusiasm within me. I loved martial arts and boxing, two sports mum, inherently opposed to any 'violence', completely abhorred. I had always felt an affinity towards contact sports - or at least since the early days, when dad would wake me up at 4 in the morning to sit with him, wrapped in thick feather duvets and watch world championship boxing matches - broadcast live from around the world - on our little black and white TV he would wheel next to his bed and then fiddle with the rabbit ear antennas until the picture was perfect. I got to see the greats that way: Mohammed Ali, Joe Frazier and Larry Holmes and many more. Just dad and I awake and warm in our blankets, watching these great bouts with the volume turned low. Magic.

But when it came to my own pursuit of sports, much like with most of my spare time activities, mum had the final say. The only exception and what I am assuming was ultimately a compromise, was my enrolment in the local small-bore rifle club. There, one of my childhood friends and I would attend weekly air rifle target practice; something I enjoyed immensely. The club was quite active and frequently traveled for tournaments, to which I was always allowed to come along. Eventually though I lost interest as one had to be 18 or older to graduate to the next caliber. Plinking away with the relatively harmless single shot air rifles by then no longer held the same attraction. In Germany, people primarily socialize in associations. In fact, there is an old and true saying that the moment more than two Germans get together they form a club. Back then, it was the main vehicle for social interaction from an early age. And mum and dad spared no time trying to find one that would peak my interest. I tried handball, soccer, basketball, Judo and who knows what other sports, but few held any lasting attraction over the years; until I discovered weights, that is. While dad was still in Indonesia, dad's brother often took me under his wings. Despite being my Godfather, he hadn't been around all that much in the early years, probably thanks to a less than happy marriage to a woman I had struggled to think of as my aunt the entire time. After the divorce though and as I became a teenager he took more of an interest and in the absence of dad kept me busy in the gym. We would work out regularly, usually followed by a dinner in a Greek or Yugoslavian restaurant, where meat portions were generous and tasty; an added bonus for a growing teen with an insatiable appetite. As it turned out I was quite apt at building muscle, too, and I could soon measure up to older guys in the gym both in terms of weights used and size.

I know dad had gone to the gym during the tennis off-season and while on contracts elsewhere in Europe here and there, but he had never really pursued the activity as a hobby. He much more enjoyed outdoor activities than grinding away in a sweaty dungeon. My uncle, I hate to say, was rather vein and maintaining his outer image was as important to him a breathing. From his neatly trimmed mustache to his choice of leather jackets and jewelry, his image was of utmost importance to him. The 1980's somewhat glitzy gym scene therefore suited him well and he would regularly sip a glass of champagne between sets with the gym owner, a former power lifter, and his buddy, before flexing his newly acquired muscles in his leather jacket for the benefit of my new aunt on the way to dinner. I liked his attention and the fact that he and the others in the gym treated me like an adult. I felt empowered and respected, but more importantly I was able to spend time in the company of grown-up guys. One of the side effects of dad's long work hours and contract work away from home was that I spent most of my time with mum, who loved me dearly and spoiled me rotten, I'm afraid to admit. But I was lacking live male role models. I knew how to iron, how to sew, heck, I even knew how to knit! But I missed out on a lot of the rough and tumble, the banter and competition that ensues when you throw a bunch of males together. Maybe that is why I developed such an affinity towards movie heroes like Sylvester Stallone, and Arnold Schwarzenegger and loved reading about soldiers, war, and guns. By the age of 16 at one time, I even wanted to run away and join the foreign legion; an endeavor that never took shape beyond imagining myself crawling through the sand dunes of Morocco, while lying on my bed in rural Germany.

The fact remained that I increasingly grew distant from dad over a period of time. I was now 18 and as mum and dad had always done, they made sure I had everything I wanted and needed. Soon I got my driver's license; not a cheap undertaking in Germany, where a minimum of 30 expensive hours in a driving school were mandatory. And with the license dad bought me my first car. I may have been rich in assets, spoiled even, but I would have given it all to have the kind of relationship with dad, which we would only have much later and which, thanks to bastard Lewy, was cut ever so short.

The newly gained freedom of movement beyond the limits of our town, also brought with it a greater distance from mum and dad than before. To some extent I guess this is a normal development the world over: as sons grow to be adults and try to find their place in the world, the ties to parents loosen and only time can tell whether they remain intact at all in many instances. As an only child, these ties had always and would for the rest of my life, remain close. But for that period mum, dad and I later looked upon as my "rebellious years", they almost came to breaking point.

In as much as mum and dad had lived a very active social life, their life in general was bound by written and unwritten rules and narrow social norms established in German culture. Things had to be immaculate, straight, aligned and in full compliance with laws, regulations and the expectations of society. "What will the neighbors think?" was often the benchmark, the watershed between what was acceptable, and what wasn't. Most of our neighbors, mum and dad's friends and acquaintances were what you would call rather well off. There were lawyers, doctors and other well-paid professionals, company owners, insurance brokers and real estate investors. In Germany, one's job mattered, as did one's social standing. And either were easily endangered by non-compliance with social norms. Underneath it all, things were probably far from squeaky clean, but to the outside, an immaculate image was to be maintained at all times. From keeping the sidewalk in front of the house spotless, the lawn trimmed and car polished to ensuring one's fashion was up to date yet still conservative, children attended the right school and the next capital purchase was in sight and suited for mention at the next social gathering, everything went according to norms and conventions. Few ever broke these rules and if they did were either viewed with suspicion or downright disdain, sure to be shunned in the long run. Perhaps not outwardly visible, but I imagine there was a lot of pressure beneath the polished façade and success stories exchanged over beers at the clubhouse. At least this is how I slowly had grown to see things and as a result distanced myself more and more from mum and dad's life. But I felt that wasn't enough. Probably more subconsciously, I felt I should go in as much the opposite direction as possible. It was time to rebel against it all in my own way. I guess I couldn't understand how we could live so free from all this in Indonesia and how mum and dad could so easily slip back into the prison of the conventions imposed by a society which seemed excessively materialist, elitist and even chauvinist by comparison.

During dad's long absences mum had always sung his praises, telling me about his successes, how dedicated he was and about the enormous respect everyone had for him both in and out of work. But dad never shared any of that with me. He never talked about these things. Somehow, it was as if my mum had the inside track but I did not. The only measure of his successes away from home, from my perspective was the amount of money dad spent on us and me specifically. Throughout my youth, much of dad had therefore remained somewhat of an enigma and I was left to draw my own conclusions based on what I observed and what I heard from mum. Of course I remember dad doing "dad stuff" with me, like taking me to the movies in nearby Frankfurt, where on one of the biggest screens in Europe we watch films like Star Wars, take me along on hikes with a group of his closest colleagues or for a bit of cross country skiing during winter. But he never opened up or talked about anything other than what we were doing at the time. I cannot recall a single conversation today where dad would have sat down with me to give life advice or share his views on things as he really saw them. It was just not how he did things.

Somehow, I had always felt like an observer, with commentary from mum providing the only insight into dad's character, activities, and thoughts beyond what I saw at home. When life in Germany returned to "normal" after Indonesia, the feeling of distance intensified and combined with the added freedom that car ownership brought with it, I found myself drifting away from both mum and dad and their conservative lifestyle. I fell in with a new crowd of similar-minded people. Now over 18, we were technically adults, although one would not have guessed the fact from our behavior. We listened to Heavy Metal, went to Rock Concerts, drank heavily, and were too cool for the rest of society of people or "sheeple" that blindly followed what in our eyes were anachronistic social conventions. One of my new friends had a small studio flat in the North of Frankfurt, easily an hour's drive away from home, where sometimes up to 10 of us would spend the weekends drinking and listening to music at full volume. Initially on Friday and Saturday nights, but soon enough even on weeknights, we would drive downtown were an acquaintance had a hard rock pub, where we would drink and talk until the early hours of the morning. And even when everything closed, we would still sometimes sit in the small foyer of a 24-hour vending machine store, the only place sheltered enough and open at that hour, and jam away with some of the musicians we got to know over time. Some of them actually went places in the industry later, but most of us were just in it for the fun of it. My increased absences were not lost on my parents, whom I sometimes saw but at the breakfast table as I stumbled back in the door after another long night out. Few words beyond the necessary were spoken during that time and my parents' discontent was palpable.

To this day I don't know why dad never said anything. I remember some arguments, but those were mostly with mum, who expressed how disappointed dad was at my behavior. In any case, despite my rebellion and his disapproval, in yet another act of kindness, one day my dad said: "The boy needs a proper place. He is too old for the loft." And so he had plans drawn up to create a fully independent one bedroom apartment in the basement, with a separate entrance and even a little courtyard opening into our front garden. It was an expensive undertaking and in his usual manner, dad spared no expense to make it perfect. Within a few months, I moved from the attic to the brand new basement apartment. For all intents and purposes I was now officially "independent". I still don't know why dad did this for me at a time when all I seemed to be able to do was cause him grief. For all I know he knew that the time had come to let me go, having realized that I was indeed different to what he had perhaps aspired his son to be, while at the same time keeping me close enough to perhaps instill change or at least retain a little of what he knew me to be like from before. He never talked about it. For some reason his generosity had the opposite effect. Of course, I appreciated and thanked dad for creating the apartment, but at the same time I couldn't shake the feeling of having been cast out, all be it into a quasi "golden cage": My parents above me, living the life I by now had so little in common with and me below, the wayward son. In my parents' defense, I was rather opinionated and hardheaded at the time and I guess there was little point in talking to me, but I don't think dad ever tried either.

Throughout my teenage years, the only thing mum and dad had insisted on without compromise was completing school with a university entrance certificate. "You can do anything you want with your life, but you have to finish school" was the credo presented every time my little teenage mind came up with other ideas. Now that I had done so and thus was no longer bound by their condition, the wheels slowly came off and I was on the brink of derailing. I had part-time work at a green grocer and a video store and gave university a try, but at the time it just wasn't for me. So one day, on the spur of the moment, when the green grocer asked if I had ever thought about becoming a chef and in the same breath had mentioned that he knew someone looking for an apprentice, I jumped at the chance. Mum was horrified. Her son was throwing his life away. Dad remained silent. But I did pass and within 2 ½ years became a qualified chef. Of course, the partying didn't stop in an industry notorious for alcohol abuse and after hour festivities. Among like-minded, I enjoyed the time as an apprentice and each week at technical school, located in the same part of town where only a year earlier I had still been partying with my heavy metal band friends, the other chefs and I would sit at a pub just across and order round after round while skipping what we thought were some of the more superfluous lessons. I guess the fact that despite this I passed the exams in the end is more of a credit to my natural inclination towards cooking than actual time spent in class.

Dad and my relationship remained distant throughout. I took up odd jobs as a chef for family friends who owned restaurants and eventually even leased the restaurant of the very tennis club mum and dad spent most of the summer at. My private life hadn't changed much from before: it was messy, chaotic, boozy and full of parties. It was like a perpetual roundabout that was too fast to get off. I was good as a chef, but I let distractions get in my way at every turn. There were successes, but eventually my heart wasn't in it and my lifestyle caught up with the business, it being a case of too much at the wrong time. The wealthy club members were penny pinchers, extremely demanding and at times even abusive and I had no patience for staying in a society I had long come to despise. During the summer season I sometimes slept on a bench in the restaurant as between finishing up the night before and getting up for the next day's business there was not enough time to go home. Club members would insist I stay open until they had their fill, sometimes into the early hours of the morning, while club members playing tennis in the morning demanded I open for them. Prices were virtually fixed and profits marginal. It was a losing battle and something had to give. Then came winter. The tennis courts became unusable and sessions were only possible in the single court hall next door. Business scraped by at a loss most nights and apart from the meager profits of a few traditional social occasions, there was little money left over. I was better off working as a chef again. My interactions with dad were limited to club related matters at the time and we saw very little of each other, except for when he was at the club and ordered something. He was a senior member and I was the publican. He supported me where he could in his role, but it was also an uncomfortable position for him to be in, as I was increasingly losing interest in the business.

I again worked odd jobs as a chef, including some catering for friends and family, something I must say I was rather good at. There was one special occasion where dad showed true pride in what I could do. It was his birthday and mum and dad had declared an "open house" for the day, meaning friends and family could drop in at any time and catering would be supplied from morning until night. We had BBQ's set up, a big Paella dish and even a Kebab station, along with a cold buffet of meats, cheeses, and seafood. Dad videotaped the event and it became one of the most talked about parties for several years to come, resulting in a number of extra catering jobs for me. Dad of course loved the attention at his birthday parties, but I think what he loved more was an event coming together in perfection. And this was one of those days. He would put his arms around my shoulders in front of people and proudly announce that I was the one who had made all the food. It was the first time I can remember him presenting what I had done with pride. What I had done! It was one of the best days ever. The overall distance continued though and things were about to get worse, but for that one day for some reason it was as if it didn't exist at all.

I had lost my driver's license in the course of one of my many escapades, having been stopped at a Police checkpoint and done for driving under the influence. Mum and dad were away on holiday and it was my uncle, who came to my rescue at 2 in the morning when I had to leave mum's car by the roadside. I should have recognized it for what it was: a low point. But somehow it didn't register at all. I could have even gotten away without suspension, as I had been less than a decimal point above the limit, in which case normally only a fine was issued. But I never so much as wrote the letter that was required, nor appeared for the charge. I felt so dead inside, I couldn't have cared less. From then on, I walked everywhere, rode my mountain bike, or used public transport. It was annoying, but it hardly registered. Even when I took a job at a Greek restaurant more than 12 kilometers away, I would either walk or ride a bike, often not getting home until the early hours of the morning. Thus, I spent more and more time away from the apartment and saw mum and dad very little, the distance ever-present, ever growing. To some extent, I think they had given up, hoping that maybe I would eventually round the corner of this crazy road I was on, or deal with the fallout as and when it came. And come it did.

Growing up, we always had dogs and one could say we really were a dog family. Both mum and dad loved them, as did I. Some of the stories weren't happy ones, like the first dog, a Dachshund which destroyed all wooden doors and subsequently had to be given away, or the Boxer which went for my throat out of jealousy the day I was released from a stint in hospital and which likewise had to be passed on to another owner. And then came a poodle mix, a little black thing that looked like a black Flokati carpet, which one of our Denmark holiday friends had given to us. She became our first, longest, and most loyal pet. For thirteen years, the dog was as much part of our life as any closest family member would have been. In the absence of siblings, it was like having a brother or sister to play with and we all loved her beyond words. Eventually, as most well cared for dogs do, she became old, almost blind and in the end could hardly stand. It was hard to watch and caused me a lot of grief. After all, it was the first pet I had truly been close to and which was on the verge of death. In an act of mercy, mum and dad made the decision to have her put down and that same afternoon we buried her in our back garden. I dug the grave and dad put her in it. I don't know if mum and dad ever realized how deeply her death affected me, but it was never really spoken about and shortly after mum and dad declared that they would never want another dog as it was too much hassle and heartache. But I felt the gap that was now there and quietly resented their sentiments. I think that was one of the main issues that caused much of the rift between dad and me over the years: Mum spoke with me often, but she always looked at things from an emotional standpoint and seldom from a purely rational one. Dad rarely shared anything about his feelings, thoughts or otherwise.

My grandmother hadn't been well for a long time. She had grown slightly demented and for a while had not been able to take care of herself or my grandfather anymore. The decision was made to move them closer to my uncle, so that he and his second wife could look after them a little easier. Growing up I had loved my grandmother beyond words. As a child, I spent extended holidays at their roof apartment and days in their little garden out the back, helping her or just splashing around with a garden hose, tasting the gooseberries, plums, cherries and other fruit she grew herself. She spoiled me rotten and in addition to the endless supply of chocolate bars and toys, she would take me on short day trips to the zoo or the museum of natural history. In the evening, I would stand on a small crate so I could watch her cook Schnitzels, sausages and pretty much anything else I liked over the wood-fired stove. She poured all her love into me. More so than she had done with her own two sons, my dad and my uncle. Mum regularly lamented the fact but in the end gave up maintaining the peace, since with my grandmother, resistance was futile in these matters. I wonder how dad ever felt about it, having gone without much of what was bestowed upon me during his own childhood. But as far as I was concerned, my grandmother was a saint.

Then, one day during what we would later title my "troubled phase", came the call that she had been hospitalized. Things were not looking good. I hadn't seen her for a while. The last visits had been awkward, with her barely responding to questions, failing to remember things and often just blankly staring into space. Their new apartment was nice, but it had lost the ambience of a true home and today I often wonder whether it was this dislodgement from the small flat they had occupied since after the war, and the feeling of loss that came with it, that may have contributed to her accelerated deterioration. In any case, the family gathered next to her bed, at a hospital about 30 minutes' drive away from home. Her eyes were closed and her skin had taken on a pale and flat complexion, but she was breathing long labored breaths. Mum, dad, my uncle, my aunt, and I sat next to her for hours, quietly speaking with her, letting her know we were there. I wasn't able to speak. I was horrified. After many hours, the doctors informed that it was simply impossible to predict when the hour would come and it was decided to send me home for bit of sleep. I don't think I was even in a condition to respond and just went along with it. The thought of my beloved grandmother like this was all too much. You know, you can legally become an adult, but that doesn't mean you are in any way equipped to deal with these circumstances. It hits you like a ton of bricks and there is nothing you can do: on the outside a grown up, but on the inside a child in the face of the unthinkable. Shortly after I awoke at home by myself the next morning, the call came. It was mum saying "it was time" and that I should jump into a taxi.

When I got there, grandmother's breathing had become even more labored and gasps were but intermittent. Her eyes were pale and half-open, but her face was emotionless, almost like a mask. Her skin tone now had a tint of waxy yellow. I wanted to be anywhere but here. I wanted to run, just run. Mum led me to her and I leaned over so that she could perhaps see me. "Robert is here, mum. You see, he is here. It is Ok to let go now. It is Ok to let go", Mum whispered in her ear and then encouraged me to say something. I had a brick in my throat, I think "Hello Oma", was all I managed to stammer. But no sooner had I said it, my grandmother drew her last few breaths. First one, then another one, then nothing, then one last deep gasp. I can still hear the air leaving her lungs as her half-open eyes grew lifeless. This was and still is one of the hardest moments of my life and still today, I don't speak about it. I was in deep shock. Nothing had and perhaps nothing could have prepared me for this and it deeply affected me in the years to come. But back then psycho-social support was a foreign term and I don't think anyone thought to even ask the question. Everyone was left to deal with his or her own grief. And it was no different in my family. The funny thing is, I don't even remember seeing dad cry. Much in line with his upbringing, I don't think he liked open displays of emotion or perhaps I have just blocked out the memory, who knows.

There had been other deaths during my teenage years: One of my closest school friends suddenly died of heart failure in the arms of his father. Another friend drove his motorcycle into the back of a truck. Both were buried in the same part of the cemetery as my grandmother and for a good while during my rebellious phase, I would pay them the occasional nightly visit, sitting there quietly amongst the graves, taking swigs in their memory, from whatever I was drinking. But grieving was a solitary affair and took place in private. No question was ever asked whether I or anyone else for that matter was Ok or how I felt about it all. I truly felt alone in my grief. Death was cold, cruel, and as casual as a stroll in the park in how it took its victims. It was my first glimpse at the reality of a world, which for better or worse I would come to know much better much later in life, but one I had been shielded from thus far. My generation had "no future" as a slogan. Against the backdrop of the constant threat of nuclear war, we were confident that little what we did mattered as it would all end in a giant ball of fire one day. Luckily, that day didn't come, but the sentiment impacted much of our outlook, along with our actions. Given the sheer enormity, the seriousness of the threat it was incomprehensible to many of us how our parents could continue living in the old ways, adhering to the same conventions and values, when in all reality the entire world was dancing at the edge of a giant, whimsical volcano. The prospect of death, of such permanent separation from everything we love, was deeply troubling and my grandmother's death only deepened my feelings of Angst, help- and hopelessness. I cannot recall ever talking about any of this with dad. I assume today that he himself had a hard time coping, but it was impossible to tell. There were times when I just wanted to shake him as if to wake him up to what I could see and how I was feeling, but the line of communication wasn't there, the connection had been disrupted and so we just continued our parallel lives.

In addition to working two restaurant jobs, I befriended a local biker gang the members of which were regulars at the places I worked. They had a compound just outside town and I soon became a regular guest at their clubhouse. It provided yet another mysterious and rebellious atmosphere that was right up my alley and very much aligned with what I had become accustomed to in terms of parties, camaraderie and the strong man image I had aspired to even as a kid. My beard grew longer as did my hair and for nights on end I would sleep on the old and cracked leather couch in the main room of the club house, while the gang's "president" was smoking weed and hash and watched cheap action films. In summer, I helped the gang with their public events, which they used to boost legal revenue.

I was in charge of catering and we smoked ribs, made burgers, and immersed ourselves in the heavy-handed biker image. I relished the company of these foul-mouthed guys with their patches, their boots and their hardened exterior. They were outlaws, they were unlike anything I had ever encountered, and by then they perfectly fitted my aspiration to set myself apart from my parents as far as possible. The feeling of being feared was powerful and a reveled in how outsiders looked at us during the many open door parties. There was always a certain electricity in the air, an underlying tension and fights would break out regularly since it didn't take much for one of the members to take offense to something an outsider said. Sometimes members would start fights just because they could. I wasn't patched yet and as such not a fully-fledged member, but the president, a tall lanky guy with a red beard, a bandana and a booming voice, had taken a shine to me and informally declared me as "Ok", meaning I could come and go as I pleased and take part in all their activities. The one thing I hadn't done was "take the test" though. But since this usually involved something quite illegal such as theft or bodily harm, given the privileges I was already enjoying I was eager to delay it for as long as I could, ideally indefinitely. I may have enjoyed the company, the image and the sense of adventure, but I certainly was no criminal and had no intention of ever becoming one.

Most of my time though was spent working as head chef at a local restaurant; a job I thoroughly enjoyed. I was in charge of the daily lunch menu, the prep, as well as developing new dishes for the main menu. I was the only permanent chef, with the three other positions covered by students working part time, which gave the kitchen an entirely different, much more relaxed atmosphere. During my apprenticeship our uniforms had to be clean and ironed, out scarfs tied correctly, our chef's hats crisp and our work shoes polished. We followed the rules of our master chef and cooking took place within the confines of classic cuisine. Here, I was the only one wearing a chef's jacket (my boss felt it would add to the place's image) but everyone else wore printed T-shirts, jeans, and sneakers. Beer was free while on duty, and so round after round would pour into the kitchen, be it in response to our own orders, from benevolent waiters or sent into the kitchen by satisfied customers as a sign of appreciation. Everyone was jovial, there was a lot of laughter and we all ate and drank what we pleased. After cleanup, we would take the party into the pub as guests, but enjoying the same privileges in addition to a decent hourly wage. Part of the place's appeal was that everybody knew everybody. If your mate worked in the kitchen or behind the bar, you would bring your own mates along to see them. And so half my former schoolmates and their friends were usually to be found drinking Weissbier and intermittent shots. My regular hours were from 10am to 6pm, but I always started at 8 or 9 and with kitchen staff having a rather relaxed approach to showing up for work, there was plenty of overtime. As a result, I generally worked 6 days and sometimes more than 90 hours a week, essentially getting paid for being creative, doing what I loved and partying with my friends all at the same time. The owner was a great guy as well. On occasion he would have a tantrum when after a messy night not all prep was done or the kitchen spotless as he always expected it to be, but for the better part he was in on it with us and often hung back after he finished his own day to have a few rounds with us.

But regardless of how much I partied, how much I worked, at the end of the day I would have to face returning to the downstairs apartment and the loneliness I just couldn't shake. It was as if I needed all the noise around me to just drown it out. The loneliness I had felt for a long time. It had a stranglehold on me and I had not found a way to escape it. Each time I would return to the apartment, all I felt was dark emptiness, a foreboding and a brooding sadness that came with the distance that had grown between my parents and me, particularly dad whom I now seldom spoke with, despite more or less living in the same house. Today it seems like a crazy idea, but at the time getting a dog seemed like a good idea. Not only had our old dog passed away, but when I had asked if we could have another one, mum and dad had also forbade me to go down that road. They had rarely ever forbade anything, but in this instance despite my pleas had been unrelenting in their refusal. Between the loneliness, my disdain for my parents' lifestyle and what I now believe was a deep disappointment in the emotional inaccessibility of my father, I felt anger rising at their unjust decision. I felt as if, in a sea of material things, they had denied me the one thing I truly needed: companionship the way I used to know it, at a time when things had been happier. It was an anger at my father, an anger at my mother and my own inability to reach them. Initially, a couple of years earlier my rebellion had started secretly with a small tattoo on the back of my shoulder; something that mum and dad likewise had spoken out against and which they wouldn't discover until years after. But now it was in full swing. I had friends who owned pitbulls. Known as fighting dogs and feared for their propensity to "snap", owning one was almost like belonging to a secret society of people who knew things others didn't. I had spent time with their dogs, watched them go through obedience drills, played with them, and had come to know them as likable, loyal, and friendly creatures. One day a friend of mine told me he had seen one in an animal shelter. He had taken the dog for a walk and thought he might be right for me. I wasted no time in accompanying him to see for myself and as far as my love for dog goes, this was love at first sight. He was a Pitbull pointer mix, tall and well-built with a head the size of a calf. He had a scar running along the underside of his neck, indicating that someone might have tried to train him for dogfights, or so it was speculated. His demeanor though was anything but aggressive and it wasn't hard to see how someone with such intentions would have been sorely disappointed. Walking him was like trying to hold on to a locomotive leaving the station. He had an energy I had never seen in a dog and eventually I took to tying him to my wrist while riding my mountain bike. Much like a horse and carriage, but at breakneck speeds he would pull me along the gravel roads leading through the nearby forest for kilometers on end, afterwards collapsing in a heap on the couch. He slept next to me and, his body when stretched out almost as long as mine, would lie on his back and snore for hours. I loved him and from what I could tell he loved me, too. I felt a sense of belonging again when I was with him, almost as if he and I were alike in a sense. Both alone, disappointed and with nowhere to go in this world. But the good times weren't to last. I worked long hours and wasn't able to give him the attention he deserved and needed. Mum and dad were clearly and, given I was acting directly against the expressed instructions to the contrary, angry at my decision to get a dog and swore to never ever as much as do anything for it. This was particularly saddening as their demeanor was in such stark contrast to how they had treated our old dog. For all intents and purposes, our previous dog might as well have been human, it was treated and loved so well. Yet, this dog that meant so much to me, was not worthy of even the slightest bit of affection, let alone as much as acknowledgement. Initially I tried to bring it to work with me and the pub's owner reluctantly agreed that I could tie him up behind the kitchen. But people ended up being afraid to even walk past him due to his size and fearsome looks and so I had to leave him at home. Long periods alone are never good for a dog, let alone for a dog with emotional issues like the ones he had and within a short period, he began to take out his frustrations on my furniture. Each time I returned I was greeted with more sofa stuffing and torn up bits and pieces. I reacted badly out of frustration and helplessness. Punishment understandably, had little effect. I will never forget his sad eyes, as he was literally "standing" at the window each time I left for work and the mix of accusation and relief in his eyes whenever I returned. I pleaded with mum and dad to perhaps feed him while I was gone or even just occasionally let him up into their part of the house, just so he could have company, but they were unrelenting. I believe in the end there were a couple of occasions where mum gave him something, and even nights where my parents felt so sorry for the animal that, against all their grudges they allowed him to spend a few hours in the living room. But overall they stood firm in their resolve – or at least didn't admit to secretly yielding. And so each time I was at work I felt bad for him being back home alone and each time I came home I got angry and frustrated when he had yet again torn to shreds anything and everything in his sight. With the growing guilt came more booze and with more booze later nights and the problem just kept getting worse. Even though he had not shown any aggression initially, he hated other dogs to the point where anything on four legs within eyesight became the object of his wrath. Not so much of a problem when I had him on a leash, although it did take all my energy to hold him, but if he managed to squeeze past me through an open door or otherwise broke free it was almost impossible to control his rage. The final straw came one day when a little girl walked a St. Bernard past the waist-high wooden fence that separated our property from the public sidewalk. I had just opened the door, when he came darting out with lightning speed, heading straight for the St. Bernard. He leapt the fence without as much as breaking stride and immediately tore into the other dog. I heard the girl scream as she watched the much larger dog getting attacked by mine. It took all my power to tear the two apart and at one point I feared for my own life as my dog's eyes showed a blind fierceness and his attack such a viciousness that told the intent to kill was the only thing left in his mind. Bloodied and whimpering the St. Bernard was ushered away by the traumatized little girl before I had a chance to do or say anything while I still struggled to contain my frothing dog. It didn't take long though for the owners to make themselves known and I can't remember how, but I talked myself out of having to pay for vet bills. Perhaps acknowledging the fact that letting a little girl walk a St. Bernard wasn't a good idea to start with helped, but who knows. The incident could have just as easily turned out much, much worse and despite my standoffish rough exterior, I secretly thanked God that the little girl had been left unharmed. I had never before and have not since seen an animal change like this in a split second from a docile, loyal pet to a raving violent lunatic beyond all control and it scared the hell out of me. I realized that between his likely traumatic past and the changes since I had taken him into my less than ideal care, that day he had crossed the point of no return and safety for anyone around him could no longer be guaranteed. He would have to be condemned to spending his entire life on a short leash and could never be trusted alone in a room, let alone free outside. Of course, my lack of attention played a big part, but I somehow also blamed my parents – in retrospect probably quite irrationally so. After all the love they had professed for dogs all my life, and the care and affection they had bestowed onto our previous one, they had withdrawn it all when I had needed them to show it most, despite my pleading and asking. Our old dog had been treated to a life of quasi-human quality and yet this one wasn't worthy, despite having done nothing to deserve anything less. I felt as if my parents' refusal of affection and empathy for the dog was symbolic for the overall situation, rather than a reflection of how I had gone and was still going about things. In a way, I felt both my dog and I had been cast out. I could see it suffer under the circumstances, caught between remorse and the overwhelming, uncontrollable urge to tear to shreds anything, inanimate or living, that came into its way. And thus I had to make the one of the hardest decisions of my life. Returning it to the shelter would have crushed its spirit even further and under the circumstances, it would no longer be adoptable, in all likelihood leading to one inevitable solution for resource-starved shelters: euthanasia. I took him to the vet, explained the situation and he, too, having looked over the dog, agreed that there would be no other way but to euthanize him. It broke my heart. It. Broke. My. Heart. And as I held this animal I had loved so much and whose demons, whose conflicted soul were so close to my own, as he slipped away forever and his body went limp, I felt something crack inside me, opening a void so deep and with such force that it was almost audible. And out of that void rose an anger so destructive that it threatened to consume me.

I lost control of just about every aspect of my life. I turned into a shell. Nothing mattered anymore. I worked longer and longer hours, drank more than ever before, and started smoking hashish each night, just to be able to get to sleep. My furniture, thanks to the dog's efforts, had been reduced to a lumpy futon bed and an old bowling alley bar chair without legs. I no longer cleared out the rubbish or cleaned the apartment. I no longer wrote poetry, something I had done for many years to channel my emotions. Now these were on the loose, attacking and all-consuming much like my dog had done just days prior. I was going downhill fast. My anger, hurt, rage, and sense of loneliness continued to build and build and I was helpless to stem their flood. Robotically and half the time semi-anesthetized, I continued to nurture them, neither bothering about consequences, nor caring where I was headed. Suffice it to say the situation was quickly becoming untenable and eventually something had to give. And give, it did.

One night, I can't remember any particular event that had triggered it, the dam broke. I had been drinking, sitting on the cold tile floor and listening to music at full volume in the basement apartment, when out of nowhere the flood of emotions took over and released a rage in me, I have never again experienced. I felt helpless, abandoned, lonely and hurt beyond such measure that I completely lost any and all sense of reality and gave into the anger that was now overflowing. I threw glasses and punched walls, howling, crying and yelling like a madman. I proceeded to smash the glass of each and every picture frame on the wall with my bare hands, my fists soon cut and bleeding. I punched, kicked and tried to destroy every object in the place in an all-consuming fit of crazed fury and hurt.

Suddenly in the midst of this, through the fog of rage I could hear banging on the front door and dad yelling for me to open up. At that moment, I refocused my anger on the one I had felt so abandoned by. Through the years all I had wanted was for him to understand me and to be proud of me, but dad had been emotionally inaccessible and often simply not been there. He had been painted a

79

celebrity of unattainable status, revered by all and out of reach. Mum glorified him, rightly or wrongly and had always made sure I had the most glowing impression possible of my father. I am sure he too had weaknesses but in my mother's portrayal, he was flawless. Mum adored dad and her praises were only surpassed by her devotion to him. How could I have ever lived up to this? How could I have achieved worthiness in his eyes? I didn't need mum's praises, I needed dad's warmth and acceptance. I opened the door, in underpants and T-shirt, crazed and bleeding. "Have you turned completely antisocial!?" Dad yelled, his own anger clear and undeniable. Instead of answering, I just raised my fists and challenged him. "Come on, come here if you want some of this!" It was all I could shout through my tears. Wanting to slug it out with him once and for all, challenging all he stood for, I waved my fists around readying myself for the fight. But dad did nothing. He just looked at me and without so much as another word, shook his head, turned around and walked away, leaving me behind in the doorway, fists raised.

I stood there, stoned, disarmed and speechless, when suddenly a realization hit me with nauseating force: I was pitiful. This, I, was *pathetic*! With the few words he had spoken and not just turning down my challenge, but barely acknowledging it, dad had in an instant exposed my deplorable condition. No slap in the face could have hit harder. For the first time, he had seen my emotional state in all its ugliness and both anger and disappointment were written across his face as clear as day at that moment. Here I stood outside in the cold night air and looked on as he stomped back up towards the front fence and then back along the main walkway to the ground floor entrance. I shouted at him angrily to come back and take up the challenge, but he never so much as glanced back. There and then it became clear to me that while I had wished nothing more than to shake him, wake him up and let him know how I felt, in how much pain I was and how I wanted his and our life to be different, I had instead overshot the mark. I had gone too far. And although I knew that I had finally gotten through to him, I learned that there was something far worse than dad's distance: his disappointment. All I had ever wanted was for him to be proud of me, to show me that I did something right; not through some gesture that needed interpreting, but looking into my eyes and telling me so.

Instead, I had gone down the path of antagonizing him to the point where his love was now clouded by disgust for what I had become. Yet in a perverse way, he had also acknowledged what I had set out to do: to distance myself from his way of life as far as possible. And in the process I had not just reached the end of that road. I had possibly irreparably overshot the finish line.

It was the lowest point in my relationship with dad and an incident I still regret even now that he is gone. In typical "dad fashion" we never spoke much about that night. Instead, both him and I went on to repair our relationship and then built on its ruins something more special and beautiful than I could have ever imagined; the fact that we were able to do so after all this no doubt a testament to how much he had always loved me, something I sorely wish I understood then as I do now.

But with many things in life hindsight usually precedes insight and thus events must often reach conclusion on their own before we can see the sum of their parts. This is probably more true in youth than in other age. I don't consider myself daft or particularly slow on the uptake, but it took me the better part of my adult life to understand what happened that night and that perhaps without its emotional carnage, the great relationship that dad and I would go on to build and which grew with every year of our lives, may not have been possible.

## Chapter 5 - That which does not kill us...

Although I kept working at the pub and hanging out with 'misfits', I started cleaning up my act. Mum and dad sat down with me for a chat briefly after the events of that fateful night and something of a truce was managed. Dad even went a step further and booked an adventure holiday, just for him and I, which even today after more than a decade of professional international travel, remains probably the best trip of my life. I sense he did so to repair things and to give us the time together he probably realized we had been missing out on. I still admire him for this, especially because doing so would have taken a lot of forgiveness and reflection, but most of all unwavering love for his son, despite what had happened and what I had done. It showed a strength of character and devotion that few of us would be so lucky to possess.

So that summer we set out on a three-week backpacking trip to Malaysia. No holds barred wall-to-wall adventure, just dad and I. We started out in Kuala Lumpur were we ate anything and everything at street restaurants, from spicy squid for dinner to delicious roti canai for breakfast. We then made our way across to Sabah where we spent a few days exploring its coastal capital Kota Kinabalu, savoring the foods of the night markets and open-air seafood restaurants, swimming on its nearby islands and looking at museums and historic sites. We shared rooms and did nothing but talk together, experience new things, laugh and drink Tiger beer. We traveled inland, first by minibus and then up a river by boat. There we explored the bat caves of Batu Punggul, crawling through guano and marveling at the thousands of bats that fluttered all around us. We spent a few days staying with a family in a traditional longhouse, were guests at a wedding ceremony and the following feast, drank homebrewed booze out of communal urns watched cockfights and washed ourselves at the muddy banks of the river. We caught a backbreaking ride on the bed of a pickup truck back to the city and then crossed the state by bus to Sandakan on its eastern coast. We explored Chinese temples, ate Lobster Thermidor and soaked up the atmosphere of the bustling streets. Visiting the Orangutan sanctuary was one of the highlights, reminding us of days gone by in Indonesia where we played with "Leila" our own little Orangutan each day.

We then spent three days at a research station. Although not really a tourist place, they had two guestrooms reserved for visitors and non-scientists could book themselves in and take part in hikes exploring the surrounding rain forests. We were issued with green colored leech socks and after each hike, we would pluck the critters from our shoes as they traveled up our legs and into every opening in the clothing in search of a meal. There were old burial sites in the vicinity and many other sights and the daily treks up and down the steep hills together with the extreme heat and humidity nearly brought us to our knees. It was truly a feeling of "we" and "us", just dad and I seeing all these wonderful things and sharing what we had seen each night over a few Tigers, eating freshly caught baked fish while sitting on the Veranda of the research station's common room, overlooking a river and the seemingly endless expanse of the rainforest.

Our trip culminated in a climb of Mount Kinabalu, an unforgettable experience if ever there was one. On day one we made our way to the base camp hut, where we spent the night in bunk beds in what during the ascend had turned into freezing temperatures. At two in the morning, we then climbed to the summit and watched the sunrise as icy winds howled all around us and made us seek shelter behind rocks wherever we could. Normally the way down is always easier, but here that rule didn't apply. About 13 kilometers from the summit back to the park entrance, the entire way down consisted of uneven and often unstable footholds utilizing natural formations of sheet rock or tree roots or crude steps carved out of the mountainside. It wreaked havoc on our knees and the last third of the hike we had to take each step sideways, our knees swollen and aching from the constant pounding they had received. That night dad had booked a four star hotel and muddy, unwashed, sweaty and our packs covered in dust, we looked like aliens as we checked in at the marble reception desk of the lavishly decorated hotel lobby. Inside the room, we literally collapsed. Our knees no longer able to support us, we moved around on all fours for a while, dumping the ant-infested contents of our packs in the bathtub for a good soak. We laughed at ourselves that night until our bellies ached and tears ran from our faces!

The last couple of days we spent relaxing in the city, before making our way home the way we had come. Apart obviously, from the incredible things we got to do and experience, this trip single handedly changed the course of dad and my history together and I immediately knew how special it was, especially in the context of what had happened before. It was the first time in my life that dad and I did things as equals and where he didn't hold back about anything. We talked and laughed and it was as if things had always been this way between us. It is hard to say whether bad things have to occur for good things to happen. But I guess sometimes this is true. It was at least in this instance and we never looked back from there. I still have the videos that dad shot during our trip, his running commentary on all of them. With the old tapes ailing I have long transferred them to digital format and I carry them with me always; a reminder of dad and who he was and how a single act born out of love for his son redeemed both me and saved our relationship.

Whilst things between my parents and me continued to improve, the rest of my life had grown stale in the process of my escapades. I lived in a small town, worked in a small town and night after night saw and talked to the same people. There was no progress in sight and even my hangout with the bikers no longer held the same attraction. I was still heading nowhere and our Malaysia trip had once again opened my eyes to the fact that a whole world lay out there beyond the boundaries of my current environs and company. I think the turning point came when one day working in the kitchen, I heard a commotion in the pub. The sound of smashing plates and furniture being overturned came crashing through the swinging door to the main guest room. Through the small server window, I could see one man aggressively pushing around another, the latter much smaller man clearly just trying not to engage. I quickly recognized the bully as one of the gang members and knew that if left to continue, the situation was not likely to end well. I stepped out into the room and called him by name, asking him to stop but he wouldn't yield. Instead he turned towards me in a flurry of profanities and told me to stay out of it; something which under the circumstances I did not see as an option, as he had begun kicking the other man who was already down on the ground. The rest of the guests were frozen in place, sitting in front of their meals. Conversation had ceased and everyone was holding their breath, but nobody came to the man's aid. To cut a long story short, knowing that some members had a tendency to carry weapons I quickly ran back to the kitchen and retrieved a baseball bat we had stored back there for worst-case scenarios. In the end though I didn't need it. I had been boxing for several years and having thrown each other back and forth a few times I landed a punch that sent him several inches off the ground before collapsing in a heap and getting dragged off premises by one of his companions. There was applause, pats on the back and several rounds of drinks for having saved the day, but I knew that I had done something dangerous. I had knocked out a patched member; an offense that would no doubt eventually have dire consequences as revenge would need to be had. My suspicions were confirmed a day or two later when the second in charge of the gang visited me at the pub at lunchtime and gave me fair warning that the man I had punched would be seeking retribution and that he was known for carrying a knife.

A couple of weeks earlier I had received a letter from an old friend. Originally from New Zealand, her, her brother and I had gone to school together and our parents had remained close friends even after their family had moved back home. She used to be like my sister during those school days and I had always been very fond of her in a brotherly way. In her letter she had said that she somehow sensed I wasn't doing so well and invited me to visit her and her German husband and explore the possibility of living in New Zealand. Given how my life was going, this seemed like a prudent move. I handed in my resignation and packed my bags.

This time I was the one leaving and I think both mum and dad had always known that the "bug" would eventually get to me. Our world there was too small after what I had seen and where we had lived. Dad even threw in $5000 Dollars to help me on the way. The view through the rear window of the taxi the day that I left is something I will never forget. Dad with a painful smile, his arm around mum and her crying, somehow knowing that this was it, that their son finally had left home. I still can't believe how much sorrow I had caused them through the years and still stand in amazement that each of my missteps and hare-brained acts of revolution had always been answered with nothing but love.

The next few years would result in an ironic role reversal, with me writing letters and making phone calls to mum and dad and the two continuing their life back in Germany.

Towards the end of the 90's dad was able to work out that, with the help of the savings schemes he had paid into throughout the years, he could take early retirement without suffering much of a loss as a result of reduced pension. By then his time at the company had taken its toll and I think he was very much looking forward to leaving this part of his life behind. In addition, I had since had a son and they felt they were missing out on life as grandparents. Thus, the decision was made for them to also move to New Zealand and dad began planning the "project" in his usual meticulous manner. The plan was for us to take over a Motel and operate it as a family. Between his various savings schemes, the sale of the house and the hard fought-for payout of the company pension insurance, dad had accumulated a sizable nest egg and between his investment and my hospitality skills, we figured we would not just be successful but also generate a sustainable livelihood for us all.

Soon after mum and dad arrived our broker introduced us to an elderly couple keen to lease out their 10 unit, 3 conference room property set in over 12,000 square meters of perfectly landscaped surrounds, right next to a farm park and other tourist attractions. It seemed perfect for what we were after and everyone brimmed with excitement at our new life as business people.

Mum and dad soon found a house a couple of kilometers away; a single story 3-bedroom with large garden in a quiet neighborhood, just as they had dreamed. Things seemed perfect.

Dad as usual loved keeping busy and between the Motel's expansive lawns, helping out with other aspects of the business and taking care of their own property he was busier than ever, but more happily so. He would spend days on the ride-on lawn mower, neatly trimming the grassy slopes leading up to the highway, often until dusk. In true form, he wasted no time to become active in associations and through his contacts in the local Rotary Club and others our conference business was doing well. Dad even organized an Oktoberfest for the club. We got in a German musician, I produced an original German buffet, and the evening ended up being such a success, that for years after people would come up to dad in the street and ask when there would be an encore. As long as I can remember dad had always had a pair of original Lederhosen, along with a traditional felt hat and other uniquely German accessories, which he would wear with pride on such occasions and which always garnered a lot of interest in German culture. That is when dad was truly in his element again, entertaining people, singing songs, laughing, joking and ensuring everyone was having a good time. The outfit was part of him as much as his gardening gloves and I don't think I could ever look at a traditional outfit without immediately thinking of him as he would stand in the middle of the room, holding speeches, toasting or dancing and laughing as the music played on.

The books for the Motel as it were though, had been thoroughly cooked by the previous owners - more and better than a pot full of Sauerkraut - and so despite the burgeoning conference and events business we were enjoying, profits from the accommodation barely helped break even at the end of each month when the lessors demanded their pound of flesh in the form of rental payments the size of which was in gross dissonance with actual revenue. We were getting by, only just. We all worked from morning until evening and sometimes even during night, when weary travelers occasionally turned off the highway in the wee hours of the morning in search of a place to put their heads down for a while.
The enthusiasm we had all felt just over a year before quickly dissipated and was replaced by the constant fear of whether we would make ends meet. We were of course, but not nearly enough to make our efforts financially meaningful and certainly not in the way the lease had been sold to us.

And then came the one thing that set it all off. The one thing that nobody except our fraud of a broker could have foreseen: One day two men walked into our small reception and identified themselves as representatives of the "crown". The land authority agents were quick to explain that they were there to take first measurements for the planned highway expansion and that this was but a courtesy call to let us know they were starting soon. Flabbergasted at what I had heard I challenged their right to do so, but the level of arrogance and condescension I encountered in return quickly led me to calmly farewell them and take a moment to digest the fact that their demeanor was one of someone who's words are backed by actual authority. To say that we were dismayed at the notion that our tranquil surrounds, the very bit that attracted guests and conferences to the business, was about to be compromised sent cold shivers down my spine. Dad had sunk virtually all that was left of his nest egg into the business. Sure, there were some minor life insurance policies due for payout a few years later, but overall this was pretty much it. This money represented his life's work and investing it for the benefit of us all spoke of his trust in my abilities; something I had longed for so desperately during my youth. Yet in a divine gesture of irony, the very thing that we had hoped to build together was now about to be ripped apart. Many phone calls, sleepless nights, lawyer's appointments and investigative efforts later, the feared facts became reality. Old correspondence and handmade drawings in a property file held by the owner's solicitor showed that the broker had full well known about the upcoming construction. Not only that, but he had deliberately deceived us when we had asked the question during the viewings, stating that but the highway's shoulder may be widened to allow for a footpath at some stage; something we had actually seen a benefit in.

The enormity of the project that the so-called crown now presented to us was far more invasive. Out of the 12,000 square meter, we would be left with less than 5000. More than half our land would be used to add lanes to the highway, as well as a new traffic circle and underpass. In addition, construction would take around 2 years, during which the entire area would be transformed into one big project site and access to and from the property made possible only through temporary makeshift paths. And to top things off, as we were owners of the buildings and chattels only, but had only leased the land, the crown opined we were not entitled to compensation of any sort. All of it would go to the owners instead. Even our claims for loss of business fell on deaf ears. What the crown wanted, it got.

In another ironic twist, our lawyer turned out to be the owner's lawyer. A conflict of interest if ever there was one. Luckily, he could see the validity of our case and eventually managed to get a faction of the overall compensation paid to them by the crown reassigned to us. It was but a pittance though, and laughably small given the amount they were recompensed for a property we were working for them at extortionist rates.

Regardless, what it all amounted to was essentially a death sentence for our business. We were left with three choices: carry on the business and suffer the long costly slope of decline that would lead to financial ruin, sell the business for whatever someone might be prepared to offer or walk away and count our losses. Battling on and walking away were not really options dad or I were willing to entertain at that point either and so we decided to try and sell. Naturally, now that the crown had laid down the plans and a timeline for the project we could no longer hide the fact like our broker had done before and would have to give full disclosure, which in turn meant tipping any potential deal in the favor of the buyer. Buying the property from us would be an act of mercy and only someone with no knowledge of the industry or finances would be dumb enough to even consider putting their money into such a lame duck.

Yet people like this apparently do exist and within a few weeks of anxious waiting and praying for an expression of interest our broker came up with a guy willing to take a look. We polished and cleaned, patched up paint and made the place look like it was ready for a presidential inspection. Before long, the day arrived where the potential buyer would come for a first viewing. Waiting for him on that day was a real nail-biter and I don't think dad or I slept for days ahead of the viewing. This was do or die, the lucky escape from the clutches of slow financial erosion or the fall of the axe. No other buyers, not even a few "nibbles" had been forthcoming and none were expected after what had been extensive efforts to generate interest.

The day came and finally a tall man in his 50s, well built, with a big potbelly stepped out of an expensive sedan in front of reception. After him came his tiny Filipino wife and their young daughter, following in his footsteps, which he took with almost regal authority. First impressions never lie and this was a man, who clearly thought highly of himself and had ultimate trust in his own abilities. He barely listened to what we were telling him that day, spending his time poking his nose into this room and that, paying only vague attention to the information we were providing to him. Much to our delight, even during the walk around the property, which led squarely across the land claimed by the crown and during which we explained the plans in the exact words the government agents had relayed the project to us, he never so much as flinched and even looked like he was tempted to laugh off our concerns. He was very sure he knew everything there was to know and we didn't, as simple as that. But hey, we didn't have to like him, we needed to sell! We briefly showed him the architectural drawings, which naturally belied the actual invasiveness of the process over the following two years and as is often the case somewhat embellished how things were to look after completion. Obviously, the fact the project had put us, the seller on the back foot and it was clear to see that we had no desire to stick around for the construction. We couldn't afford to look desperate, but we needed to sell to this man, come rain or shine, come the crown or even Queen herself.

The viewing didn't last long and we sighed a collective sigh of relief as their sedan pulled away and disappeared onto the highway.

Within a few days, the unthinkable happened: he made an offer! Our initial excitement at the news though quickly turned to disbelief when we saw what was on the table. His offer was below half of what dad had invested. Out of over $450,000 dad had put into the business, we were to get $180,000 thousand back if we accepted, minus fees and other deductibles.

Dad was very quiet during that time. I can only imagine what went through his head. We were in shock. What had started out on the premise of new beginnings was about to be crushed, the fruits of dad's lifelong hard work about to be slashed into less than half with the stroke of a pen. Looking back at how dementia works in many cases and how early onset is often triggered by such traumatic events but evades diagnosis for many years after, I can see how this was the second such incident that ultimately would have contributed to dad's illness. The first time, he nearly lost his company pension and had prevailed only at enormous emotional cost. But this time he would lose no matter what and we both knew it. For dad it was as if life itself was suddenly in freefall. He who had built safety net after safety net to ensure a prosperous, comfortable and long retirement, now found himself sitting night after night with a calculator, working out how much mum and him might have left for the rest of their lives and pondering why and where in all of this his well-developed ability to flawlessly plan had deserted him. The anguish and guilt I felt were beyond words and the hatred for both our broker and the landlords was immeasurable. We were hogtied, helpless, betrayed. And whether rightfully or wrongfully so, I felt deeply responsible for our, for dad's misfortune. The whole matter actually drove me to the edge of suicide. My marriage had long become more of a dutiful connection, bound by the routines of everyday life and the need to raise my son and our outlooks on life and our aspirations had slowly become irreconcilably different over the years. Now that the business was about to go down the drain things fell apart on that end as well.

Yet again, dad and I, much like before when I was younger, never sat down and talked about how we felt. Sure, we expressed anger and disappointment during our business meetings to find a way out, a magic bullet to solve our problems, but we spent of those dark hours brooding and despairing by ourselves, no matter that we felt the same. The only difference this time round was that we were in it together; we had become a dad and son unit, one that had trust at its base. Perhaps therefore these talks weren't quite as critical as they would have been the years prior. We now understood each other better. But I still wished dad had opened up more. The stress of the situation was plain to see in his face, but we were both so absorbed in misery, that neither was able to reach across.

The worst moment for me came driving along the highway one day, contemplating my failure as a son. My failure to protect dad's aspirations and dreams for his retirement and having let him down yet again in the process. Mum has always insisted that dad never felt that way and dad certainly never gave so much as an inkling that he might have, but that didn't matter. I had wanted to shine for dad, show him I could achieve; no, more than that, I could show him I could be as good as he was during his professional days. And yet I had failed him again. I felt worthless, an utter waste of space. I saw the pillar of an overpass approaching and was determined to aim for it and end it all. A suitable punishment for my failure and surely a blessing I thought, so deep was the shame I felt at that moment. It was only at the last second that with all my power I forced my hands not to turn the wheel towards the concrete pillar. The vehicle passed under the bridge and a flood of tears streamed down my face. I pulled over and completely broke down that day. Once again, nothing was ever the same after this. And yet, much to my amazement and contrary to what I had been telling myself, my relationship with dad didn't suffer. Instead, it perhaps grew even stronger. We quietly shared this devastating defeat and never really spoke of it. The scars ran deep for both of us.

The papers were soon drawn up and we sold the Motel to the big man and his little entourage.

As expected, they did not fare very well and soon began making noises about compensation claims and lawsuits, but nothing of the sort ever eventuated. We never looked back and over time even the pangs in the pit of my stomach each time I drove past the property along the freshly built highway expansion, subsided.

It was as close as it has ever been and likely ever will be that I have come to suicide or in fact murder (our landlord). Some say time heals all wounds. I don't necessarily believe in that. With some, I think we just put on thicker bandages.

I am certain that the experience caused dad to examine his priorities in life, perhaps even his life's path itself. Either way, in the years immediately following he became much more relaxed about just about everything. Sure he was still quite pedantic when it came to mowing the lawns, creating schedules for DIY projects and continued to organize events at the tennis club and volunteered at the Rotary club, where his dedication, planning ability and logistical skills earned him both recognition and awards, but being forced to sell the business and in the process losing much of his savings I think had caused him to let go of certain things. Hard to put a finger on it, but I think it may have been the realization that everything, no matter how well planned, was still impermanent and ultimately subject to events outside the realm of his control.

Which is also why I guess he ended up focusing on the things he *could* create *and* control, like his garden, ever-present home improvements and the likes. While it is hard to say whether the change in him had come as a result of an epiphany or they were the first, and virtually unnoticeable signs of his illness, is not for me to say. It is all too easy to interpret the past and wrongfully so at that, based on what color goggles one chooses to wear and I don't want to do dad the injustice. He has suffered enough of the latter.

Following the trauma of the business sale, dad and my relationship endured. I took on a new career, separated from my wife and moved to Wellington. I would still visit on the weekends and dad and I would spend most holidays and many weekends together. We would still go on the occasional hike and dad took up mountain biking with a group of his rotary friends; not a small feat, now that he was in his mid-sixties. His life became simple, uncomplicated and finally, from what I could tell, enjoyable the way he had wanted it to be.

Sometimes friends or acquaintances from Germany would visit and mum and dad would host them, with dad becoming their instant tour guide of the local attractions like parliament, the Wellington cable car, Mount Victoria and others. Over several German travel seasons which normally fell smack in the middle of New Zealand summer, he became so good at it that he could do the standard tour almost with his eyes closed and was always eager to provide facts, figures and anecdotes about their new chosen home 'downunder'. Mum, too, was more at ease with their life now and things began to look like real retirement, apart from dad's relentless drive to stay active of course.

During our time in the Motel we had gotten a puppy, a huntaway cross, as I had always harbored the desire to again have a dog around and relive some of the fond memories I had of the old "Flokati" companion from my youth. With the sale and my separation there was little room in my life for the dog now and I dreaded to make the same mistakes that I still sorely regretted. Oddly enough, mum and dad welcomed the dog and over time it became dad's closest buddy. The two would go on long beach walks, play ball in the yard and sit next to each other on the couch watching TV in the evening. It was a lovable dog and totally dedicated, especially to my son. Watching the two grow up together evoked memories of yesteryear, not just for me, but for mum and dad also. Looking at the two rolling around on the floor and chasing each other around the yard was as if history – the good parts - repeated itself; a glimpse into a time capsule of very happy days. Even dad now got into the midst of it. Now as a grandfather, with all the pressures of working life and the painful burden of keeping the company or the business alive lifted he could be the father he had perhaps always wished he could have been when I was little; a change and role that would became even more prevalent with the professional change I was about to make. After the business debacle, I had changed careers from hospitality to security and had made the transition rather successfully, ending up as a security coordinator and later analyst for the American Embassy for a number of years. Having gained the necessary acumen, I was lucky enough to secure a contract with the Australians as a security advisor in crisis-torn Timor Leste. I would finally step into the overseas contract shoes of my father and I was quite proud of it. The contract came with a handsome monthly salary, something that had always eluded me and I think dad was truly proud of me, or at least that is the impression I got from a man who still rarely verbalized his feelings. I think me finally coming into my own gave him a sense of relief. I don't believe he considered his job done until I would do so, probably not least since several situations had arisen well beyond my 18<sup>th</sup> birthday where he had bailed me out of a pickle, readily each time and without questions asked.

I think it was mum and her tendency to react to everything on an emotional level first and rationally second, and the importance she places on making sure everyone in the family not just *feels* one way or another, but the fact that she will not relent in her questions until one articulates one's feelings in great detail, that slowly, eventually caused my father to open up, becoming better at expressing his own feelings over time. Initially hugs from dad were still a bit awkward and his "I love you" always rushed and not as confident and clear as his usual speech. But mum certainly stayed on the case and eventually he would express his love for me openly and with a big smile on his face or say it clearly over the phone and I cannot put in words the feeling it gave me when he did. It was something I miss hearing today more than anything. There is a photo of dad at a café, smiling broadly into the camera as he leans over a cup of coffee. It captures his essence so well, that we even used it for the little pamphlet we had made for people attending his funeral. The glint in his eyes that it managed to capture was a testament to the irrepressible joy that he would radiate in those happy moments.

During the next few years working for the Australian Embassy in East Timor, I would take every opportunity to come home and see mum and dad and each return felt like a celebration of life as the very nature of my work often brought me face to face with the uglier side of humanity, in a country that was still reeling from a recent crisis. In addition to better pay and position, I think the move also meant that by going through a similar period of my life as dad had when he worked in Indonesia, we both now understood each other even better. After all, some insights in life are revealed only once you walk in someone else's shoes. This was one of those occasions. I tried to time my returns so that I would be present for birthdays and holidays and the times we spent together were always more than special. Despite the challenges of work, the fact that I no longer struggled from paycheck to paycheck and was able to not just pay my own way, but now occasionally buy or do nice things for mum and dad to some extent made me feel redeemed a little and I thoroughly enjoyed seeing dad happy with where I was going.

Over Christmas, we would have barbecues almost daily and dad even relinquished his hold on the pole position: controlling the barbecue and cooking the meats. He had done so for as long as I can remember and usually only taken a step back when social commitments during parties had meant he wasn't able to tend to it himself.

But now he freely handed over, standing next to me with a glass of wine in his hand and chit chatting while I was grilling the steaks. And afterwards, without a word, he would clean the grill and restore it to pristine condition. It was still his baby and although he had come around to sharing when it came to cooking, meticulous maintenance was still something he would have never entrusted to anybody else; rightfully so perhaps as I have never had his eye for detail and his level of perseverance when it came to matters of getting things picture perfect. I guess that had been and for the rest of our lives would remain as the big difference between dad and I: I was a "good enough" kind of guy whereas in his eyes "good enough" went against everything he had stood for most of his life and an thus attitude he could never approve of, let alone taken on board. But I think he, too, knew this and had for the better part accepted it as a point of difference between himself and his once wayward son and as a result was now able to look past it in favor of appreciating the relationship we had come to develop. But cleaning the barbecue or similar tasks would remain his domain for as long as he lived, or at least until he became ill.

The other benefit of my overseas contract was that finally I could do for dad what he had done for me back in 1993 and so in 2009 I organized another "no holds barred" holiday for dad, my son and I. I met both in Bali before taking them with me to Timor Leste so that they could experience the environment I had written and talked so much about. We attended "Australia Day" celebrated by the expats and resident troops in a big beach event. Dad met the ambassador, my colleagues and friends and we had an incredible time drinking beer and watching the armed forces play cricket. We went on a one-day scuba diving excursion with a barbecued lunch, organized by my good friends Ann and Wayne, the owners of Dili's Free Flow Diving Company. Although sadly, dad was not able to cope with the heavy equipment at that stage anymore, he enjoyed swimming, roaming the beach, and watching one of the many documentary crews Ann and Wayne frequently hosted. We munched on freshly grilled Tandoori chicken, played with the resident tame potbelly pigs that were always up for a snack and had an all-round unforgettable day. Next, I rented a four wheel drive vehicle and we drove inland taking in the coastal landscape from viewpoints in the hills and snacking on local fare offered at roadside markets. For lunches, we visited all the places I had told dad about. Indonesian fare was always dad's favorite and we dug into goat sate and spicy grilled fish at every opportunity. For dinner we would eat at some of the better restaurants owned by expats I had come to know as friends over the past couple of years and we sat with them drinking beers, with dad listening to their stories and reveling in the atmosphere. We attended bar nights at the hotel, listened to live music, and got a little drunk over one to many Australian Four X beers. Dad and my son were staying in my small two-bedroom place at the hotel where I had taken up residence for the remainder of my contract. It was close quarters but our three generations got on like a house on fire. It was almost like a sequel to dad's and my journey back in 1993, only that that could probably never be surpassed and even trying to do so would be next to impossible.

A few days later, we flew back to Bali where among other things we went river rafting; quite a scary experience as I sat behind dad, holding him by his life vest as the rocking boat and raging torrents threatened to throw us overboard. It was at that moment that I realized for the first time that physically dad was no longer the man he once was. He remained active, sure, and could probably have still out-cycled me any day of the week, but age had certainly begun to take a hold; something he probably would have never admitted to but which was definitely the case on this occasion. For the first time in my life it felt as if part of the reigns dad had held all my life, were slowly being handed to me.

I had watched my grandparents age of course. But then again grandparents are supposed to be old and I had never given age a second thought, not even when they passed on. It was what grandparents did eventually and something many of my classmates and friends had gone through just as I had. But by some naïve notion I had never even thought of the possibility, let alone the reality that the same was true for most of us: that we would age and that what was once strong and youthful would eventually give way to old age and frailty. Of course dad was far from frail at the still relatively young age of almost 70 then, but the few signs of age that started shining through on that trip, as subtle as they were and as much as dad's energy and refusal to yield belied them, weighed heavy on my heart.

The rest of the trip we visited wildlife parks, rode on the back of elephants and ate Indonesian food from local stalls wherever we could, something where dad was always truly in his element, often reminiscing about his time in East Kalimantan over a plate of Rendang or Sambal crab.

It was a fantastic holiday and the first and unfortunately last time our three generations ever went on a trip together.

After my separation and divorce mum and dad had taken my son on various overseas trip, with dad in the process, as much as it pains me to admit, becoming a father to my son much more than I had ever been, but time never again allowed for the three of us to travel together.

Following my time in East Timor, I was able to secure another contract with the Australians, this time in Nairobi, Kenya, and thus my work led me even further afield, with regular returns becoming more difficult.

The previous year an unfortunate incident had taken place, whereby our beloved dog and dad's close companion in a quirk of character had bit dad on his throat, piercing the skin and causing not a grievous wound but a wound nevertheless. She, too, had aged and with it her character had begun to change. I happened to be visiting when the incident occurred and it was a frightful experience which unfortunately broke all trust between us and the poor animal. My parents had loved her as much as I had and she had become a family member much like our original family dog that had been with us throughout my childhood.

But now she was scared somehow and becoming increasingly paranoid and the incident was something we simply could not let stand. My son was still young and it was feared that next time either he, dad or mum might not be so lucky.

We all knew what needed to be done, but neither dad nor mum had the heart to do it and so it fell to me to once again make the heartbreaking trip to the vet to have her put to sleep. It was as if a time tunnel had suddenly opened up and I was right back at that moment in Germany all these years ago, reliving the pain and anguish, the utter sense of despair I had felt the day I had made the same trip with my beloved, but troubled dog then.

I know in my heart that it was the right decision, but as with many of life's hardest decisions, knowing something is right doesn't necessarily come with self-absolution and a tattoo with her name on my lower leg is a symbol or my internal struggle to reconcile the two even today.

Unlike back in Germany though, when mum and dad had sworn off getting another dog, within less than two weeks another, this time eerily identical one to the one we had just had to euthanize, was in the house and the pain of loss was quickly turned into love for the new arrival. Once again true to form and although I could see how much the incident had hurt him, dad and I never spoke about the events after and as again he never expressed how he felt.

Around the same time, mum and dad had begun the process of selling their house; a giant step for the two, who had loved it immensely since they had bought it shortly after their arrival in New Zealand in the late 90's. Dad's green thumb was visible all over the property. He had spent years cultivating and transforming the large, but previously rather neglected garden into something that even passers-by would stop and behold. He loved his fern corner where he had created a small piece of native bush, along with the long flowerbeds that lined the fence and the small vegetable patch out the back near the garden shed. Year after year he would sit at the computer and read about native plants and their requirements, carefully plan new garden projects and take great satisfaction from the creations that would go on to flourish as a result of his gardening skills. And yet, ever so slowly and barely noticeable, the kingdom that was his garden had started to take more out of him than he was still able to give. Along with the maintenance demands of the large property, which exceeded their needs for living space, it became evident that within a few years the house they had adored for so long would become a burden at first and eventually unmanageable. Dad, as ever, was quite pragmatic about it while mum quietly worried about what their future might hold and they thus soon made the decision to find a new, much smaller place. I think this is something I still admire about dad today: Where other men of his caliber would probably have closed their eyes to the reality of the toll that age takes on all of us, dad's eyes were fully open to it and instead of trying to fight the inevitable, he acknowledged it and adjusted accordingly. Where others may have seen defeat, dad saw new opportunities to create, a new project to tackle, which would instead reinvigorate and enrich their lives. He simply carried on. They soon found a small two-bedroom townhouse with its own, much smaller garden and dad wasted no time to completely remodel it, just as he had done with the gardens of every house they had owned.

Dad seemed happy to have a new challenge, and with less time needed to maintain the property, he now focused on his other hobbies like cycling, playing tennis, managing the tennis club bar, lawn bowls, daily walks along the beach to collect drift wood for his garden, and of course watch every sports tournament under the sun, often into the wee hours of the morning.

Dad had a seemingly limitless supply of energy, it was merely his body that began to let him down here and there, and aches and sprains became part of daily life. He mentioned them, but never complained and mum spent days and weeks at a time nursing the injuries he continued to self-inflict on account of his "never give up" approach to whatever he did.

In fact, if there was one trait, one characteristic that defined dad, it was his capacity to do whatever he had set his mind on to the extreme, stopping only if either successful or defeated by his own body. There were times this would drive mum nuts, but it was his dogged determination that had made him who he was, and which even later as he became sick would be the last thing to go, literally. Whatever dad had in mind, dad pursued without compromise.

Meanwhile it was as a period of change for me also. I had stepped out of government contracts and started working for humanitarian agencies, covering operations in conflict zones and other insecure contexts in East Africa and other parts of the world. I had met and soon got married to my intelligent and beautiful wife in Kenya, her family welcoming me with open arms. For all intents and purposes and despite my international work, it looked like Kenya would become my new home. Life had been turbulent, but at last and although thousands of kilometers away from mum and dad, it had somewhat stabilized. I deeply regretted not being able to have both

99

there for my wedding in Nairobi and my then fiancé and I spent many a night weighing up whether to hold it back in New Zealand. In the end though much of the family and friends were in Kenya and mum and dad, despite their desire to attend, simply could fathom neither the long journey, nor giving their dog, their "second child" to a kennel for the duration.

Instead, we both visited them soon after the wedding and it was an amazingly joyous occasion to see dad sparkle as he embraced his daughter-in-law and my parents pulled out all the stops in welcoming and spending time with us. Dad took an instant liking to Sharon and the two got along like a house on fire, with dad showing off the various mementos and sharing many stories of his former life of travel. I could see he truly loved her like a father and it breaks my heart that they had so little time together before things took a turn for the worse.

Even in the later stages of his dementia, when at times he failed to recognize even mum or me, her name still produced a faint smile and when we visited him at the rest home his eyes always glowed in recognition of her face.

In mid-2012 something occurred that mum believes was a key trigger for dad's illness and looking back I actually agree with her, as dad was never the same again after.

They had been receiving their pension from Germany for years without issues and despite the financial setbacks suffered along the way, mum and dad were doing just fine, finally enjoying their hard earned retirement. Unbeknownst to them though, fat cat bureaucrats in Berlin in their infinite wisdom had at some point decided to pass regulations, which would impose income tax on all pensions. They had done so without as much as notifying any of the thousands upon thousands of German pensioners that now lived abroad. Until one day several years later, that is. A stern letter arrived, advising my parents of their failure to meet tax obligations no one had ever bothered to advise them of before, in the same breath demanding back tax payment of over 35,000 Euros.

In the generation they had grown up, if the government wanted something you complied, no question asked. You didn't question, you didn't protest and you certainly didn't try to evade.

And it was in that mindset, which still very much prevailed with mum and dad, that the letter and its demand were received as something they had no choice but to comply with.

The authorities might as well have stabbed dad in the heart.

With the opening of that envelope their savings, the last bit of what remained of their funds, which dad had managed as if his life depended on it, not least because it somewhat did, would be scooped up and pocketed by the state, never to be seen again.

They needed it to prop up their pension, to maintain the house, to keep life the way it was.

After a lifetime of saving, working and fighting hard for where they were now, the threat of their remaining years spent unable to make ends meet opened up right in front of them like a black hole. They were devastated. Dad was barely able to speak. In her emails mum expressed how worried she was about dad's health, and the way the stress of the situation caused his blood pressure to spike.

They spent days and weeks researching and gathering all manner of information related to their plight. It was a time that zapped dad of much of his strength and perhaps even to some extent broke his will to live at one point or another.

After months of anxious communication, exchanges, letters, and engagement of specialized tax accountants and attorneys, in December 2012 mum and dad then finally received a letter advising them that they were not liable after all and that all they had to pay was a small penalty for late submission of some documents.

Although both their and my relief was tremendous, the damage had been done and the whole affair had left an indelible imprint on dad.

After his passing, when we tidied up his files and his computer we found that much of the order and organizational talent he had maintained for years and which he was known for by all, had given way to confusion much earlier than his physical symptoms had indicated. In fact, I am now convinced that the very beginnings of the full onset lay in these events of 2012, almost a full year prior to their first physical manifestation.

And then, one day in August 2013, it all began. None of us knew, least of all dad, what would happen in the course of the next three years and the deluge of sorrow that was about to descend on our little family.

You could say there was life before and then there was life after August 2013. And bastard Lewy made sure the one after would never again resemble the one before.

Mum had always been the communicator, writing letters and greeting cards to friends both abroad and in New Zealand and keeping me updated through regular emails about their lives and whatever new developments were happening in their community. When called to the phone during one of my calls from wherever I was at the time, dad would always stay somewhat factual. He preferred live conversations and therefore usually had mum, who had much more of a knack for telephone chats update him on developments. He always finished his turn on the receiver with "Na dann, mach's mal gut Junge. Ich hab' Dich lieb" ("Ok then, so long boy. I love you"). He also rarely wrote.

And in turn, much like she did on that fateful day as well, mum would continue to keep me updated about their situation, first here and there and then daily as dad declined and I continued to weigh the need to maintain our livelihood against the need to return and support them back home.
It was a constant balancing act for several years, one hard decision after the other. Whether they were right or wrong is not for me to judge. It is but for dad to determine. One day perhaps, I will see him again and it will surely be one of the first things I will ask, because it is a question that will weigh on me for the rest of my life. But I am leaping ahead.

Mum's regular emails and skype messages now form a voluminous body, a quasi-journal of dad's illness from beginning to end. I have searched the internet time and time again, read articles and blogs, watched documentaries and reviewed similar publications narrating the journey of dementia patients, of loved ones going down the same long and rocky road that dad's illness would end up following. Many of them describe the onset and course of the condition in great detail, but most stop at a certain point, usually when it comes to hospitalization and those last tough miles that the families must endure before being released from the clutches of this cruel, malevolent ailment.

I understand why they stop short of describing these details. After all, these are intimate, highly personal moments over weeks and months. The suffering endured by patients in the end stages is not something that is easy to talk about and even harder to put into written words. Perhaps it is also a prospect best left hidden from many, who at the beginning of the Lew Body Dementia rollercoaster still live in hope and blissful ignorance of the last stretches that bastard Lewy ultimately keeps in store. During the late stages we noticed that even nurses and doctors never gave us the full picture of what they already knew to be the end game, as if to spoon-feed us each piece of bad news in order to not let us choke on the many traumatic events they knew were to come.

But when it was over, it became clear to me that denying us the gift of insight into a future already known to the professionals, they had achieved the opposite to what they perhaps had aimed to achieve. Instead of allowing us the time, while we still had time, to come to terms with the full horror that awaited dad and us, they condemned us, with the best intentions, to a death by a thousand cuts made by piecemeal information and avoidance of hard truths.

My emotional constitution has never been the strongest and I must admit that I have been known to cry when faced with events of far lesser magnitude, but I have always preferred to hear a hard truth, than to endure endless tip-toeing around it. I also believe I am not alone in this.

It is therefore, that I decided to translate these journal entries, originally written in German and put them together into one volume for those who might be at the beginning, or somewhere along their own journey with arch enemy Lewy Body; so that they may gain strength from knowing the hard truth and prepare themselves and their loved ones for it; a privilege unfortunately for the most part denied to both us and dad.

# Part II - The Rollercoaster

## Chapter 1 - TIA

"Nothing is more frightening than a fear you cannot name."

— Cornelia Funke

31/07/2013

"Dear Son,

Unfortunately, today I have something troubling to tell you:
Around lunchtime, just before midday, dad said he didn't know what
was happening, but he felt extremely dizzy. His face and head were
very red. I got him to sit down and got the little blood pressure
monitor…it showed 190 over 110! I immediately called the doctor
and asked whether I should call an ambulance, but they said we
should instead head to the practice instead. So we went straight away
and they asked a lot of questions, even about his parents and their
medical history etc. Dad is now on diuretics. They do this to alleviate
potential water retention. Our GP is still on holiday but he returns on
Tuesday. Now we will have to go for a blood sample and we will
discuss results next week. Of course, we are changing our eating
habits a bit. Dad doesn't want any coffee at the moment anyway.
And no alcohol. Together we will surely get his blood pressure down.
This evening already it is a little lower. Please don't worry, but I
thought I need to tell you about it. As I said, it will be Ok. We look
after each other. I will keep you posted."

*Upon receiving the news I somehow knew that things weren't going well at all –*
*probably worse than her letter disclosed, especially considering mum's lifelong*
*propensity to protect me from bad news by downplaying adverse events and instead*
*blanketing them in words of optimism. Dad had been seriously ill all but perhaps*
*twice in his life and even then they had been physical injuries, in one instance*
*resulting in blood poisoning. This was something different and unheard of, despite*

*the close calls with blood pressure he had had the year before during their brush with the German taxman.*

*I booked a flight and as it turned out my arrival was timely:*
*The couple of days that it took to arrange my return trip from Kenya, was all it took for matters to get much worse: While I was on my way dad suffered an episode.*
*Much like a few days prior, he started feeling faint and dizzy while retrieving something from the garage. Mum had come to his aid but was unable to stop him from passing out on the floor. The ambulance was called and he was hospitalized overnight for observation.*
*Something sinister had officially announced its arrival. But it would be months and more until anybody, including the doctors would finally be able to shine a light on it. For now though the questions far outweighed the answers and we were all very much afraid as a result.*
*I spent the next 10 days with my parents, to observe and to make sure everything was as good as it could. I accompanied dad to the doctor and to his other appointments as they were trying to figure out what was happening with him. He, too, looked worried although when prompted he would brush off any concerns with a silly joke or two. He was not the kind of man to give in to fear; fear I am sure he, too, felt.*
*The diagnosis was eventually a TIA, a Transient Ischemic Attack: caused by a temporary disruption in the blood supply to part of the brain, usually by a small and temporary blood clot, resulting in a lack of oxygen to the brain. Dad had struggled with varicose veins on the back of his leg for a number of years and we figured either these or simply his eating habits had been the culprit. Prognosis was good and the doctor said it was a common occurrence with most patients making a full recovery without any further issues. Dad received blood thinners, watched what he ate and both he and mum carried on.*

15/08/2013

"Dear Son,

…We asked the practice several time whether dad can still drive the car and they promised each time (4 times!) they would get back to us. Until now, we have had no information, but I am following up. Dad had enough of waiting and drove to the gym to speak with the trainers there. He would love to go there again regularly. The owner is also a physiotherapist. Dad brought back a long questionnaire,

105

which we'll fill in today. He also needs approval from the doctor as well as his own physiotherapist. It is a ray of hope for dad that he now knows exactly what he needs to do: two to three times to the gym each week and then walk Rosy [the dog] on the other days. Some of my friends told me that their husbands, too, have had a TIA. It is incredible how many people have had one. Even Aunt Marlene in Germany, upon hearing about dad, immediately told me about quite a few cases in her neighborhood.

I now bought a pill organizer for all the medication and I helped dad with it and explained everything carefully, just to be sure we don't forget one or the other medicine…"

15/05/2013

"Dear Son,

Just a quick update: Dad just got the Ok from the doctor to drive! It was a relief for him and we straight away drove to shop for carpets…"

16/08/2013

"Now I can finally write. It is just after 4pm now. There was one earthquake after the other today (Strength 6.7, 6.2 etc. down to 3.8 and back to 5.8). Dad was out walking and thought he had had a second stroke. He was very depressed of course. He didn't know it was an earthquake and he was barely able to walk straight. Of course, there was huge relief when he found out the cause and that it wasn't what he had thought. But at that moment he felt as he had two weeks ago when the TIA started…"

17/08/2013

"Today we had a somewhat eventful day. After getting up in the morning dad sat at the breakfast table and said he felt exactly the way he had two weeks ago. I took his blood pressure, it was ok, but he had an unnaturally red complexion. This time I called the ambulance immediately and when I described the symptoms, they came straight away, arriving only 10 minutes later. It was 9.15am. The paramedics checked dad over thoroughly and opined it may be best to take him to hospital. Of course, we were all rather anxious.

Dad was transported lying down and TJ [my son] went with him. At the hospital they again checked dad over for hours, including a CAT scan (luckily we didn't have to pay the $1,600 they normally charge, as it was an emergency covered by public health). They now suspect that dad did not have a TIA as originally thought, but instead an actual stroke. But we will only find out conclusively next week, when they will do an MRI.

Now it's just after 5pm and we are again at home. We've eaten something and are able to slowly calm down. Until all results are in dad has been advised against driving, but he can go for walks (nothing vigorous) and live as normally as possible. I will do the driving and walk with him, so that he feels safer during his walks.

I am quite angry that our GP's practice didn't instruct for him to be tested at the hospital straight away, but there is no point in getting agitated anymore, we are looking ahead and try to "stay cool". In some way the treatment at the hospital was a relief for dad, as he felt well taken care of among all the examinations and questions.

The neighbors also showed us a lot of affection and brought flowers. Of course, nobody in our little street had missed the big ambulance. It was quite an overwhelming day.

Dear son, we know we probably caused you a lot of anxiety, but we had promised to report what is happening. Right now, all is Ok and dad and I are getting on with things just fine. As I said, for now it's important for dad that he gets the right treatment so things can improve and I think he felt genuinely touched by the outpour of empathy from everyone around. I wish I had nicer things to write about. But again, as for now all is Ok."

19/08/2013

"To bad I missed your call as I was out thanking neighbors for the flowers.

Dad had a very good day yesterday. He went for a walk (he understands that he should not exceed half an hour per day) and then he spent the rest of the day gardening. The fresh air helped him immensely.

Also one of our neighbors visited. She had had a stroke some time ago. She now pops in here and there and talks about her experiences. These talks are lifting dad's spirits, and he is determined to do everything to recover. The day yesterday really motivated us. We start each day afresh and make new plans. We even spoke with your cousin, who as you know is a nurse. He, too, is giving us advice and explains the odd thing or two we don't quite understand. We will scan all the hospital reports and he will try to find out more, although it is all in English anyway. Most of it are scientific descriptions and formulas, like a secret language we can't decode. He will be of great help though, I'm sure.

My friend Beatrice is an optometrist, but she had originally studied general medicine so has a little knowledge about these things as well. I had a very good chat to her also. She said dad's former team members from the tennis club are worried as they haven't heard from him for some time, but we won't tell them just yet. Only once we have the final results will we do so. But in any case, all the empathy makes dad feel much better…"

20/08/2013

"Thank you so much for your call earlier, which did us a lot of good. The depression which dad has at times now is part of the overall course of such an illness (stroke), but I am doing everything I can to get him out of it again whenever it happens. I have some experience with my sister in these matters. Today it lasted through the morning, but became better as the afternoon went on. And since we know where the depression is coming from, we are much better able to address it. Please do not worry yourself; we will get a handle on it…"

22/08/2013

"Thank you again for your phone call, which we really appreciate very much as always und which means a lot to us. They are the highlight of the day for dad. Today was a good day, even though it didn't start out that way. It rained heavily in the morning and dad was a little bit, just a little, depressed. But after we watched some Formula 1 and talked about the race and did our morning puzzle from the paper, I was able to convince dad to go shopping with me. Dad liked coming along and it was a good way to get him out and about again among people. We also went to the library and after a bit of hesitation dad got interested in some books and so we took out a whole bunch of them. I was extremely happy that dad showed such interest. Later, a friend from the tennis club visited and gave dad a card signed by all of his friends, along with some homemade fudge as a present. They were both engrossed in conversation, which again was great for dad! And then your call…dad is being spoiled. I am happy for him…."

25/08/2013

"…We had a beautiful summer day. 19 degrees. Dad and I prepared lunch together and then dad did some gardening. He rests intermittently and I make sure he doesn't overdo it, but by now even dad knows himself that for the moment he still can't keep working non-stop. Health-wise dad is doing quite well, here and there he gets a little dizzy, but pretty much only when he stands or works for too long without taking a break. He has to find his own rhythm for work again. His blood pressure has normalized. Of course, we can't expect everything to instantly return to the way it was before. It takes time. But we are happy that things are looking up and progressing. Even the sadness, the depression is a thing of the past, which I am especially happy about…That was pretty much it from our Sunday – Dad is just watching a crime series "Pater Brown" and is reading a book during the commercial breaks. He must like it because he hasn't gotten stuck into reading that much for a long time. A good sign, isn't it?"

26/08/2013

"Thank you for all the attempts at calling us and your mail which I just received. Our day started as usual: Breakfast, Coffee, and then Norbert took his diuretics and a little later I took his blood pressure. We were surprised that suddenly it was only 88 over 65. By now, I no longer sit and wait of course and so I called the practice straight away at 8 o'clock and asked what to do. I have to say, our GP's clinic is really very good. First they gave me advice on what to do as the doctor hadn't arrived yet. A little while later, we got a call telling dad to stop taking the diuretics. He is instead supposed to take a lot of liquids and otherwise rest up and not do anything strenuous at all. The doctor advised that we should come and see him on Wednesday morning. Right now, I am watching dad like a hawk. He keeps getting dizzy, but our neighbor (the one with the stroke) called and told us that with her these dizzy spells lasted for months before they subsided. Of course dad wanted to bring out the rubbish bins and do some gardening as well, and so I had to get a little firm with him and explained that these things are just not possible today. Eventually he relented. The doctor said that as soon as the blood pressure normalizes he may continue with things as usual. Just not today. Instead, we watched TV and played Scrabble. Early afternoon the pressure was again a little high. I am happy we have the Scrabble game, and as we make up our own rules Dad often laughs out loud. A good sign, isn't it? And since his pressure had been low, he was allowed to drink a strong coffee, which he enjoyed, I think. Now in the evening everything seems Ok again. Blood pressure 128 over 81. We assume these variances were the result of the diuretics…"

4/09/2013

"This afternoon we received a letter from the hospital in which they advised that dad's MRI appointment is on 18 September. Dad and I are of course very relieved, that finally they found an appointment slot for him. Accordingly we are in high spirits, despite the recurring winter weather, which is not very pleasant at the moment…"

7/10/2013

"…Thank you so much for the birthday surprise. I read out your email to dad straight away and he was very happy. We are now eagerly waiting for the book to arrive, which was a surprise for dad as he didn't know I had told you about it. Today dad mowed the lawn again for the first time and after that worked in the garden for a long time. And he felt good doing so. It's still a little strenuous since he hasn't worked out for the last two months, but he is elated that he is back to normal. He just has to push himself to write emails again, which he is determined to do. As promised I will write to you as soon as we are back from the doctor's appointment tomorrow…"

8/10/2013

"We just got back from the doctor's and a good lunch after that. The MRI report confirmed that dad did not have a TIA, but instead a stroke, all be it a rather mild one. The stroke originated in the center of the brain and the doctor explained in simple terms that it was the same as an accident at an intersection that connect several main roads. Nobody knows where the blood pressure variations come from, but the doctor doesn't want to start with heavy medication. Instead, he wants to observe dad for the next 4 weeks. I am sending emails to his practice each week with the blood pressure values so that he is informed. If these remain high, we have to go back. Otherwise dad should resume living a normal life, even playing Petanque found the doctor's approval and dad should socialize a lot in order to keep busy and distracted. In a nutshell, there are no real constraints on everyday life. Of course, he is not supposed to overexert himself, but he can manage that quite well by now. All physical activities are good and the doctor also commended us on playing games together every day like Sudoku, Scrabble, and other Computer and memory games. You know I, too, feel that dad is doing much better. We just have to watch the blood pressure. According to the doctor, dad also has to learn not to let news, good or bad, excite him too much or let them eat away at him and instead perhaps become a bit more indifferent. But that's easier said than done.

I just spoke with dad about how he feels now that he has the result. Dad is a little disappointed on one side because it was an actual stroke and not a TIA, but on the other side relieved that he now has an explanation in black and white of what has happened. Dad says it is his goal to leave this whole stroke story behind and focus on other things again. He also doesn't want to talk about it with others anymore. It's the only way he can create distance to the event. Something that is important, so that he can free himself up for nicer things and can stop brooding. Of course, I will help him with it. We started with this straight after the appointment. We went to a nice little Café and I enjoyed a very good lunch and even a piece of cake with coffee after. Dad was more disciplined and only had a cup of coffee. After that we rented a few movies, and even a thriller for dad. In a moment "Bonanza" starts. We won't miss it and these shows from the old days make us laugh every time..."

13/10/2013

"Again thank you for your call this afternoon. Dad was in the garden when the phone rang. It was a nice surprise. Even though it was Sunday we had a day that was busy both work- and visitor-wise. As dad told you he worked in the garden, pulling weeds and dug out a whole bush including roots and drove everything to the rubbish dump. In the morning, he was at his new club to watch a Petanque competition. Yesterday he was at training and met many new people, who straight away invited him to play along. He also went for an hour-long walk and the training in the afternoon lasted another 2 ½ hours. Dad is getting fitter and fitter, which I really watch with joy..."

15/10/2013

*Much to my surprise, I received an email from dad. He rarely wrote and on the phone, our conversations had usually been very brief, as he preferred to listen in on my calls chatting mostly to mum on the second phone.*

*This would be the last written piece he would ever write to me and although its contents may not be particularly exciting, they clearly showed that his capacities at the time were still intact and that his writing and computer skills had not suffered from what was still thought to be a stroke. This would soon change...*

"Dear Robert,

As you know, we had recently mentioned that we wondered whether the book "Children of the Milky Way" is available for purchase somewhere. And indeed you, dear Robert, managed to get the book "The origins and history of our home galaxy" and had it sent to us via NZ Post. At the time, we had thunderstorms during the night and day, which is why the book was kept dry at the post shop for us. Our letterbox was flooded. It was a real joy for me to hold the book. And now I am sure this nice surprise will fascinate me. One of our friends already ordered the book through the library, but of course in English, which would be a little hard to read for us with all its scientific terms. Through the book I realize, how inconspicuous we all are here on Earth and how small Earth actually is. I can't wait to start reading it tonight (Will give the Lee Child thriller a break). This afternoon the rain and wind finally stopped so that I could go for my daily walk. I walked along the beach and from there towards the estuary, then back across the golf course before heading for home. I walked for 2 hours. Had it been drier this morning, I would have gone to play Bocchia instead. I already met a few members of the club. The atmosphere there is very friendly and I enjoy going there.

Dear Robert, thank you so much for the lovely surprise today. Mum keeps you updated about everything that is happening here. So there isn't much new, since we have hardly been out of the house. The next few days, showers are forecast, but then it is supposed to be sunny again. Then it's back to playing "Petanque", which it is called here. I became a member yesterday.

As you know, I gave up tennis, voluntary perhaps, but for good reason. But I haven't canceled the membership, instead I will remain a non-playing member for $10 in annual fees. That way I can take part in the social life of the club and can still be with my friends.

The annual membership at the Petanque Club is also very reasonable: Only $75. And for that, I think it will be a lot of fun.

Tonight I can really feel my upper legs. Because of my hike at the beach, my muscles are protesting. Well, I have taken a break from sport for this long and so now, I have to catch up on exercise. The GP is right when he says, "Use it or lose it". And with that I will close for today. The book is waiting.

I am looking forward to your next mails and will keep you updated on my progress.

For now, know that I am thinking about you a lot and wish you could be here.

Your Dad."

*We were all at the very beginning of a rollercoaster and didn't know it. Dad's illness was deemed but a temporary setback, had gotten a name, and life slowly began to return to the way it had been. But as with all rollercoasters, going up is*

113

*usually followed by a jaw-dropping plunge. And the one bastard Lewy controls is no different.*

26/10/2013

"I wasn't sure whether I should write, but after speaking with TJ and him saying, "Oma, dad wanted to know *everything* about what is happening with Opa and you promised you would", I knew he was right. But we just don't want to create too much anxiety for you. You have a lot on your plate right now. So I am writing now ahead of our phone call tomorrow, so you already know what's been happening.

The week prior, I had called the ambulance, because dad felt quite unwell. They were the usual symptoms like dizziness etc. The blood pressure varied. The ambulance took him to our GP's clinic. Dad was allowed to go home after his check-up and after a while, he started feeling better. The next week, meaning last week, he fluctuated, sometimes feeling well, sometimes not so well. But yesterday morning dad told me that he could only sleep sitting down, because he had trouble breathing. And suddenly the signs of another small stroke were there. I immediately called the clinic again and they said to call the ambulance. They came, again checked dad over very thoroughly, and stayed in phone contact with the clinic throughout. But nothing further was discovered and they advised to prop dad up in bed with more pillows so that he could breathe easier. These difficulties could stem from fears and from the depression, which dad still has frequently, (he thinks he is a burden now, which in turn saddens me very much). Anyway, dad slept relatively well and the breathing problems seem to get better. When I returned from shopping, dad opined that perhaps one of his eyes may have been affected. He couldn't see that well on one side. So I called the optometrist and got an appointment even though they were about to close. They really checked dad's eyes over well. Luckily, both eyes were ok. The fact that he can't see that well out of one eye, something which is really minimal, could be age-related. Technically, he doesn't even need glasses but since it's somewhat of a borderline case, they might help a little. Next Tuesday we have another appointment with our GP and later we will make another one in regards to the glasses. Dad also finally went to the dentist and can expect 4 sessions. But he is glad that he managed to push himself to go and thinks it's a competent doctor. At the moment dad's health has improved a little and he is weeding in the garden. Physical movement is important for him. We still often go for long walks.

One has to have much patience with a stroke like that and it can take a long time before the body has readjusted. That our life can no longer be the way it used to is obvious. Dad and I are happy we have each other. We can talk about everything that is happening and help one another. These talks are especially important during these hours of depression. Dad agrees now, that he can't do it all himself anymore. But for every task there is help. We are better off here in that sense than the people back in Germany. Sometimes we go for lunch at a café or go window-shopping. We get books, which dad might be interested in from the library and we talk about what we read and jointly choose our TV shows…Now you know what has been going on. But you should know also that we are managing the situation well. We know the signs and help always arrives within minutes. The paramedics insisted that we call them, whether at night, on Sundays or holidays. They prefer to come even if the patient improves, rather than arrive too late. I just read this mail out to Dad, and then came his interjection: "I am in the best of hands!" Whom he means by that, I do not know, but it sounds good anyway…"

27/10/2013

"Dad is resting a bit and so I am hoping to write a few lines. I have thought long and hard what to write. Dad would be upset, if he knew that I am writing, but I think it's necessary. It's not that he is fatally ill, but his health is changing quite a bit and even his face looks different. Dad does not have a lot of strength. We walked for half an hour and he was quite fatigued. Under no circumstances can dad know that I am writing this to you, as otherwise he may not trust me anymore. Of course, I also don't want you to drop everything and come here, but might it be possible for you to spend Christmas? Of course, I'll leave it up to you. When you called yesterday, dad said again that he doesn't want you to come since you are only just getting used to the new environment. I am in a bind and don't know what the right thing to do is…"

*The above email referred to several instances where dad became both very tired and at times refused to take the medication. I would call almost daily and each time tried to talk him into taking the pills, which he increasingly became averse to. His mood during that time also swung regularly from „normal" to depression and being upset, followed by periods of drowsiness and just wanting to lay down in bed, something he had always abhorred until recently. There would be several mails and calls from mum of this nature, virtual cries for help as managing the situation would eventually became harder and harder. This was but the first of them.*

27/10/2013

"Your call meant soooo much to us and dad and I talked about it for a long while after. After this truly sad Sunday were TJ and I sat at lunch without dad and dad stayed in bed…after your call the evening was a total reversal: Dad very much took to heart what you told him and subsequently took the prescribed medication. The last night, it's now 4 am, he has spent sleeping and snoring away soundly, which is a good sign. Dad told me you were planning to come. I can assure you that after his talk with you (and the medication) he is certain that things are looking up and going by that I think he was even happier about your call than if had you just come straight away. He would probably have found it burdensome, since it would have excited him even more. The last thing he wants is for you to disrupt your new beginning in Myanmar. He is so happy that you are doing this that just hearing about it he already feels better. The fact that you are planning to call as often as possible in the next few weeks gives him a boost. Perhaps, taking these pills he will get better soon. I think he also accepts now, that he sometimes has to take on advice from us in order for him to get better. Your call was a big success and I am grateful that you talked to dad. I only peeked into the room here and there, so that dad could speak to you in private and without me. TJ also called in the evening and chatted with dad a bit. Together all this worked wonders and I very, very happy and glad. I know each

116

day is different from the next, but obviously, the talk constituted a positive turning point. Again, you can't imagine how glad I am. Dad spent the entire evening much more positive than the last few nights.

Dad just got up briefly. He says he has slept very well, for the first time in a long time. He's gone back to bed and wants to sleep on a bit. You see, you are the best medicine for him…"

*Based on the events that had prompted my call, mum and I agreed that it would be best if I wrote to their GP prior to their next appointment and describe what was happening. The following is what I wrote to him that day:*

27/10/2013

Dear Dr. Stephenson,

Over the weekend I received several messages from my mother and my son regarding my father's health, which were all quite disconcerting.

I subsequently had lengthy discussions with all, especially with my father, and was able to establish the following:

He seems to be relatively OK physically, but it is his emotional/psychological state that is causing considerable stress to him as well as to all involved as he struggles with severe bouts of depression on a day-to-day basis; so bad in fact, that he told me that he thought this whole 'thing' would kill him, that he did not think he would recover from it and that he thought he had lived long enough. Consequently he has started to make 'preparations' by showing my mother what to do around the house etc. My son, who is just about to sit his final school exams, has been witnessing this also and had a break-down on the phone to me today.

I was also able to establish that my father did not take the medication originally prescribed to address his anxiety and bouts of obsessive thinking, for fear of side effects. I have advised him that the benefits in this instance will far outweigh the possible side effects and he has finally agreed to take the meds. I am very fearful at present not only of the effects of my father's psychological state on himself, but those around him; including my mother who is at the point of break-down. I was therefore wondering whether there is anything else that can be done to help my father, such as the prescription of anti-depressants perhaps? He seems to react well to the talks I have with him over the phone (I try to do the same with my mother and son as well), but that of course is just a band aid solution. I have asked both my father and mother to explore the possibility of anti-depressants with you during their next consultation; in actual fact, from what I can tell, my mother could potentially also be a candidate for a similar prescription (depression runs in the family on her side as well, and I do worry about her well-being). Thank you very much for taking the time to read this. Both my parents have great respect for you as a person, your advice and of course competence as a medical practitioner. I am hoping that perhaps getting my father out of his

118

psychological state, even if it means through medication, will provide the momentum he (and the family) needs to turn this around. I know that in all likelihood they present themselves well during the consultation, "putting their best foot forward"...but behind it all things are far from OK.

I just thought you should know this.

Thank you so much for your assistance.

Warm Regards,

Robert Landeck"

29/10/2013

"Today we had our appointment with Dr. Stephenson. He had read your email and we think he appreciated your letter. The visit went very well. Because of your mail, which he had printed out, he was able to address things very differently with us. He took time to explain to dad what "anxiety" was and how "anxiety" can impact the body. And that's exactly what it was like last weekend when dad wanted to stay in bed. Dad was impressed by the explanations and apologized for not taking the medication because of possible side effects. Both the doctor and the nurse explained very clearly how these medications work and what the names etc. mean. He prescribed 20mg of Citalopram Hydro bromide, of which dad has to take half a tablet each morning. It may take 4 to 6 weeks before they take full effect but dad is just glad that there is help. He stopped the previous anti-depressants. Dr. Stephenson opined it will be possible for dad to get back to his former self and that he would even be able to drive again, which due to medication is not recommendable at present. We talked for almost half an hour. It gave me hope as well, since I now know what has been happening with dad these last few weeks and why he has had these anxiety attacks and depression episodes. And I also now know how to handle it in future and what to do. But as I have said, your calls are so incredibly important for dad's recovery and the talk today was almost medicinal for me and improved my mood. The future now looks a lot rosier for all of us and I can't begin to express, how happy I am about it....While we were waiting for the prescription we went to a café for lunch. There, we took time to "calm down" from the positive excitement and the joy that things will get better."

*Over the next few days, the new-found positivity endured and although dad still had some bouts of depression, the hope and confidence that the new medication would increasingly take hold and improve things, helped both to cope much better. Their life, it seemed, once again gained new momentum.*

3/011/2013

"Everything is as usual here. Dad had a so-so day today, but we have good and not so good days. Our neighbor who went through this herself visited Norbert today and talked to him. It really helped dad and the two got along famously. I am very happy that we have both found a friend in her. This morning dad trimmed the hedges again, perfectly as always. This afternoon he went to play Petanque. He had a lot of fun. In the meantime I did some Christmas shopping. Tomorrow dad and TJ will mow the lawns. Tuesday it's Petanque again, Wednesday and Thursday dentist's appointments and Friday Dr. Stephenson. I am playing taxi and the week is flying past. I will keep you posted."

4/11/2013

"...Not much exciting stuff going on here. TJ and dad worked in the garden for one and a half hours. Dad is impressed how well and cleanly TJ works. TJ has invited us to his graduation on Wednesday and the dinner gala on Thursday, which we will also attend. It is quite exciting, but also a little emotional when we think about the fact that his time at school is thus coming to an end. Dad had a better day today than yesterday. You see, it's still up and down a lot, something that is likely to last for a few more months yet. But we are learning how to handle it. Friday is another appointment with Dr. Stephenson. Let's see what he says. I will let you know straight away. Dad is just watering the flowers. Incredibly dry weather at the moment. A challenge for dad... Tomorrow it's Petanque and then a visit to a sick friend..."

120

6/11/2013

"I just wanted to let you know that today and tomorrow we are busy with TJ's graduation at his college and so will be out of reach for a bit. Here everything is as usual. Dad's anxiety medication dose was increased from half a tablet to a whole tablet and that is seems to help him. Dad is sleeping more soundly – no nightmares – and even during the day it's now no comparison to what it had been like. Dad regrets that he didn't agree to these tablets sooner. It would have saved a lot of issues. But as I said he is better now and we are very much relieved. Yesterday I called the stroke foundation und they gave me the number for a specialized stroke unit at the health department. Their boss is a former Rotarian, whom we even had over for dinner a while back. Now we will get an appointment for a field officer visit, which will be very interesting for us. You see, dad is feeling much better and now we can pursue all manner of things to achieve optimum results."

09/11/2013

"I am writing just in case the telephone connection won't happen today. Last night for the first time dad took the pill against his terrible nightmares and slept through the whole night. No dreams. What a relief!!! Because of these pills he takes a little longer to "come to" in the morning, but that's something we gladly accept. Straight after getting up he takes his "day pill", which counteracts the night one. The type of medications they have today is just incredible and Dr. Stephenson really is a great physician. Should the nightmares return, the dosage will be increased slightly, otherwise it will remain at half a pill. There are actually not that many medications dad has to take: one in the morning to thin his blood, and one to be able to "start the day". Then in the evening one for blood pressure normalization and half a tablet for his nightmares just before bedtime. And that's it. I hear from others about the sheer number of prescriptions they need to take – seems very odd. Dad is in the best of hands in terms of medical care and I am relieved that they don't pump him full of all manner of drugs. He will need to take the 'nightmare pill' for a little while and then the doctor will stop it. Same with the day pill. We are in constant contact with him. Every 5 or 6 days I am writing an email to the practice, containing blood pressure levels (noon and evenings) and inform them how dad is getting on so they know what is happening. That's working really well. Now you are up to date again..."

10/11/2013

"This afternoon I wanted to give you a "clinical update" before our phone call. Today dad had one of his not so good days. It could be that the night pills are not agreeing with him. Dad was suffering from severe depression. It really wasn't good, so I called 111 immediately and they referred me to the team medical practice – emergency department. So I drove dad to the practice, which is manned by an emergency doctor on weekends. He determined the pills were the reason for dad's confusion and depression. I know this from my sister Marlene and know that patients need to change medication quite a few times before they find the right one for their condition. Anyway, he is to stop taking the medication immediately and is getting a different one, at least in the interim. Tomorrow morning I will call Dr. Stephenson and see about the next steps. Dad is in bed now and has been sleeping for a while...You see, every day is different. Yesterday he was relatively ok and today: exactly the opposite. We just have to take each day as it comes. That was also the doctor's opinion. For dad though this is incredibly hard to accept what is happening with his body. We just hope that this new pill will work. I am sorry that now sometimes I have to send news like this – I pray it will be different again at some stage."

11/11/2013

"Today was a day of ups and downs. Dad had a restful night. The new sleeping pill worked within minutes. It worked so well that I had to remove his specs from his nose – he had already dropped his book. Getting up this morning was no problem at all and we had a very good two hours while we had breakfast, did our daily puzzles (which wasn't possible the last two days) and put up the Christmas tree. Then suddenly, within seconds, dad's mood dropped to below zero. Norbert got a burning sensation in his chest (could be indigestion), felt weak and just sat there, not wanting to talk anymore. I suspect it may be the day pills Norbert isn't taking to all that well. Since I had

122

promised the practice to send an update about the weekend and Norbert's status anyway, I wrote an email straight away. A few minutes ago, I got a call from the nurse, who told me that Dr. Stephenson wants to see us tomorrow at 10am. I will let you know what he says.

This afternoon, after dad slept for a few hours on the sofa he felt better and we have just started baking cookies together. Dad is rolling dough balls and then flattens them on the baking tray. He has recovered and we can laugh again here and there. So perhaps the day will end on a nicer note than it started…"

12/11/2013

"We have just returned from the doctor's visit. Dad didn't have a very good morning today, meaning he was suffering from heavy depression again. Dr. Stephenson recommended to keep taking the sleeping pill, the aspirin and the blood pressure medication for now. He says he has to seek additional advice from a specialist for geriatrics. He doesn't want to make any mistakes. It is a mystery to him and he cannot pinpoint what is happening to dad at the moment, since all the tests show that it was just a small stroke. Especially these sudden changes. We will monitor how dad will continue to handle these pills. After all, it seemed that the sleeping pill really works. Dad slept all the way through a second night and only when he takes the day pill he starts to decline. But of course I could be wrong and the cause lies elsewhere completely. Regardless, we will try it for another 3 days without the additional pill.

Now, a few hours after taking the day pill dad's condition has improved. He is even reading a book. When dad comes out of these bouts of depression, he is very positive, but of course, when he is in their grip things look very different. This afternoon TJ will come to help mow the lawn. That's also very good for dad. He loves spending time with him…

We now have Dr. Stephenson's personal email address, so we can reach him anytime."

13/07/2013

"Here my morning report: Dad slept very well thanks to the sleeping pill and upon waking felt relatively better than yesterday. We watered the garden and had breakfast. Then a wee while later his depression returned – only today it wasn't as intense as it was these last few days. When it started, we decided to go for a walk with Rosy. After that dad went to bed again and slept for around half an hour. I quickly went to do some shopping and when I got back, he was trimming some bushes in the garden. We were able to talk a lot despite his depression. Then we watched some TV, after which dad tidied up in the garden and this evening we will watch old TV series, which always make us laugh. I am writing all this in such detail so that you can see that today was very different when compared to the last few days. And I am very thankful for that. Of course, for dad things aren't right yet, since he desperately wants to be well again, pretty much instantly. Then I need to explain to him that that's just not possible and why and that he has to be patient, which in turn makes him a little grumpy, at which we both usually laugh a little. But these moods are very, very sad. It's only days like today that lift me up and perhaps dad a little, too."

## Chapter 2 - Shadows

14/11/2017

"Another update from us, so you know what's been going on before we speak on the phone:

Last night was again very good for dad. He slept long and well. Only after getting up, he felt down. He didn't see me straight away, since I was in the living room at the time, and thought I had left him. Why he has these thoughts, I really don't know. After about an hour, he felt better and watched the NZ vs. Mexico soccer game. But only until halftime, then things took a turn for the worse again for dad and he went to bed. After a few minutes, he called out to me and told me that the "ghosts" or "dark shadows" were fighting him again and he couldn't do anything about it. I got him to get up and we went for a little walk to the nearby duck pond on Rahi Rd. It was good for dad, but the depression stayed – not quite as bad, but it stayed. We had lunch, watched TV – Dallas and Bonanza. Dad nodded off here and there. Now he feels better and the sadness is gone. It's a constant up and down. Meanwhile dad told me that he's just not interested in anything anymore, really. Neither the newspaper, the radio or TV, nor even the computer are of any interest to him, and so I try to come up with different things for him to do so he is distracted and kept busy. I wrote to Dr. Stephenson earlier and am waiting for his reply, which u no doubt will take a while since he wanted to reach out to the geriatrics specialist first. Just now dad went to the bathroom and said that it was probably time he shaved. That is a very good sign and an indication he is feeling better again.

Dear Robert, please do not worry about these mood swings. I am learning more and more how to handle them. These swings are likely to continue for a while longer and Norbert just needs support. I hope I can provide that for him. Anyway, he keeps saying that he is happy to "have me". And this a very nice thing, isn't it? I also don't leave him by himself at the moment and instead go for walks with him, accompany him everywhere and take him shopping with me, even if he just wants to stay in the car."

15/11/2013

"...This morning we watered the garden, had breakfast and (for the first time in days) did some puzzles from the newspaper as well as Sudoku. I was so happy that dad participated. Later I had to go shopping and then it was lunchtime. As always, we watched a little TV and then dad and I drove to the landfill to drop off all the green waste from the garden. Then we went to the hardware store and garden center. Dad showed me a lot of things there. Back at home, we had a little rest. Dad had a very good day today – a little depressed in the morning, but since then all has been ok. The sleeping pill still works well for dad. I am now convinced that stopping the Day- and Night-pills was the right thing to do. Of course, we know that each day is different, but at the moment things are going quite well. I also received a reply from Dr. Stephenson today, which I will forward to you shortly.

Dr. Stephenson's email:

"Thanks for keeping me informed
I have written for an urgent review by the specialist but not heard back yet
we just need to be very supportive
Norbert needs to be encouraged to do things as you are doing and we need to slowly rebuild his confidence
Brent"

*Then, a day later somewhat of a turning point occurred. I had to make some difficult decisions in relation to where to go next and whether to secure a new contract or simply spend some time at home in NZ. I wrote to mum and dad asking for advice. Not for help, just advice on what they thought I should do. It had been a difficult year both personally and professionally and sometimes getting sound advice from mum and dad, the kind I had sought so many times before, simply seemed the right thing to do. Dad had always been very pragmatic in the way he had provided answers; problem solving was his life. Each problem became a project and I had always been able to rely on his honest feedback. And yet this*

126

*simple email, describing my situation and asking for advice on upcoming decisions now obviously threw things into complete disarray at home. Bastard Lewy may have still been in disguise, but it didn't stop him pull the levers that would continue to change the way dad was able to interact with me and others from this moment onward:*

15/11/2013

"Dear Robert,

It is a little difficult to write this letter, but I think I simply have to. I wish dad hadn't read your letter from last night. Despite the sleeping pills, he hardly slept until 4am. And when he slept he had terrible nightmares, which threw him back into deep depression. He dreamt and believes that he can't help you – that he just can't do it and the "evil ghosts" are fighting him and Norbert thinks he has to give up. I have taken him into the living room and made him a relaxing tea. Now he is lying on the couch because he thinks there he is further away from the evil ghosts in the bedroom. I have turned off the lights and check in on him every 5 minutes or so and try to calm him down. Maybe I will succeed in getting him back to sleep so he can rest. These waking nightmares are terrible. For the foreseeable future and until he has settled again, I will have look at all mail, letters, emails etc. by myself first and only give him things to read which don't agitate him. If you need advice, please time your mail so that I can be at my computer early in the morning. Then I move the mail to my personal folder and delete the letter from dad's computer.

Please understand dad: he really wants to give you advice, but can't change your situation. And that is terrible for him."

17/11/2013

"Thank you for the call yesterday, which was really good for us.

We went shopping to Briscoe's – a big sale was on and after that, we bought some cake for afternoon tea. Dad was distracted, which helped and so the rest of the day was good as well. This morning the sky was grey and it rained. When it stopped dad went for a brief

127

walk, but was feeling quite faint. He is now sleeping on the couch. TJ invited dad to come along to one of his basketball games, but at the moment he's just not interested in anything at all. Let's see how he feels after his nap. Maybe things will improve.

A little while later now. Dad went to bed and wanted to sleep, has drawn all the curtains and I even had to close the door. I think he may have one of his not so good days today. I wish I could distract him a bit, but on days like this I there isn't much I can do. It will change again I am sure, maybe even after a little sleep."

17/11/2013

"We had a few visitors today and had lunch together with TJ, which dad liked very much and it helped lift dad out of his depression. We all prepared it together and had a lot of fun. TJ fried some eggs etc., I made a salad and dad helped set the table. As I said it was all-round enjoyable and I am happy how different dad reacted today. Now we tidied up together and we will see how the day progresses. I am just writing this little mail so you know that things were looking up here today compared to earlier in the day.

19/11/2013

"A few minutes ago we returned from our appointments today and I wanted to write you straight away. The first appointment was with Dr. Stephenson, which again went very well. He took a lot of time with dad and spoke with him in detail. Norbert's nightmares have now slipped into daytime, along with accompanying depression. One dream was: Dad didn't know how to help himself anymore, and so he took the car and drove up into the nearby hills. There "someone" tried to persuade him to drive over the edge. But dad didn't want to. It must have been a terrible dream. In any case, dad has now been prescribed a pill for daytime, of which Dr. Stephenson says it will take two or more weeks to take full effect. I am to write to Dr. Stephenson every few days. This morning dad really was in a bad way. On the other hand it was good for the doctor to see him in this condition, which Norbert often tries to "disguise" or hide. The second appointment was at the gym, regarding strengthening dad's

128

muscles again. Dad had a long talk with the trainer, Barry, who seems very competent. He asked very specific questions and is going to speak with the doctor about any aspects he should pay particular attention to. I called the practice to give permission to share dad's information. Initially dad will go half an hour twice a week. Later perhaps 3 times, until dad has recovered enough to do the exercises by himself. So right now dad is busy all week except Mondays. Tuesday Petanque, Wednesday gym, Thursday Petanque, Friday gym and Saturday and Sunday Petanque. In addition all the doctor's appointments. I think dad will enjoy going back to the gym and we all hope it will bring good progress for him. The field worker from the stroke foundation will be here in an hour and we will get even more advice what else we might be able to do. Once a month dad will go to their meetings. It's a social affair (spouses can come along) with various activities like indoor bocchia, card games, lunch outings etc. etc. It all sound very good. The most important thing at the moment is to get dad out of here so that he spends time among people and is distracted.

19/11/2013

"This afternoon the stroke foundation field worker dropped by. We were given a lot of information and received all manner of reading materials. But we will take our time and read it tomorrow…The talk was very interesting and dad was able to speak about his condition. We feel well looked after. There is a lot on offer for stroke victims. Dad is not even tired tonight; we are both still very excited. I am even more tired than he is, but then again I have only been getting 4 or 5 hours of sleep each night. Now I look forward to the first night on the sleeping pills Dr. Stephenson prescribed for me. There was something nice from this evening that I wanted to tell you: Dad has a few problems remembering all these pills. So he keeps asking me constantly which ones he has to take when and for what (of course we have a pill box, with compartments for Morning, Lunch, Afternoon, Evening and Bed). But it is preoccupying dad to the point that he gets very confused (after all he has never had to take so many pills before, except the odd Panadol). I told him he should only try to think ahead as far as the next pill. So far, so good. Then, a little while later he again came to me and said hesitantly: Gisela, you already know what I want to ask you, don't you?" "Of course", I said, "it's about the pills!" – You can't believe how much we laughed at that moment. It was the first time we were able to laugh about something like this. I think it's a small step forward."

20/11/2013

"Today has been the best day for dad and me since end of July. It was fantastic: Dad did not feel dizzy or faint and wasn't sad at all. He slept well through the night and was well rested in the morning. I drove him to the gym at 11.30 and stayed during this first session. The trainer was very good and dad was happy. He walked on the treadmill at fast speed for 20 minutes. The trainer was impressed. Before that dad did a few exercises to straighten his posture again. Dad didn't even sleep this afternoon!!! I went for a walk with Rosy and when I got back at 5, dad was still busy in the garden, had clipped the hedges and kept himself busy with all manner of things. Now we have just finished watching soccer. Another half hour and it is bedtime. All round a great day. This afternoon someone from the stroke foundation called and again invited us to their Christmas party. Isn't that nice of them? I think dad now really feels well cared for and looked after. I hope that he can soon have many of these wonderful days."

23/11/2013

"Too bad we couldn't talk today, but I am glad I went to visit my friend Erin. Her husband Dan is gravely ill and they don't know how to go on. He has been in hospital since Thursday night. He has dementia and quite severe at that. He couldn't walk anymore, kept falling down, became incontinent etc. etc. It's terrible. Erin had to drive to the hospital in Penikoru again this afternoon. She couldn't take the dog because it was just too hot outside. So I offered to dog-sit so there would be no "accident" while she was away. We are so glad that we have our neighbors who are happy to take Rosy anytime. When dad had his stroke and our life initially became different to what it was like before, you could see that Rosy didn't know what was happening and felt confused. When dad lies down in bed for a nap some afternoons, she lies next to him and stays with him. She is very compassionate. Erin is not very impressed with Penikoru. She says it seems like a hospital you would otherwise find in a developing country. Straight away on the first day, someone stole Derek's wallet. But, and that is probably the most important aspect, she said the doctors are very good. I didn't get back until 5, but called Norbert a few times while I was away, to make sure everything was Ok. He told me you had called. Now he is outside watering the garden."

26/11/2013

"I have a favor to ask: if you are planning to call today, please delay until evening. I am waiting for Dr. Stephenson or the nurse to return my call. Norbert was not all that well today – it could be that he is constipated. Unfortunately, he only told me about it just now, that he hasn't had any movement in days. It could also be that he's not that well because of the medication. The nurse said she will call back as soon as she's spoken with the doctor. Dad is resting at the moment. Please don't worry, constipation is uncomfortable, but there are quick fixes and then dad will be Ok again."

131

## Chapter 3 - Lewy Tips His Hat

28/11/2013

"Dad had one of those not very good days yesterday. If it had to do with the rainy weather – I don't know. He was worried – as he often is – about money that might not be transferred from Germany into the account here and was imagining the worst scenarios, i.e. how we would be able to keep the house without money. We couldn't pay the council rates. To cut a long story short. He was completely confused. I tried to calm him down and even logged into internet banking and of course, there was no problem. I had to explain the process of money transfers to him until he remembered. After that, I said to him jokingly: You gave me a fright with your worries! Dad then laughed as well and said, "And how it frightened *me* when I got these thoughts!" Then we laughed together and felt relieved. Later I took dad to the gym, which made him feel good. Back at home, he slept for two hours. In the afternoon, we decorated the small Christmas tree, but after half an hour, he had to lie back down. In the evening, he was in good spirits and we watched basketball. Dad seems to go through a particular cycle each day: After getting up it's possible that he will take some time to come to. Despite this, we do our morning puzzles. Sometimes he just sits with me, but I try to persuade him to participate. These puzzles are important brain training. Then he usually starts feeling better until lunchtime, when things go downhill until late afternoon. Then things improve radically until bedtime. As I said, yesterday was not a very good day. But by now I have learned to handle it much better. It's also important to recognize whether dad needs to be nudged towards being active, or whether he really needs his rest. Something he doesn't like at all at the moment are crowds. He often stays in the car when I go shopping. But that, too, can change again from day to day. Yesterday we received a letter from the neurologist, who is also a psychologist. This doctor will visit us on 10 December here at home. I don't even know what he wants, but Dr. Stephenson has initiated the appointment and will explain it to us next Monday. I assume the doctor wants to assess dad at our place, so Dr. Stephenson can getter a better insight into dad's illness.

Dad had forgotten that we were to have such an appointment and now I have to keep explaining to him why it is important. Eventually dad then agrees. I am hoping the day today will be better than yesterday. Unfortunately it is raining which dad doesn't like at all. I will have to get creative. I have started renting movies here and there from the DVD store and dad really enjoys watching a movie in the evening. Seems he has found a new hobby. I'm happy about it."

1/12/2013

"These last few days have been a little stressful here at home. It is often difficult to gage dad's mood. For example, today we went for our walk along Kahai River and I asked him several times whether we shouldn't turn around and go back. But dad wanted to continue. So we walked just over an hour. When we got home he was spent and went to bed for several hours, didn't want lunch, only wanted to sleep. Late afternoon he went back into the living room and at least ate some fruit. Then we had a two (!) hour conversation, whereby dad kept insisting that he wanted to work in the garden: roll out the hose, water the plants, roll up the hose etc. I know it sounds so trivial, but in the end, I actually lost it for the first time and told him: Go do the damn garden then and then go back to bed. I felt sorry straight away, but it has happened so often in recent times that dad overexerts himself and is then unable to do anything at all. I do try to take each day on its own merits, but sometimes that isn't easy. At least he ate a hearty dinner. His eating habits have changed when compared to even just half a year ago and he normally eats very little now.

Dear Robert, I have grave concerns that this wasn't just a stroke…But we will have to wait for the doctor's visit and assessment on 11 December. Dad has changed a lot during the time following his stroke. You will surely see it for yourself. Our neighbors and friends have said so too. I fills me with a little bit of fear. Nevertheless I will think positive for now and that, too, helps."

2/12/2013

"It is hard to put what I am trying to say in words. But I will try:

133

There are so many small things each day, which confuse him. For example, this morning at 5.30am he got up and got ready in the bathroom, because we have an appointment with Dr. Stephenson at 9.30am. When I asked him why so early, he said it was because he still wanted to lay down for a bit, but had wanted to avoid the run on the bathroom when *everyone* wanted to get ready later. I still have to look out which pills he takes and when, even though we have a box with compartments for every day and every dose. He gets the days confused. He remembers appointments, but gets them mixed up. As I have said, every day is different. Some days I feel like "Thank God, my Norbert is back", but more often now I feel terribly sad about what is happening and sometimes get a fright. Of course, I try not to let on how I feel and try to be as "normal" as I can. Every little niggle makes dad feel terrible. Yesterday he said there was "rumbling" in his stomach, so he immediately took two Panadol and antacids. But he only told me about it later, so now I have to stay watchful. The problem is that dad cannot accept that he is not well. He even wants to give up the gym, which we had had such high hopes for. He says the trainer demands too much. I offered to talk to him, but dad doesn't want me to. He only wants to play Petanque once a week now. He says working in the garden is more important. But he can't do it all alone. TJ has to do the lawns instead. But at least Norbert can see that by now. Dad doesn't watch TV off his own bat anymore, but instead most of the time sits on the sofa and just stares at nothing. He is sad. I try to get him some movies from the store. But even that only works on good days. Newspapers and the computer are also no longer of interest to him. I read emails to him. I do the bank transfers also, because it has become too hard for dad to get the numbers right. In summary, dad barely participates in daily life anymore. Robert, In know I have not written all that direct, because I don't want dad to see what I am writing, in case he suddenly stands behind me and tries to read this mail. Und when you reply, then please don't make reference to my personal letters. Perhaps try to describe in a roundabout way what you want to say. I don't want to make dad's condition worse. Our neighbors and friends have already approached me about dad and likewise opined it could be the beginning of dementia. I have also read that dementia and stroke "go together". It would be terrible for us all, but I want to get the best for dad out of each day. And I will not get angry again the way I did last night."

02/12/2013

"We just got back from our appointment with Dr. Stephenson and I wanted to write immediately:

When the appointment ended, I asked Norbert to go ahead, because I just wanted to ask a quick question. Norbert left the room and I asked Dr. Stephenson to tell me very honestly, if he thought that Norbert was experiencing the onset of dementia – Hallelujah, it's not the case!!!!!! Norbert's depression is so severe though, that he experiences and displays similar symptoms as dementia. Now I have the task to be firm and not to allow certain things, for example staying in bed too long during the day, skipping meals etc. Even when it comes to physical activities, I should nudge him to go to the gym and not allow dad to let himself go. It was again a long and extraordinarily good conversation for dad, which subsequently propelled him to a "high". Dr. Stephenson repeatedly and patiently explained to dad why certain things aren't working the way dad wants them to. He also tried to convey to dad how well he was looked after by his son and his family.

O, Robert, I am soooooo relieved, that this isn't Dementia!!

I am hugging you and the world at the moment"

## Chapter 4 - The D-word

4/12/2013

"Good day dear Robert,

Yesterday we went to the stroke foundation's Christmas party. Dad was completely knackered afterwards (met too) and went to bed, depressed. His depression remained until late this morning and still hasn't left completely. Dad got so agitated about all these unfortunate fates of the stroke victims gathered there that his blood pressure went almost as high as he did when he had the stroke. This morning it is almost normal again, but for the next few months, we will no longer attend events. Dad likes visitors at home, but not too many, which allows him to chat in a relaxed atmosphere."

6/12/2013

"Just one more thing: dad had an exceptionally bad day today. He didn't want to get up and simply *gave* up. I immediately called the nurse, who spoke with Dr. Stephenson. I should leave dad be for now and call back in the afternoon to see how he is then. Dr. Stephenson mentioned that he may get these really bad days here and there. We have to be patient. Meanwhile I have noticed that I cannot mention to dad anything that is even remotely different from the normal routine. Dad even agrees. He just doesn't understand many things at the moment. Dad currently has to take antibiotics for a sinus infection the dentist cleared out. Now dad has to take these pills three times a day and gargle with salt water. You cannot imagine how difficult it is to explain this to him over and over and over again. I just have to be on the lookout that he takes the right pills at the right time and that he actually gargles with normal water and only a little salt. I try to remain factual and pragmatic, but sometimes that is not easy. Please don't worry about it though because Dr. Stephenson and his nurse make sure I am Ok. And I actually *am*, under the circumstances. Tomorrow, maybe even already this afternoon, things might be different and dad feels better. This changes without warning at any time. Something to get used to. Now I will get the house in order. I never know if maybe the paramedics have to come or a doctor, or, or....so I better keep it tidy."

7/12/2013

"Don't know what to write as subject

Dear Robert

Yesterday was not very nice here. No, not the whole day, just the afternoon. It started when I had to get some shopping done. Dad and I called each other every few minutes while I was away, so he knew where I was and I knew he was Ok. At least he sounded it on the phone. When I got home dad told me he had already taken his evening pill – it was only 2pm. These pills pose an insurmountable hurdle for him in general. I calmed him down and told him it wasn't so bad to make a mistake here and there, but that it might be better if I locked away the pills in future. Dad agreed. Then we were talking about something and I noticed something was quite off. To cut a long story short: Dad didn't recognize me anymore – he told me that only after a few minutes, after he had looked at me as I was sitting on the sofa, when he saw my feet, my arms etc. he actually realized that *I* was in fact Gisela. Before that, he mentioned Gisela a few times, but didn't know where to place the name. You can imagine how I felt. I tried not to show how sad I was and instead changed the subject. But dad could not remember friends, their names etc. It was horrific. I then took his blood pressure and it was 108. We drove him to the emergency doctor and they checked him over thoroughly. It was not another stroke. I think in future I will have to anticipate more of this. Dad was allowed to go home and after we sat together for a while he got better and better and was able to resume normal conversations. We talked about the situation for a long time – dad knows exactly that something isn't right and that we somehow need to handle it. I kept reassuring dad that we will get through this together – and I mean it, too. Dad and I sat together and cried a little, then we felt better.

I would have loved to write about something cheerful, but we can't choose what happens in life."

*On 8 December, Mum had to go to see the Inland Revenue Department, a drive and subsequent appointment that would take several hours. TJ volunteered and stayed with dad for the day. It was the first time that someone other than mum had the opportunity to observe and be with dad for an extended period and without any "filters" which both mum and dad were very good at applying; not to deceive, but purely out of hope that this was but a temporary condition. During these hours, the true extent of dad's deterioration for the first time became known and I received a message asking me to call urgently. What I heard convinced me to immediately leave work and head home.*

10/12/2013

"Thank you so much for your calls and your offer to help. We had already given you a rough outline of what was happening in terms of neurological testing. The neurologist was very, very competent and so was his nurse. He fired off questions, one after the other to dad. I was very proud of dad, how he reacted and answered; everything in English and well-articulated. Many New Zealanders would have struggled. The two ½-hour test demanded a huge level of concentration from dad and he got through most of the questions with flying colors, even sometimes not so easy ones. But of course there were small intermittent things, which showed us what was really happening. For example, dad was supposed to copy simple geometric shapes, a task which as an engineer he would have considered child's play. But instead he couldn't complete this test today and gave up on it. Of course, the diagnosis dementia was a shock for us all, even though we had suspected it a little already. But naturally we had pushed it aside. It's not something you want to admit straight away. Dad accepted the diagnosis with great composure and was overall in good spirits, even afterwards. We talked all afternoon. Dad asked questions here and there and I tried to answer as competently as I could. Later we went for a walk, which helped. We now know that we have to embark on a new chapter in life and we want to try to do it as best as we can. Nobody knows how slowly or quickly this illness progresses. But it was a shock in how many areas dad has suffered a decline. It is unbelievably sad. Although I couldn't sleep last night, I am still not tired. It's is just too much to cope with all at once. But we promise you to make the best of every situation. It will take quite a while to "digest" everything. Dr. Stephenson wants to see me as well. He wants to prescribe something to help me remain calm during the day. As you can imagine I am close to tears most of the time at the moment. Oh, one more thing: when you get here we would like to begin the process of power of attorney. It's better if you're there for this, because you can explain it well to dad. How great it would have been to have something nice to report from today. But unfortunately there wasn't anything nice at all – except perhaps our evening walk."

*I arrived two days later in emergency mode, in time to witness what was bastard Lewy's most aggressive assault on dad since his "stroke". Dad had been hospitalized following another episode while I was still in the air somewhere over the Pacific and so my first trip was straight from the airport to the hospital. He recognized me and seemed relatively Ok, albeit very confused. Luckily, he was released again a day later, as physically he was again mostly fine. The decline however I witnessed on a day to day basis following his return home was simply so unbelievable that what I saw and heard made me doubt my own sanity and for the sake of retaining it compelled me to take notes, as I was sure nobody would believe me even if I tried to describe what was happening.*

*In the following therefore, a few of my notes of days spent with dad following my arrival in December 2013 and over the Christmas holidays:*

"Dad gets up and says 'it looks like home here'. I explain that he *is* at home.
He has his coffee. We try to give him the half pill he needs to take, but he refuses.
He says he wants to go, doesn't want to be at home anymore.
I remind him of the nurse's visit and how he had said he wanted to stay home.
He says he doesn't need pills and wants to leave.
I say he can leave, no problem. He says he wants to go for a walk and that he wants his freedom.
I ask for him to take the pill and to go for a walk after. He says he doesn't agree to taking pills and that we are trying to force him. I am adamant that he must take it to feel better and he says we must break his teeth and beat him or he will not take it.

We leave it at that. I offer for him to go for a walk but now he doesn't want to go. He then walks around in circles in the living room. 5 minutes later he wants to go for a walk. I say he can go. Instead, he asks about what I am writing. I say I am writing work emails. He says I am writing an 'idiot letter' for the doctor... He then asks to go for a walk again. I say he can go. He then asks if he can lay down. I say he can do that as well. He asks 'and what then?' He then talks about the garden and what happens if he doesn't want to do the chores. I say it's ok not to want to do them and that we can get someone to help. He asks 'and then?' And so it goes on and on.

7. 35 am: He walks in circles again. 8 am dad asks for coffee and keeps monitoring me closely. I make the coffee and he accuses me of trying to poison him and asks if I put something in his coffee. I offer to switch his cup with mine, but he doesn't want to, all the while accusing me that I put things in his food and drink. I say I find this quite offensive and that if he doesn't trust me, to get someone else to make his coffee. He gets upset and says he is joking; yet a few minutes later, he asks again. 10 minutes later, he asks us not to treat him like a slave as he is the only one doing any work around here and he would like an apology. He also says mum isn't talking to him, although she has just spent the last ten minutes doing so. He leaves the room to lay down but returns a few minutes later. He says he now wants to take the pill, so that it is "finally all over" [sic: death by 'poisoning']. I place the pill in front of him and say it is his choice to take it or not. He takes it (1 pill). The rest of the day goes reasonably well, after administering another 1/2 tablet at lunchtime. In total, we do the following activities: walk on the beach 20 minutes, lawn mowing 30 minutes, gardening 40 minutes, evening walk 20 minutes. I even take a photo with dad as he seems as good as new now.

*Sunday –*

140

Dad takes 1/2 pill in the morning and is reasonably ok. He then does gardening for too long, but doesn't want to stop. Takes 1 pill after lunch. This has no effect and he slips away into depression, suicidal thoughts, and confusion. Two notable differences: his death wishes are more violent (wants us to stab him) and he tries to take the car. As of 4pm he sits on the couch quietly and occasionally talks about money.

4.30pm he gets up and starts looking for his phone. He then proceeds to make calls to mum's cellphone from the bedroom. He cannot understand why she is not answering. He says he is trying to call "the house" [sic: their home]. We give him the number [their own landline number] and he calls his own landline from his own landline phone. He cannot understand why it is just ringing and keeps experimenting with the two cordless phones. In the end he says he is trying to call his mother (grandma died in the mid-nineties).

The rest of the evening he spends talking about projects, money, the garden and that we shouldn't abuse him, that he is not a slave etc. etc. We all go to bed early.


*Monday-*

Morning, just after 5am: he gets dressed except shoes and wants to go for a walk. Mum persuades him to sleep another hour. 6am he gets up and is unhappy. Mum goes shopping and after 10 minutes, he gets up and goes into the garden...per chance I see him disappear onto the road and walk away from the house. I wait 15 minutes and then go looking for him. I find him on Livingston Ave. He says he has come from visiting his friend and asks what I am doing there. I say I was out walking and saw him so thought I would join him. He asks what the place is called where I have come from. I say home. He says there is no home here. We walk to the lake and sit down. He says now "we" have done *it* and when I ask what "it" is, he says we are all liars and that he doesn't have a family here, and that we

141

swear at him and are out to get him. He also says that there are two different Gisela's and that I will get into trouble if my wife Sharon finds out. I try to tell him there is only mum, and he says age difference doesn't matter. He says he just wants to be with his family in Germany. When I ask him which one, he says the one near Frankfurt. I say that's mum but he is adamant that it is not us. I then ask about his brother and he says he prefers to be with him in Germany. He then goes on about us imprisoning him and that he just wants to sit there and never go back. When I ask back where, he says the place. I ask if he means home and he's again says there is no home and that we have taken everything and that we don't really live here. We sit quietly until mum arrives with the car. It takes all the powers of persuasion to get him into the car and to breakfast... Incidents and surreal situations continue over the next two days.

*Walking the dog* –

TJ goes for a walk with the dog, but forgets poo collection bags. Dad follows him with bags and when he meets up says to TJ: please think about it. When TJ says about what, dad says please don't kill her, think about it first.

*Underpants* –

Dad accepts new underpants! Then an hour later, he sits there crying. I ask why and he says in German that he can't believe we treat him this way. I ask what he means and he says the underpants, why are we making him wear these funny colors like red and blue. I say he doesn't have to wear them and we can put them away. He gets agitated, calls me a liar and an idiot, points at mum and tells me I should tell my wife (not sure what I am supposed to tell). I say my wife is in Nairobi, but he just repeats himself, accusing us of treating him like a slave. He then gets up and walks out of the room.

142

For the last 3 days, he has left suddenly without notice on several occasions, just wandering about.

*24 December -*

Christmas Eve dad gets dressed and ready for dinner. Then dinner is up and he disappears. I find him in the bedroom. He is in his underpants, crying. He says he can't afford to pay for dinner. He is convinced there will be a big bill he can't pay. I tell him I invite him and that I will pay for everything. He gets dressed again and joins us for dinner.

*Thursday-* Boxing Day

In the morning dad says he has had enough and that he doesn't need food anymore because it's all over. I say let's wait and I'll make dinner anyway as I am sure he will get hungry again. He gets upset and leaves the room, only to come back into the living room emptying out his wallet and tossing the contents into the room, then ripping it up into pieces. He then goes into the bedroom and proceeds to throw things about, after blocking the door with the dog's bed. He tosses mums jewelry around, puts on all his rings, breaks his alarm clock etc. He stays like this for over an hour. When he comes out, he asks me to arrest him. I say he hasn't done anything wrong and it's ok. He gets dressed, walks outside and stands in the front garden, then walks to the end of the fence and sits in the grass. After a while, he calls the landline on his mobile. I pick up his call and he says he can't walk anymore, that he is at the gate and if we can pick him up. I say ok and so he walks back into the house. He gets changed and we pick up his belongings from the floor. He says he needs a new wallet... Now a period of calm has resumed, interspersed with nonsensical conversations. His latest delusion is that the council will build a walkway right through their garden. He patrols the garden measuring where this will be. Long periods of him standing and staring, interspersed with the four

143

topics: money (mainly that it's gone, how the bank works or who is contributing what), garden (he is a slave, he wants to do more, he can't do it, doesn't want to do more etc. etc.), the 'system' ( who is in it, who doesn't belong into it, what points are awarded for what, that it's not fair etc.), conspiracies (we all lie to him, the phones have been reprogrammed, the second Gisela has an affair with Rob etc. etc.), self-destruction (how to die, that he wants to die, that everything has been taken away from him and that's why he wants to die, that it's the end, saying good bye to friends etc. etc.), appointments (when, where, how, completely unrelated to daytime or what has actually been agreed on. Example: he wants to go for a personal trainer session at 6am in the morning, go to the optometrist on Xmas day etc.)

Today, Thursday, 26 December 2013, is the first time in my life that I am afraid to be alone with dad, because in don't know what will happen next and if I can handle it."

*Following dad's outburst during which he locked himself in their bedroom and started destroying things, it became clear even to mum that the situation had gone beyond "manageable" at least for us as non-professionals and within the confines of their own home. Dad needed 24-hour supervision and assistance of the kind neither mum nor I would be able to provide. At the same time the changes were occurring with such ferocity, that this was increasingly becoming a psychiatric emergency. An unimaginable decision had to be made: to admit dad to the emergency psychiatric ward of Penikoru Hospital, less than two days after Christmas. It is impossible to put into words the thoughts and the feelings, what this step meant for mum, for me, for all of us. Dad was no longer able to remain home. Despite the terrible situation, we were still confident that this was but a temporary setback and hopeful that with the right medication dad would be able to return soon.*

*In the end, his stint at Penikoru hospital would last three months.*

## Chapter 5 - Scrambled Words

*By early January, my leave was up and although I really wanted to stay and in perfect hindsight probably should have, there was little else that I could do to support mum, who quickly developed her own routine around her visits with dad. The drive to Penikoru usually lasted around 40 minutes, which together with time spent at the hospital took a good chunk out of each day. Mum diligently prepared food and brought dad lunch each day, so that he wouldn't miss his favorites and to give him a much needed change from the hospital fare on offer.*

*Penikoru hospital, in keeping with its charter as an emergency psychiatric ward, featured an assembly of some of the worst mental illnesses you could ever witness. There was a lot of moaning and screaming, a lot of fits and seizures. People here were unwell in the truest sense of the word. We knew dad simply didn't belong in a place like this and even if on some level he perhaps actually did, then not in this particular facility. He seemed far too well when compared to the other patients, far too well-groomed and "together", at least to the extent that attribute could be applied under the circumstances. He seemed like a man with a broken finger in an amputee ward. Unable to leave and with the surrounds being very "hospital-like", dad spent most of his time in the clinical surrounds of his room. Most of the time he would already be waiting for us inside the entrance when we arrived and just as often he would accompany us to the exit, waving us off behind the glass doors. They were heartbreaking moments for everyone, day in day out. And yet, just as many times he seemed to just accept and contently returned to his room after we left. No tears, no inkling that he may have felt the way we did.*

*To this day I wonder whether dad was actually fully aware, but had resigned himself to the way things were or if he had simply lost the connection to the world around him that would have allowed him to feel anything at all. For his sake and our own sanity, I still try to convince myself of the latter. Anything else would be just too unbearable.*

*Now it was time for me to return to work. I would not see dad again for a while, but assured mum that I would return as soon as possible or anytime she felt unable to cope. Saying good-bye to dad was different this time. Having witnessed his decline over the last three weeks there was now an uncertainty, whether or not he would even recognize me again the next time we met. Following my departure, mum's and my email and Skype correspondence resumed.*

15/01/2014

"Good morning dear Robert,

Thanks to you doing the driving to Penikoru and me looking out, I didn't have any issues getting there and back. Yesterday I brought lunch for dad. All the trolleys were in use and so I had brought a tablecloth, which we spread across, his bed and had a "picnic". We both enjoyed it. I made potato salad and meat patties and passionfruit with yoghurt as dessert, along with some kiwi fruit. Dad couldn't stop eating, he liked it so much. I will do this more often now, since I cook for myself anyway, I might as well bring dad something, too. The first part of the visit – lunch – went very well. The second part was a little sad, as dad had a few lucid moments and consequently told me about what he believed was happening to him. He asked: "Gisela, am I now an Idiot? I just can't find the right words anymore and then I say things that are completely different from what I actually want to convey. Then people often look at me strangely and I get the feeling they think I'm mentally disabled." For example, he knew that he asked me about the "water kicks" [his old bathroom slippers]. He knew that it was simply an impossible word, but he couldn't find the right one. He stumbled across his words and you could see him concentrating in order to find the right one. In the end, I tried to help him and asked whether he might mean his sandals. He told me about other words, which he just couldn't find a substitute for. We then wrote down the ones that came to his mind, along with the actual ones he was trying to say. We will do this every visit now. Maybe it will help him a little. I know our neighbor, Gay, who had a severe stroke a while back, said that she also suffered from loss of vocabulary, and how she felt when people didn't take her serious because she wasn't able to articulate herself. She told me it took months before it all came back to her. Some words disappeared forever, but it's hardly noticeable now. This being taken for a mentally disabled person when you are not, is terrible. That's why I, too, hope that dad might improve over time. But apart from these difficulties the visit was very nice and dad was very much "awake", in a good way. He asked me where the plane you are in might be right now, asked about TJ etc. Then he asked about the flowers in the garden, which he worries about and was very happy to hear that you helped tear out some of the withered bushes. The occupational therapist has also "taken action". Dad is now in charge of looking after the flowerpots in the unit's little garden. She also brought dad a puzzle book with instructions in English, since he likes solving these kinds of things. Some he did straight away. I will get an English/German/English Dictionary today, since often he knows a word in one language, but not the other. Dad's grammar is very good; he knows how to write the words, so perhaps a dictionary will be of help. Today I have to leave a little earlier for my visit as the therapist and I are going for lunch and then for a walk after. Last night dad called as usual and it was again a good call, with very few "slip ups".

P.S.: Dad had already explained to the staff why you couldn't come. He told me the Chinese doctor had said that she had some good talks with you and must have made some compliments as well. Dad told me he is very proud of you and that that's what he told everyone as well. He is sad that you can't be there, but fully understands that you have to go back to work and that your work isn't possible here in NZ."

16/01/2014

"Yesterday the therapist went for lunch with us. Dad clearly enjoyed it very much. His voice picked up and he never complained about the long walk. For the way back, Jill got the car though, so he wouldn't overexert himself.

Yesterday dad tried Tai Chi for the first time. A teacher comes on Wednesdays and holds classes for those interested. Initially dad complained that his muscles were too weak, but after the nurse and Jill spoke with him, he said he'd continue. I just finished my evening call with dad, who was still in relatively good spirits. The only thing he can't manage is the fact that he only has to dial our phone number to call me and that the phone number of the hospital has

147

nothing to do with it. So we went back and forth with the explanation, but by tomorrow he will have forgotten. Otherwise, he felt well physically after our outing today. Jill said it should be Ok if in future I took dad out for a walk and also visit the hospital café, which would make a huge difference. Back home I got a call from yet another nurse who wanted to make another appointment for an assessment. When I asked her what kind, she wasn't able to answer. I don't even know what the doctor's name is. I really don't want dad to be used as some kind of guinea pig, so will certainly protect him from that. The call irritated me immensely."

*For the next two weeks things continued in a similar way. Mum drove to Penikoru every day, dad seemed to stabilize and was getting help with the difficulties he was experiencing. They often took him out for walks and things "normalized" in as far as that was possible. His memory issues however continued, while doctors were trying to find the right balance of the medications they frequently changed.*

02/02/2104

"Today I spent two hours with dad at the hospital and we had a great time. We spoke a lot about his illness and what had happened. I get the feeling the medication is finally taking effect and dad was in very good spirits. He remembers his time at home when his health declined and even the incredible things he said to you in the kitchen once. He told me that he never really wanted to do that, but that his head told him otherwise. He also knows how he behaved in relation to the pills. He even demonstrated what he recalled. We were on a walk through the park at that time and we literally had to stop because we had to laugh so hard. Dad said he only learned at the hospital how to take the pills properly and that today it wasn't a problem anymore. He now knows that back then he thought we were trying to poison him and says he witnesses similar behavior from others at the hospital sometimes. He knows that without the meds life would be much, much worse and says he is glad such meds are even available today. Of course, I didn't mention to him in detail the things that had gone on during the last days he was at home. But he recognizes that they were hard times for us, but also that it was simply impossible for him to change his behavior at the time. He even said, "Who knows, if I hadn't acted so stubbornly in the beginning, maybe I'd be much better today."

I told dad that you got your job back in the Philippines. He didn't know that you had taken leave without pay when you dropped everything and came back. He is very happy the organization took you back and said he was proud of you. It was the first time that we managed to talk about his illness in such detail and dad never once gave me the impression that he didn't know what I was talking about. Quite the opposite: I was impressed about what he knew, remembered and the thoughts he had. For a while now I have been thinking that apart from having lost such a big part of his vocabulary he has actually improved considerably. By now, I also understand most of the time what he means when the words he chooses are perhaps the wrong ones. But dad is very intelligent. Everyone in the unit likes him. He participates, helps other patients and even brokers peace between quarreling patients. As you can see, it was a great day!

"6/02/2014

"Here everything is Ok, more or less. Today was Waitangi Day and so we visited Norbert in Penikoru. He is very confused at the moment, after the last few days which had been so good. I guess it was to be expected, but of course, these ups and downs are not nice. Nevertheless we had our lunch together and went for a walk after, during which attached photo was taken."

10/02/2014

"Today I didn't visit Norbert. I had an appointment for the car to get its warrant of fitness and so it got too late for the drive as I would have hit rush hour. Instead we spoke on the phone a few times, but dad was very confused; even the duty nurse could not figure out what Norbert wanted. He really was in "another world". Earlier, around 5pm he called and said he wanted to advise that we could take the flight at 8.05 tomorrow morning. He couldn't provide any other explanation. So I tried to distract him and told him I would have to think about it and that I would call him back around 7pm. By then he probably won't even remember, but he seemed ok with it for the moment and the nurse said it was probably for the best. Tomorrow I'll go again, but a little later in the day as the patients go on field trips on Tuesdays. By the way, dad says 'Hello'."

11/02/2014

"I can understand that it's hard to think about dad and not cry. Believe me, I feel the same. Just this afternoon it was like that again. I met the occupational therapist after my visit with dad and she asked me how I was coping. I don't know what happened, but I just started crying. She took some time out with me and we talked outside on a bench in the park. She said that dad's illness is truly cruel, as it allows him to come back momentarily and become the person he was, which is very confusing for family members; these sudden switches, this up and down, between "normal" and then the sudden drop is just too much to comprehend. I have tried to read up on it online but have found nothing that can help us."

12/02/2014

"Dad wasn't well at all today; physically, yes, but mentally he was very much gone. Kept asking about the price for flight tickets to Penikoru, asked when my flight was and told me the departure lounge was in the basement. When I told him I had come by car, since it's only 35km, he asked who was going to pay for that. When he heard we are paying for the fuel ourselves he opined the hospital should pay for it, along with the airfare. Well, tomorrow is another day and things may be different."

*Dad's ups and downs continued. His delusions increased but were never violent or suicidal; not like they had been when he was still at home. Mum and dad went for walks frequently and she captured many of the "happier days" during those months in photographs which still showed dad almost the way he used to be. His phone calls were always somewhat of a challenge as they usually occurred around 6 or 7pm, when his mind would enter what later mum would refer to as his "sundowner" phase. Overall dad had improved though, clearly thanks to a careful balancing of the medication; improved to the point where the difference between him and the rest of the patients had become so stark that it was simply no longer tenable and potentially quite unhealthy for him to remain in this unit, which had only ever been meant as a temporary solution in any case. It was also clear however, that dad returning home at that point still remained a somewhat risky proposition. The need for care, despite his improved mental state was, after all still considerable. Due to dad's rapid deterioration over the Christmas holidays we had never gotten round to completing the power of attorney and by the time we did dad's mental state no longer allowed him to sign the documents, which required the signatories to be of sound mind. So in addition to looking after dad, now came the paper war of securing court orders, so that not only decisions could be made on his behalf, but that mum could formally sign his release forms and get him out of an environment which had truly outlived its purpose and in the long run was likely to cause more harm than good.*

# Chapter 6 - Hope Always Floats

03/03/2014

"I met with the doctor and the therapist today, who gave me their assessment report. On this occasion, I found out that there might be a shortcut to get dad into the rest home: a temporary guardianship. The process to get full legal guardianship can take weeks and until I have some kind of guardianship dad cannot be released. We also spoke about subsidies, rest home accommodation etc. which they all explained again. After that I visited dad, who was a little grumpy. It seems he's been spoiled a bit from all the being looked after at the hospital. This afternoon it was time for him to have his blood pressure taken. You can't imagine how he pestered the nurses to have "this important measurement" taken. And since they didn't "jump" straight away he was grumbling. And he immediately went on to tell me that it took two of them to get it right anyway, since they all do it wrong. Well, he often doesn't understand even simple things anymore."

*Below is a copy of the medical report, the assessment completed on dad in March 2014. It was significant and saddening for several reasons. It removed any doubt about and thus much of the hope we had held in relation to dad's illness. It put a full stop to what had previously still ended with a question mark. Not only that, but it was also the first time in what had already become quite a history of appointments, tests and assessments, that bastard Lewy was formally identified as a possibility. In a way, it was the first time he got caught out and yet he would be allowed to sneak around and do his thing behind the scenes for some time yet before someone would finally shine a light and point their finger at him.*

1. I am a registered medical practitioner:

   (a) holding the following qualifications
   MB ChB 2006 Otago
   and

   (b) practising as a
   Psychiatry Registrar for Psychogeriatric Service

2. I examined the Subject Person for the purpose of this Report on the following date:
   26 February 2014

3. At the time of the examination referred to in the preceding paragraph:

4. The Subject Person's general health is:

5. The Subject Person suffers from the following disorders:

6. The Subject Person wholly lacks the capacity to understand the nature, and to foresee the consequences, of decisions in respect of all aspects of his personal care and welfare.

7. The Subject Person partially lacks the capacity to communicate decisions relating to his personal care and welfare generally.

8. In my opinion the appointment of a Welfare Guardian is likely to promote and/or protect the welfare and best interests of the Subject Person.

9. The Subject Person wholly lacks the competence to manage his affairs in relation to property.

10. In my opinion the appointment of a Property Manager in respect of all or any of the Subject Person's property is likely to promote and/or protect the welfare and best interests of the Subject Person.

11. In my opinion the Subject Person is not likely to recover competence to manage his own affairs.

12. In my opinion the Subject Person would not be able to understand the purpose and consequence of the present application, even if a Solicitor were appointed to explain this to the Subject Person.

13. In my opinion the Subject Person wholly lacks the capacity to understand the nature and purpose of the proceedings and would not be able to take part in a meaningful way.

14. I have the following further comments to assist the Court: From a clinical perspective Mr ▇▇▇ has a diagnosis of dementia though the aetiology remains speculative (possibly related to Alzheimer's/Lewy Body/cerebrovascular disease). The severity of Mr ▇▇▇'s dementia is of such a degree that it diminishes his ability to take care of himself. In my opinion Mr ▇▇▇ lacks the capacity to understand the nature, and to foresee the consequences, of decisions in respect of matters relating to his personal care and welfare. Mr ▇▇▇ also lacks the capacity to manage his own affairs in relation to his property. Mr ▇▇▇ is not likely to recover competence to manage his own affairs.

15. My comments are as above.

.............................................................
(Signature of Registered Medical practitioner)

27 February 2014

Psychogeriatric Service, ▇▇▇ Hospital, ▇▇▇,
PO Box 50-215, ▇▇▇ 240.

154

*I think the email I wrote to my wife Sharon that day best sums up how I felt after reading the report:*

"Hi honey,

Just to share, attached neurologist report the doctors issued to mum for the purpose of applying for guardianship. I know I am up to date with what is happening, but reading it in black and white....is sooo hard to take. I am beating myself up for having missed all these opportunities to be with dad when he was still "with us"...his 70th birthday...their wedding anniversary....all those occasions. And now it's too late. My dad and I were so close. And now it's all gone. I hate myself for this. And the worst thing is: I knew the moment would come one day, but I fucking procrastinated. And now there isn't even a way to let him know how sorry I am...because he wouldn't understand.

This is all fucked. All fucked."

## Chapter 7 - Home is not a Place

*Despite the emotions that we all went through at the time, the report also gave the whole "episode", which we still tended to look at things as, some kind of finality. In typical German fashion perhaps even, having something in black and white made it "official" and thus less confusing. Dad too was relieved that there was finally a diagnosis. His ups and downs continued, but his delusions now were harmless and usually revolved around the same themes which made them far more manageable. In addition, he continued to experience extended periods, sometimes almost entire days, of lucidity. Towards the end of March dad was even able to dictate a message to me, in which he expressed how hopeful he was that things were on the up and up, how proud he was of me and that he was confident that together we would all get through this just fine. By the time temporary guardianship and court orders had been processed, dad was in relatively good condition, to the point where he was even allowed to return home. I remember feeling a little uneasy about it since the recollection of the time prior to his admittance was still vivid, but I ultimately trusted mum's and the doctors' judgement on the matter and wasn't about to rain on her parade.*

*And so just prior to the Easter holidays in April 2014, dad was finally released and allowed to go home. A joyous moment for both mum and dad, if ever there was one, and a collective sigh of relief. Over the following weeks mum managed and dad seemed exactly the way he had been during his hospital stay: confused and often repetitively obsessing about one or the other aspect, but mum was always able to distract and talk him round; something which took much energy and patience, probably more than she may have admitted at the time.*

*Then on 21 May, came the following mail:*

"Hello Robert,

Here the email as promised, since dad can read Skype very well and I don't want him to read this message, even though he told me that it would be ok for me to write about it. All in all today was not a good day. It started with a letter from the council with a test bill for the

156

water meter based billing which would soon follow. The envelope was addressed to both of us. The form showed the average water usage for a 2 to 3 member family depicted as small drawings of people. Dad took the envelope and said suddenly: What will you do when they find out about this scam? I asked which scam and dad said: There are only two people shown in this household but there are three of us! I asked him who the third person was. He said he didn't know, but was sure there were three. I couldn't get through to him. In the end it turned out that he thinks there are two Gisela's, but he is not sure which one I am. He doesn't know my birthday, doesn't remember our wedding and says he also doesn't know which Gisela used to bring him food when he was in hospital. It went on and on, whereby dad was very calm, but completely emotionless. After some time I terminated the conversation and went for a walk with him. We sat at the duck pond for quite some time and talked: It turns out that dad still can't get over, if ever, his stay at the hospital, even though he is mostly aware of what led to it. But there is so much for him to work through: the mistrust, not just towards individuals but in general. He follows me around like a puppy wherever I go; he doesn't want to be alone. No matter where I am, even when I just pop over to the neighbors to ask for help with something, I can be sure that within a minute he is standing next to me. He has very little self-confidence, which I try to give back to him. He has a terrible fear that he might have to go back to the hospital or into a rest home. Even the fact that I now have legal guardianship [and thus the decision is taken away from doctors or other officials] does not give him any peace of mind. He says he sometimes understands it all, but when he's down like today he connects everything back to money and how others want to take it away from him. Please don't think days like this happen too often. Luckily they don't. On the other hand I am glad that dad is speaking very openly about what is going on inside him. Most of all he now needs a much slower daily rhythm. We don't invite people over and don't accept any invitations. Dad only wants to visit people he knows very well and we never go out in the evenings. Between afternoon and evening dad gets very tired and any changes during that time are very demanding for him. I also told him how I feel when he speaks of the 2 Gisela's. He says he only knows the other Gisela from phone conversations etc. etc. Tonight he said: You know, I love you, no matter of what I may be thinking "up there". That was a very nice end to the day. But seeing dad like this also hurts so much, especially when he expresses his thoughts and feelings. He desperately wants to be the way he used to be, but knows it's not possible. The only thing that can help from our end is patience, patience and more patience. The prospect of you arriving is his joy. Thankfully, his feelings for you are indestructible. He said himself that the bond between father and son can never be broken. Please don't worry about me Rob. I am able to handle it. I just want to give him back his trust. I know that not all the damage to the brain can be repaired, so I try to give him a life without fears and mistrust. As I have already said, these very difficult days have become rarer, but today I realized that it all just lurks in the background and comes to the forefront again and again. But I am learning how to deal with it [when it does]."

21/05/2017

"Your suggestion to stay at a motel is very caring and I understand why you made it. But I think it's better for dad if you stay with us. I am not sure whether he would understand it if you didn't. We can try it anyway. I think dad is also proud of the fact that we changed the garage into a temporary bedroom, which we may actually use for guests in the future. Not a lot of hassle, we just made it a little more comfortable. Having you here means a lot to dad, perhaps more than you may think. Of course he knows you will have to leave again and I am aware that won't be easy. I know I said dad needs his routine, but I also know how to take his mind of things. Please don't think dad and me living together poses a lot of issues. We have many good talks and a lot of fun watching TV. We set the table together, he dries the dishes, helps with the grocery shopping; simply put our life is actually almost normal again. I am truly impressed how much progress dad has made. He often thinks about my well-being, too. For example yesterday I asked him whether he actually enjoyed Sunday church or whether he went because he felt he had to. He said he actually enjoyed it, but only wanted to go if I wanted it as well, as not to impose on me otherwise. Dad is expressing his feelings

158

a lot more than he used to and that is giving us many opportunities for meaningful and rewarding conversations. I know our life isn't as it was before, but it is enjoyable nonetheless. I had imagined it much more difficult. I try to start each day anew. It is my firm belief that God is present, helps me and will never abandon me. Maybe we never talked much about these things, but this firm belief has accompanied me through my whole life and is my anchor. And it gets me over many of life's hurdles, much more than others could perhaps. It gives me such an enormous amount of strength, you can't even imagine. Another thing that helps is thinking positive. Not to ignore the negative or even cover it up, but it is rather an inner voice that keeps telling me what I should do or think. I know you think a lot about these spiritual aspects, so perhaps you know what I mean."

*I visited again for a couple of weeks, following the end of my contract in the Philippines and of course because it was dad's birthday on 6 June, a very different one that year no doubt. I tried my best to cope with his often very confused conversations, but overall the time went quite well compared to a mere few months prior. He enjoyed his birthday cake and the photos from that day were some of the last I took of him smiling and laughing almost the same way he had always done. I think having me there also gave mum a much needed reprieve as I tried to give them as much of a vacation as possible. The time also helped us tie up some legal loose ends. Seeing what trouble we had to go through to be allowed to make decisions on dad's behalf, just because we had not taken care of powers of attorney earlier, mum and I made sure we got papers signed between her and I, just in case. Sometimes we still needed to explain to dad who we were. It wasn't like before where he had sudden bouts of mistrust brought on by not recognizing us, but he genuinely forgot who we were. So mum would yet again, ever so patiently get out the photo albums, spread out the pictures and go through them one by one until dad's memory slowly returned or he at least was satisfied that we were actually the family we said we were. As with most holidays and family visits, the time passed all too quickly.*

*Things remained as steady as they could in the following months and in October 2014, Sharon and I visited again and spent a few wonderful weeks with mum and dad. Sharon patiently did puzzles with dad every day and listened to his often confused monologues. Overall, though he participated as best as he could and reveled in the attention he got from his daughter in law, whom he hadn't seen in over a year. The year went on and things didn't really change much. Mum and dad even spent Christmas together at home and without too many "incidents". New Year's Eve came and went and it was already late January, when the following message arrived:*

21/01/2015

"Dad's confusion has increased at the moment, so I am not taking him along on errands. It's just too hot for him to sit in the car at the moment. This morning he told me that he couldn't go into his room because there was a high-ranking cardinal sleeping in his bed. The person had arrived during the night and was very tired, so dad offered his bed. Nevertheless, I went into the room and of course there was nobody else. Dad opined he must have left. This evening he asked me where I would be sleeping tonight. I asked him whether I was allowed to sleep in the small bedroom [mum had moved there when dad returned as he was often restless and needed his peace and quiet]. He said that would be ok. The he asked who else was arriving today. And again he started talking about the other Gisela. I apparently wasn't her today. He also asked who would come and distribute the pills. But as I mentioned I can handle these situations and calm him down with my responses. At least dad had a few good hours today after changing meds yesterday. But I made a mistake, which probably triggered his confusion: Dad wanted to sit at the computer and enter the log on info for online banking. So I tried to help him and gave him the numbers, while he entered them (I know by tomorrow he's forgotten everything, but I just tried to help). He saw the accounts and was satisfied all was in order. Then he wanted to play some online games, which he tried, but soon realized that he just couldn't do it anymore. And this threw him off completely. In future, I will have to set aside computer time for him, perhaps 10 minutes, or so, and then distract him before there is overload. I still make so many mistakes..."

*Mum always had a talent to deliver bad news as softly as possible and downplay the many things that were happening in the background. Within less than two weeks, the situation worsened to a point were once again despair took over. Dad had some serious "drop-outs", becoming more and more incontinent and his*

160

*delusions about the two Gisela's more and more pronounced, to the point where mum began to fear for her own safety. He wasn't violent, but his head now told him that he was having an affair with the "other Gisela" and his approaches became as worrying and "creepy" as they were delusional. His obsessions about money, his hallucinations became so engrained that it became very difficult for mum to "distract" him, as she had usually been able to do. What I heard was more than enough reason to come back for a visit, especially when mum, on 1 February 2017 out of the blue and without any prompt whatsoever said she had transferred "a little something" into my account in case I had to book a ticket urgently at any stage. Things had come to a peak and the EMS report, speaks of what happened that day:*

# Urgent Community Care
## Care Record

***Incomplete***

## Patient Details | Incident Details

| Patient Details | | | | Incident Details | | | |
|---|---|---|---|---|---|---|---|
| First Names | | Ethnicity | Other European | Case Date | 1/02/2015 | Case Code | 780 |
| Surname | | NHI No | JJ66196 | Case Number | 086 | Case Type | Medical |
| | | | | Follow-up Case No. | | Vehicle | TGO3 |
| Date of Birth | 1939 | ACC Number | | Incident Facility Name | | Patient Status | 4 |
| Patients Age | 75 years | Phone | | | | Dispatch Code | 26C01 SICK PERSON ALTERED LOC |
| Gender | Male | Next of kin | | Incident Street Address | | | |
| Res. Facility Name | | Guardian | | | | | |
| | | GP | | Incident Suburb | | Category | Other Neurological |
| Address | | GP Fax | | ETOH | No | | |
| Suburb | | Practice | Team Medical | Accessed System Via | 111 Call | Destination if UCC transport | |
| City | | | | First Contact by Patient | | Send report to GP | Yes |
| PostCode | | | | ECP Dispatched | | | |
| | | | | Arrival on Scene | | Access details for UCC revisit | Yes |
| | | | | Patient Discharge/Referred | | | |
| | | | | | | Freedom Alarms to contact patient | False |
| | | | | | | Outcome | See and Treat |
| | | | | | | Revisit Consent | Yes |

## Vitals

| Time | Pulse | Resps | BP | SPO2 | SPO2 Mode | GCS | BGL | Temp | Temp Site | Pain | ETCO2 | Peak Flow |
|---|---|---|---|---|---|---|---|---|---|---|---|---|
| 1/02/2015 2:15:00 p.m. | 74 | 16 | 130/75 Sitting Left Arm | 99 | On Room Air | 15(m6v5e4) | 7.4 | 36.5 | Tympanic | 0/10 | | |

## Call Presentation

Dementia-Periods of confusion

## Current History

PC-Episodes of confusion

HPC-Pt has been having episodes of increasing confusion over last 2/52, seen by GP and medications adjusted since. Toady pt has had an episode of confusion-unable to recognise his wife and asking his wife to leave the house. Wife has called TM advised to call an ambulance.

SE-
CVS - no chest pain, dizziness all the time, no palpitations
RS - no SOB, no cough, no cold / flu symptoms
CNS - no LOC, no headache, no weakness, no paresthesia, vision and hearing normal for patient
GI - slight abdo pain? pt states normal, no bowel symptoms, bowels opened normally, no nausea, no vomiting
GU - no urinary symptoms

Impression-
Increasing confusion secondary to dementa (likely as it has been ongoing)
?TIA

Plan-
Assessment
Baselines
Discuss safety issues with wife as pt has previously become aggressive towards her.
D/w nurse at TM-pt has appointment tomorrow with Dr
Grandson to stay overnight-Any concerns - if pt becomes threatening or aggressive towards wife and
grandson they will go straight to neighbours and call 111 police and ambo
?longterm arrangements/respite care/full assessment

### Urinalysis

| Leukocytes | Nitrates | Protein | pH | SpG | Blood | Ketones | Glucose |
|---|---|---|---|---|---|---|---|
| Neg. | Neg. | Neg. | 6.5 | 1.015 | neg. | Neg. | Neg. |

### Treatment

| Time | ECP Drug | ECP GuideLine | EAS GuideLine | ECP Skill | EASDrug | EASSkills | Adverse Reaction | Relief | Management |
|---|---|---|---|---|---|---|---|---|---|
| | | | | | | | | | |

### Outcome

| | |
|---|---|
| Patient Outcomes | See and Treat |
| Patient Transport | No Ambulance Transport |
| Patient Outcome Unsatisfactory due to | |
| Referral Pathway | GP Surgery Appointment |

Verbal☐ Written☐     **Patient Advice**

**GP Notes**

Paramedic

Free Ambulance

Signature _AHundgren_

---

03/02/2015

"It was another difficult day here. Dad was not in "our world" at all
– except perhaps during lunch, which he ate. But he barely spoke.
He wanted to get dressed in winter clothes – it was 25 degrees Celsius
outside – and go to "his house". He also wanted to know how much
he had to pay and what a night in the room had cost. He didn't want
to sleep here as it was not his home. That's how it went the whole
day. I sometimes get the feeling he is further and further removed
from our world. He talks about nothing but his possessions. Perhaps
you can remember the time at the hospital when he would talk to
himself continuously. That's what he does all day now, but also
expects me to pay attention to what he says. Here, too, I am learning
to withdraw at the right time. This evening he demanded that I
create a list of all the pills and write down exactly what is in them. I

told him that at 9pm in the evening I wasn't going to write down anything anymore. I said to him 'let's go to sleep for today and see what happens tomorrow'. He finally went to his bedroom, but "discovered" there was no name sign on the door. I suggested he may want to write his name on the door himself, but in the end, he didn't do it. He complains that he can't take the pills himself, but then says he can do everything himself and so on and so on. Nothing was right for him today. I read online that these mood swings may last a few more days before they subside and better mood prevails. I am hoping for the best. Our dog is till incredibly caring towards dad and sleeps next to his bed whenever he lies down. Dad only pets her briefly most of the time – I believe he likes her, but doesn't recognize her anymore.

4/02/2015

"This morning it was a little difficult, but this afternoon dad, even though he wasn't really "with us", was in a good mood, wanted to help and was overall quite balanced. This morning when I went into his room he asked whether I worked here. Probably because I had stripped down his bed – he had only had a small "accident". I immediately saw that his thoughts were elsewhere. I read up on Lewy Body and about the kind of care patients need and tried to put it into practice today. Maybe that helped. His mind is consumed by thoughts about money. Whether people might come who will take away the house? What is the room rate for a room here? How much is breakfast? And so on. I hope that the advice given by the doctors online will help a bit. I will keep trying over the next few days and see if it does. For example, one mustn't object to the patients or push back, but distract them as calmly as possible or, if that doesn't work, communicate as best as possible on their level. Under no circumstances should one tell the patient that something is wrong or correct them, because they don't understand. They will get agitated and their mood is likely to worsen. Anyway, I tried this today and it was a quiet and Ok afternoon. I had to do a lot of paperwork for the taxes in Germany today. Dad sat with me patiently. I tried to get him to glue receipts onto plain paper, but it was too hard for him.

Whenever I went to my room to make a photocopy, he would follow, sit down, and watch. I wish there were more days like this."

*I had been watching these latest developments, including the ambulance callout from a distance, initially from our home in Kenya and then from my job in Myanmar. Although distance never is a good thing in times of family crisis, it can also give insights, which would otherwise be denied. The ability to look at a situation from a little further away, taking everything into account and looking at it not from within but from the outside in, can reveal developments one would otherwise perhaps be oblivious to. It was becoming clear that mum was desperately trying to keep dad at home, despite now sometimes being afraid for her own safety and the "bad days" not only far outweighing the good ones, but also threatening to consume anything and everything that was still left of their former life. Both mum and dad lived in fear: dad, during the few lucid moments he still had, in fear of going back to some kind of facility and mum in fear of not being able to control the situation enough to keep him at home. It was a losing battle, a war of attrition. I had tried to support mum as best as I could, spent time with dad and observed, but always kept quiet when it came to mum's understandable but increasingly unrealistic desire to look after dad in their own home.*

*So, with a heavy heart, on 5/02/2015, I wrote the following message:*

"Hello Mum,

I wanted to write this mail for your eyes only, since you might read my other one from earlier to dad as well.

Your reports about dad's condition naturally affect me deeply and I am fearful about the speed of these changes. Of course, I spoke with Sharon about it as well and we agreed that we will both be there to help if needed. She now has a multi-entry visa and so we can travel without all the additional paperwork. Same with me: I can travel anytime. I know you read a lot about this illness and how one should handle the condition. But Mum, and it is incredibly hard for me to write this: You have held on to keeping dad at home because you live for and enjoy the "good moments" in which as you write he returns to "our world", and which give you both focus and energy. Of course, I understand that and I admire your dedication to dad's care. But what happens if one day dad doesn't "come back" from his

165

world? I wish I didn't have to ask the question, but I think we generally speak openly enough to bring it up; which of course we have to some degree already. But what happens when this threshold is reached? It's probably difficult to determine, but when I hear about dad like the other day when he tried to get away in search of "his house", then I have to ask what would happen if he were successful and you can't hold him back. Or what would happen if one day you are unable to distract him and calm him down, because either the timing is wrong or the situation doesn't allow it? I think back with horror to the time when dad put on all manner of jewelry from the bedroom, tore up his wallet etc. My worry here is not about your ability to handle it, because I know you might still be able to. What I do worry about is that the options are forever shrinking in cases like this: now the ambulance, the psychiatric emergency helpline, or even the Police would need to be called; and once that happens the decision to admit dad to a facility or hospital will be out of your hands. And this, we already know, would not only be terrible for dad, but might then also mean that an "open unit" like Rawhiti rest home may no longer be an option. According to your latest messages, I take that dad already thinks he *is* in a rest home (his questions about costs, name sign etc.). I am deeply worried. Please tell me very honestly what I can do. I am here; ready to come back to you. I love you both very, very much and pray that something may still change for the better."

5/02/2015

"Thank you for your caring mails, especially the personal mail addressed to me. I understand your grave concerns around dad and I. You are so far away and can only rely on my reports. But please believe me, my reports are very honest. If I had trouble getting through the day with dad – I would write about it. It is true that dad's mental health has suffered a sudden decline, but despite this, I can handle things. Today for example, we had a good day and were even able to laugh together. Last night I stumbled across a webpage that covered "Capgras Syndrome". I brought up the page "Dementia and Capgras Syndrome: handling Behavior and Emotional Fallout". Capgras Syndrome named after the Frenchman

166

who identified it, matches dad's condition exactly. The syndrome manifests itself in the irrational belief that a familiar person or place has been replaced with an exact duplicate – an imposter. The write-up is very interesting and provides some help for care givers. I tried some of the things this morning with great success. Perhaps the additional meds dad is now taking in the mornings help as well in terms of his depression. But at least I have noticed that dad reacted in a positive manner to my approach to his monologues. It is so incredibly nice of the two of you to want to come immediately when it becomes necessary. But I like to assure you, I am Ok – even TJ said I was doing well and that I can handle dad. And if he wants to go look for his house, I will just join him and then distract his thoughts. And should he leave by himself, it wouldn't automatically mean he would have to be admitted. Normally patients are returned home first and then I, as legal guardian still have a say. It happens all the time that confused people leave home and are brought back. What I will do is to smuggle our address and phone number into his wallet. But at the moment it's not that dramatic. We just have to live with these mood swings. These will remain – can be of short duration or last for days. This type of dementia is so "multi-faceted", I admire the scientists which pursue their research with such patience. This evening when saying good night I asked dad whether he didn't agree this had been a nice day. His answer: A wonderful day – and what are we going to do tomorrow? I told him, I wanted to sleep first and then develop a schedule for the day. He thought that was a good idea and stroked my hand. I am writing this so you don't always get bad news, but some good ones, too. I also initially thought that dad perhaps thought he was at a rest home when he asked about the name sign. But that's not so. I think it's more the hospital and Rawhiti which frightened him a lot. He always emphasizes, regardless of whether it was a good day or a not so good day that he wouldn't want to keep living if he had to go to a hospital or a rest home. I say it using different words than this, but in retrospect, I know that the two institutions left a lasting shock. And when he has a bad day he keeps talking about how we will put him away into a rest home. Let us hope and pray that dad's health will allow him to stay here for a long, long time."

07/02/2015

"We watched the coverage of the rugby game in Wellington today. Dad also watched, but his mind was elsewhere. The day was one of the good ones, although the word "good" is probably more attributable to me than to dad. It is truly sad to see the different things that are happening in his head from day to day. Suddenly dad said: Our Rosy is gone. I got a fright and thought the dog had run away. But there she came walking around the corner from the garden. I said: There she is. But dad said no, she only looked like Rosy, but it's not her. Then he told me some confused story about Rosy and how she was being held at a kennel in a pub etc. I listened, gave meaningless feedback, and eventually got his mind onto other things. He seems to have lost all connection to our reality. You know, throughout the past weeks I have gotten used to it, but I can imagine it would be very hard for you if you were here and had to patiently respond to these irrational things, while hiding your thoughts and feelings. It takes practice to be able to handle it. Even the smallest of things, which we wouldn't even think twice about, are unfathomable for him. The only explanation I have is that dad had another TIA at some stage without us noticing it and which hit important parts of the brain. This afternoon we baked his favorite apple pancakes. Dad couldn't stop eating and smiled from ear to ear."

*The next week went by without further incidents. Mum and dad visited the doctor who agreed that it was not yet necessary for me to be there, but asked mum to email him updates, so that they could keep monitoring the meds and how dad reacted to them. He had good days and bad days. Days where he wanted to be admitted to a home so he would be out of the way and days where the fear of going to a home preoccupied his mind. Mum kept insisting that she was able to handle the situation, but I could read between the lines that it was beginning to take a toll on her as well. I began speaking with TJ behind the scenes and he too was increasingly getting concerned. Yet each time I broached the subject she would stonewall. To this day I think she felt that nobody but her truly understood dad. And who was I to argue against the sentiment? But as we had seen so many times before, brief periods of relative stabilization were usually followed by another decline...*

# Chapter 8 - Paranoia

14/02/2015

"After a few good days the mood changed this afternoon and suddenly dad's tone became quite aggressive. He asked when I would go home and shortly after accused me that I had stolen our wooden Maria carving and many other things. This went on for a while and there was no talking to him. Then he turned around and wanted to put on his shoes so he could go to the Police and lodge a complaint. I had never seen this aggressive behavior before. I then said that it might be better to go see the emergency doctor. I called them and the nurse told me to ring 111. The operator was very helpful and connected me to a special nurse, apparently trained to assess whether someone should be dispatched to assist. Meanwhile dad had calmed down, but insisted on what he had claimed. Then, when the nurse asked to speak with him, he suddenly was very nice! But the nurse wasn't fooled so easily. She gave me a number I should call immediately if dad's behavior changed, in which case they would send help straight away. This number is attended 24/7. I had a very good talk with the nurse. Dad calmed down, ate his dinner, and then wanted to go to bed early. When I suggested he should take the evening pills, he obliged. Now it's 8pm and he is sleeping. The nurse said I should get another doctor's appointment, which I will try on Monday morning. I will also write to Dr. Stephenson. I am so very sorry to write another mail like this. I can imagine how you must feel. The situation changed from minute to minute. There is nothing predictable about this illness. I am Ok so far. It is good to know that I can get help even at night, if necessary. Again, Robert: I am OK."

*Despite mum's assurances however, things were far from Ok. Dad's behavior did not change. Mum was no longer the one whom he trusted to help him make sense of the world he now spent most of his time in. Instead, she was now becoming the target of his conspiracy theories and thus his anger at times whenever bastard Lewy had dad's brain misfiring at levels not previously seen. He never lashed out or became physically aggressive, but his demeanor was hostile enough for things to* escalate to a point where a more permanent solution to the increasingly unmanageable situation was needed.

On 16/02/2015, after a long struggle and an unspeakable investment of energy devoted to keeping dad at home, even mum, who had been almost superhuman in her patience and resourcefulness, admitted defeat. Dad simply could no longer stay at home and on referral from their trusted physician, was admitted to Rawhiti rest home. A flurry of official correspondence followed to apply for care subsidies, advising the family court and get all manner of other administrative work done that was required. Thankfully, the rest home owners had known dad prior to his illness and we had made contact with them well ahead of time, so the process was uncomplicated. Mum's Skype messages from that time are no longer available, but having to check dad into the home, was one of the most traumatic moments along a road, which would have a lot more of the same in store. Mum visited dad daily as she had done the last time during his stay at Penikoru hospital and arranged dad's personal trainer to come once a week so dad got some exercise in. She and TJ decorated his tiny room to make it more 'homely'. Dad seemed to take the move well. If anything, his mood could probably best be described as indifferent. He participated in the rest home's daily activities – probably the youngest resident at that stage, he was more agile than the others, many of whom relied on Zimmer frames and wheelchairs. Many of his hallucinations now revolved around work, whereby he would keep a small leather folder with various paper clippings and conducted operations from his room which he imagined to be his "office". In his mind, the single story building had both upper and lower floors and even turned into a cruise ship occasionally. Lucid moments were now rare. Meanwhile mum for the first time since being appointed property manager for dad, had to do their annual accounts for the family courts – a costly bureaucratic travesty if ever there was one, especially since all their property and accounts were owned jointly. Public Trust auditors needed to inspect, family courts needed to approve the invasive and extremely detailed account breakdowns the system demanded – all the while completely ignoring that mum in fact owned everything just as much as dad did. It was another level of insanity on top of dad's struggle, which not only overwhelmed but also totally consumed virtually any time mum had outside her daily visits to the rest home. I tried to help as much as I could from a distance, together with our lawyer who was assisting mum back home – the billable hours in conjunction with Public Trust Audit fees, thanks to the utterly moronic requirements of the state, eventually and unnecessarily amounting to several thousand dollars. Between scanning and emailing reports and daily Skype messages with mum, I wrote the

171

*occasional letter to dad, which mum could take along and read to him. He would keep these in his brown leather folder and show them to everyone as "official correspondence" he had as part of his "important work". New and disturbing developments were dad's sudden bouts of sleepiness, which now without warning had him drop where he stood. On 23 April 2015 it was time to again contact their doctor. It was also time to book another flight home.*

"Dear Dr. Stephenson,

I hope this email finds you well. It has been some time since I have written, but since my mother and I communicate re. my father almost daily, I have been kept informed on developments. One of the recent changes is my father's inability to stay awake. He seems to fall asleep spontaneously, in some instances literally where he is at that moment. This morning for example Rawhiti staff found him kneeling in front of the bed, having fallen asleep while praying and they were unable to wake him for quite some time. As of late, this appears to happen with some regularity, albeit completely random. I googled (more or less on a whim) the connection between Lewy Body/Dementia and Narcolepsy and it appears the latter can appear in the course of the illness. One thing mentioned was potential mitigation of frequency and severity through the introduction of appropriate dietary supplements (Hypocretin/Orexin).

I know I may be way off on this, but thought I at least ask you if perhaps this is something we should consider for dad? He does seem to have deteriorated further and I would like to try everything to make things easier/better for him, even if it is for a little while.

Thank you so much for all the support you have given and continue to give to my parents.

Best                                                                 regards,

Rob Landeck"

*I arrived on 3 May 2015 and visited dad the very next day. To be honest, I was shocked at the size of his accommodation. The tiny room was barely 3 meters long and 2 meters wide – more a cell really than a room, with a single bed, a chair a small dresser and a bedside table. His world had shrunk to less than six square meters. There was a wardrobe as well, which at some point most days would become the object of his obsession. Each day we came, tidied it up and folded his clothes and each afternoon or evening he would take it all apart again, "rearranging" everything into complete chaos. He spent a lot of time sleeping, but did sit with the others at mealtimes and during activities. He still loved the little sports games they played almost daily: "bowling" with a giant inflatable ball and pins, throwing a little beanbag towards an inflatable giant wedge of Swiss cheese and scoring points for the different holes it landed in, or rolling a tennis ball trying to go through one of several holes in a board. He was still fitter than everyone else around him was and so usually beat the other residents by a mile. In fact, he was quite competitive and really took it to heart when someone else out-threw him on occasion. Rawhiti was an open unit and as such, residents were free to come and go as they chose, most of them staying in due to their diminished physical abilities. It meant that mum could take dad for lunches in nearby cafes and restaurants, take him for walks through the park or for an ice cream at the beach, all things he enjoyed immensely. There were several common rooms with TVs and comfy chairs and we would often sit together and chat away about this and that, with dad usually giving us his latest theories about his work, the home, the other people etc. which he all managed to combine into quite elaborate hallucinations. He had aged a lot over the last few months and although he still smiled when he saw me, recognizing me for who I was became more and more difficult. Sometimes I was a colleague, other times "the guy" and yet other times actually his son whom he would then introduce to everyone each and every time. It was truly tough seeing him like this and the drive home to their house was usually filled with tears and desperate attempts to hold it together. I am still surprised I never crashed the car in the process. Usually both mum and I would have at least one double whiskey when we got home to calm our nerves.*

*One of the emerging issues in May 2015, in addition to what I came to refer to as narcoleptic bouts, was the fact that he increasingly wanted to "run away". He never knew, nor was able to articulate where he wanted to go, but the urge became stronger and stronger. In the beginning, there had been a few times when as we were leaving, having already said good-bye for the day, he would suddenly try to come with us; each time an emotionally extremely challenging event as you can imagine. He would stand there, hand still on the door handle, looking at us in a state of bewilderment, while we explained to him that he would need to stay. The crazy thing was that his bewilderment was as short lived as these moments. As soon as one of the caregivers would gently take his arm and begin talking to him, his thoughts would shift and he would immediately forget about the plight, which had caused him distress literally seconds before. To this day, I still wonder whether he actually fully recognized the situation for what it was and then just "pretended" to be distracted out of defeat. He was, after all very intelligent and able to "disguise" certain things very well. It is a notion that is simply too terrible to contemplate, and yet every once in a while it still nibbles away at me....*

*Very soon, I would find myself on one of many search missions, having received another call from the rest home that dad had "disappeared", but for now things were still manageable. And yet, only a couple of weeks after my departure that would change:*

# Chapter 9 - Another Step on Lewy's Ladder

"Dear          Dr.          Stephenson,          Dear          Brenda,

I hope this email finds you well. I am writing on my mother's behalf, ahead of her forthcoming request for an appointment to discuss treatment approaches to my father's clearly declining state of health. For the last few weeks the number of instances involving dad becoming more and more aggressive in his attempts to leave Rawhiti have become equally more and more frequent, culminating in today's episode whereby it was virtually impossible for both staff and mum to deter him from using force to break a door to get out. At the same time, his inability to communicate, hold a consistent or rational stream of thought and verbalize anything but his own hallucinatory reality, means that previous approaches of reaching him by talking to him, trying to distract him or calm him through hot drinks/food etc. no longer work in these now more frequent instances. We would like to explore with you the possibility of increasing or changing his medication to reduce his aggression, as we fear that otherwise Rawhiti staff may soon find themselves unable to cope, despite their best efforts and expressed desire to keep dad at the home          for          as          long          as          possible. I know mum had previously been against treatment involving heavier medication, but she now agrees that given the stage dad has reached this          may          well          be          the          only          option          left. As ever, I am/we are immensely grateful for all the support and help you          have          given          and          continue          to          render. As mentioned, mum will be in contact regarding an appointment to discuss further."

*Dad's medication was adjusted accordingly. Mum continued her visits and even the occasional outing was still possible, most notably mum's and dad's 52ⁿᵈ wedding anniversary on 12 July 2015, which they celebrated together at one of dad's favorite cafes nearby. Dad even dressed up and groomed himself for the occasion, which of course he didn't remember. And yet the event represented one of the very few days when dad was able to recall many other things. He told mum about the times when he had run away and how he was angry at himself for doing*

175

*so afterwards. He could remember roughly how often he had run away and in which directions. He knew it was merely his brain telling him to go. He even said he enjoyed living in Rawhiti because of the company there, but that he still felt sad every day when mum left. They spent three hours together like this before dad got too tired and fell back into confusion. Regardless, it had been one of the few remaining days where they were able to chat, laugh, and sit together almost the way they had always done. The time they got to spend in this way truly was an anniversary gift from somewhere!*

*But true to himself, as if begrudging any such reprieve, bastard Lewy had other plans and so less than a week later things changed again:*

19/07/2015

"Yesterday I went to feed the ducks at Te Moana with dad and then we went to the farm park where he ate a large Lasagna and a piece of lemon cake in addition to the lunch he had already had at the rest home. Unfortunately, his mood was not that great today. He was very confused, irritated and even grumpy.

He didn't recognize me at all and when one of the care givers asked him who I was he didn't have an answer. Before we went I had to ask them to help me convince him to dress warmly. They helped him change, as he didn't want me to (since he didn't know who I was). But at least he wanted to come along. On the way, I got a little fright, because he suddenly took the gearshift into his hand and tried to move it. I was so surprised that I yelled at him to take his hand off it. He didn't mean anything by it. Overall though he really wasn't mentally present at all today; even his demeanor during lunch was different. Back at the rest home, he was restless, wandered about until one of the care givers took him along on their drinks-round, before trying to get him to sleep. I went home. I just hope tomorrow will be better, because his short-term memory is currently zero. He can neither find his room, nor does re recognize the toilet across the corridor."

20/07/2015

"My visit with dad was Ok. I think we have to get used to the idea that dad has yet again taken another step down. Today at least he

176

knew that my name is Landeck; my first name is gone. We played Bingo with the others, but dad just sits there. I place the markers for him. That way he won three times and got his chocolate fish, which he enjoys."

22/07/2015

"Dad was not in a good way today. It was good I visited, since he didn't want to be washed, even though his room did not smell very nice. He said "no" to the duty nurse and that was it. I had to sweet-talk him several times until the nurse was allowed to clean up. Dad was angry, didn't understand the situation, nor what we were saying. At least I was able to persuade him later to lie down for a bit, because he was just too confused. He also wanted to run away again today. They had to lock the rest home doors. I tried to explain to him that things can't really go on like this and that it could mean he may have to leave the rest home for another facility. But he was completely indifferent. We can only hope that the decline will then be at a point where he won't even know what is happening. But we will see. Maybe it's just a phase…I only want to think from day to day at the moment."

29/07/2015

"Today dad didn't even want to sit with the others. They had a Ukulele group for entertainment. The residents enjoyed it, but I couldn't persuade him to join. Instead, he slept and I read a book. Then we had something of a small conversation, or I'd like to think so at least. But his replies may have been coincidental as well, because he slipped back into his world shortly after. The thing he fears most is the thought that one day I might not visit anymore. He even cries when he talks about it and I reassure him each time that he is the most important thing in my life and that I would never leave him. Maybe his fear also stems from the fact that he couldn't remember who I was – at least that's what he told me last week during a brief period of clarity. He also says he can't remember us getting married. Of course, when all this is going around in his head it is understandable that he's afraid I might not return."

02/08/2015

"Today we went for a walk. You have to watch out now when walking with dad since he tends to overestimate himself and wants to keep going, but then suddenly gets tired. So I walk around the block with him as not to get too far away from the rest home. Today he made me look for "dogs that had followed him", then according to him [while walking around the block] we were suddenly at the train station in Lavington and he saw his mother, after which he spoke to Dirk Saunders [a friend of mine who died years earlier]. Dad enjoyed the walk, but I was glad when we made it back."

03/08/2015

"Today's visit was very different from yesterday. When I arrived he already walked towards me – well groomed, neatly dressed and in good spirits. We had a great afternoon; in addition, he won Bingo, 2nd prize, twice and was happy. It really is a rollercoaster. I don't know what to expect from day to day. At least for today I'm good. I gave him a lot of compliments and he glowed. He especially likes hearing that I hope he stays faithful with all these ladies at the rest home. It's just something I try to cheer him up with."

06/08/2015

"Today dad didn't want to shower again. When I got there he still wasn't wearing last night's incontinence pad and had not had breakfast. There was nothing they could do. When he doesn't want something, nothing works. At least I was able to persuade him to eat lunch and put a new pad on. He was grumpy, but complied. But I have told the staff to call me if this continues. I can still talk to him and somehow convince him – at least for the moment."

*It was time to board another flight and see what needed to be done. But before I could there was an incident during which dad, refusing to be washed or changed, held on to the care giver's wrist to the point where she had started feeling unsafe. It was another low point and things were going downhill yet again. I arrived a few days later and the changes in both mum and dad were palpable. Mum had been "on call" pretty much day and night for months now, with the rest home calling her each time dad became unmanageable. She was glued to the phone, barely dared*

178

to go out and although she would have never admitted it her nerves were clearly frayed.

Mum was increasingly 'quirky', living in this world, which now solely consisted of looking after dad. Much of what she said didn't make sense to me, she said some weird and quite insensitive things sometimes, didn't listen and had become quite forgetful; all signs of the immense stress she was under. Dad had changed for the worse. Conversation was now impossible and he used mainly mumbled words and randomly strung-together syllables made into "words" that had no meaning. He was happy to see me, but identified me only as 'the person on the photograph in his room'. I tried to have some earnest chats with mum because she was simply reading too much into what he was saying, hanging on to what words could mean just like she had done in the past when he had simply forgot and tried to replace them with others. This was different though. She got increasingly disappointed since quite often even she no longer managed to interpret what dad was saying, of course assuming that whatever he was trying to talk about still had some connection to the real world. We spent some time on the computer reading up on the illness. I was trying to nudge her towards the fact that she would need to let go of the notion that dad was still capable of rational conversation and that he would eventually slip away completely. But she wasn't ready to let go yet. The rest home though sadly was, since caring for dad who had become more and more difficult to handle was now beyond their capabilities and resources. It was a rest home for elderly with primarily physical impairments and simply not equipped for the kind of patient dad was quickly becoming. The emergency phone calls were a regular occurrence now and driving missions in search of dad were the order of the day, each time he had managed to get away. Then there were the growing number of incidents where he refused to cooperate at any level, along with some quite unfortunate "toilet-related" occurrences, which took the already busy staff's ability to cope to the absolute limit. We had tried to stay a step ahead of bastard Lewy, who secretly pulled the strings as he always did, but he was once again gaining ground and I could see we were fighting a losing battle. Mum had already researched potential facilities, closed psycho geriatric units, of which Langdale, a small hospital with a closed unit and a hospital wing, all specializing in dementia care had come highly recommended.

It was again a scary thought to imagine dad there and obviously a very emotional time. And yet, when the day came to move into his "new home", a larger room with private bathroom, he was not at all perturbed and to an extent welcomed the

179

*change of scenery, if one can even say that given his mental state. Of course the move again necessitated all manner of forms to be filled and phone calls to be made, which I helped mum with as best as I could. More assessments of dad were done, more information passed between doctors, payments coordinated regarding care subsidies and things organized and packed for his move; a virtual machinery of logistics, finance and administration – while dad spent most of his time coordinating his own but imaginary operations.*

# Chapter 10 - Beginnings and Endings

25/08/2015

"I drove to Briscoe's and bought a new chair for dad today; very sturdy and dad is able to get up from it without issues. I bought a few bigger pillows as well. Then I went to Langdale. Dad was sitting in front of the big window in the lounge and looked very peaceful as he watched the landscape. He was happy to see me and we went to his room. He liked the pillows. They let him sleep long and so he was in a good mood. Then it was lunchtime and although I said I had my own at home, they still brought some toast, pea soup, a quiche and a plate of fruit. Dad had his beloved coffee afterwards. He relished his meal. He even went to breakfast by himself as they told me. Dad has already made a few acquaintances; one lady waved over to him straight away when we went for lunch. Then dad wanted to have a nap and I said good-bye and went back to get the chair from the store. When I returned dad stood in his room. He was full of sorrow, as he had wet his pants. But he managed to get undressed by himself and I got one of the caregivers for the incontinence pads. Dad was really happy that he could undress by himself and managed to place his things on the bed very neatly. Later we even got something to drink and a sandwich and cake for afternoon tea. After some more "chatting" dad let me go and I went shopping."

26/08/2015

"I went through our house today looking for things dad might like in his room. I decided on the Asian carvings, a clock, and a carved angel, which had previously hung above his bed. Early afternoon I took Rosy and we visited Norbert. He was taking a walk in the corridor and was in a good mood. He was delighted to see Rosy and took her by the leash. He seemed proud of her when the other people petted her and told him what a lovely dog she is. One of the caregivers helped us put up the things I had brought. We let dad decide which items he wanted and where they should be placed. He chose the picture hooks and kept busy the whole time. The room now looks very pretty and very comfy with all the cushions, the small table etc. The only thing that was strange was that dad turned around the pillow with the penguins on it. There was something about them he didn't like. We even had to put up his rosary near his bed. Of course, after all this work and having to make decisions it was time for chocolate cake and a tuna sandwich. He sat in his room and enjoyed the attention the caregivers paid to the carvings. The good byes at 4pm were easy today. That's the time when he is in his 'sundowner' mood and it's time to go. By the way, when I got there I noticed dad was wearing sneakers and socks, which weren't actually his. He said now it made sense that they felt too small. I guess it happens in a facility where everyone walks around freely. Dad also often doesn't know which room is his and goes into others. The overall atmosphere is very calm, friendly, and balanced. You are right when you say that for the last two months Rawhiti probably was no longer right for dad. Around lunchtime I got another call form Langdale advising that last night dad again fell down in his room and then fell asleep where he lay. They could handle it, but just needed to advise me. Right now, I am just living each day as it comes, without thinking about what the future may bring. And if dad is happy in this new unit, then I am happy, too. By the way the staff asked me to write down some German words for everyday things, as to ease communication with dad [dad increasingly lost the ability to discern whom to speak English and whom to speak German to, so frequently just reverted to German all the way]. I will sit down at the computer tonight and start typing."

28/08/2015

"Another good day today. The new doctor called and said he was quite satisfied with Norbert's current state and that Norbert had acclimatized well to the new environment. I think so, too."

30/08/2015

"My visit with dad was o.k. Dad was a little exhausted from yesterday (no wonder - dancing). He slept till ten in the morning I was told and when I arrived he sat in the chair in front of the big window of the hallway which leads to the lounge. He was in deep sleep. After some minutes, I tried to wake him up, but he did not want to be woken up. So I waited some more minutes, then I took the bowl with the Nestle Almonds in chocolate and showed it him. That made him wake up immediately. Later we had afternoon coffee in the lounge - Rosy was the star of the home again - and I went with Dad outside for some moments, but again he was tired. So we returned to his room where Dad immediately fell asleep in his chair. I said good bye to him and everything was o.k."

8/09/2015

"The doctor and staff are still happy with dad. The doctor says that dad's behavior is typical for this illness. He now wants to administer the psych meds in small doses throughout the day instead of all at once. And when dad refuses because he thinks that they are trying to poison him, then there is a nasal spray which contains the same meds. When Norbert breathes in he receives the dosage. The doctor told dad to do whatever he feels like in the unit, meaning to sleep as much as he wants to (they hope his tiredness will subside with the new meds) and there will be no rules that apply. Dad still likes it there. Yesterday I spoke with the husband of one of the Alzheimer patients. His wife also doesn't recognize him anymore. We talked for a while and he suggested I attend a group of family members of dementia patients, but I don't think I can talk to strangers about dad yet without breaking down in tears."

11/09/2015

"Today we found something new to keep dad busy: Jenga. You build a tower out of wooden blocks and then you try to remove them one by one without the tower collapsing. You wouldn't believe how dad was able to concentrate. He was totally focused on the game – the engineer inside him came to the forefront – and he worked very precise. Suddenly he was able to focus completely and he even spoke very clearly (a few minutes prior I still couldn't understand him)."

16/09/2015

"Everything is still the same with dad. All is Ok. I took the pictures which dad had always liked at home into the unit and asked if he might want to have them in his room. I placed them on his bed and dad became positively excited. He immediately started explaining the image's background to Xalvador the caregiver and was very happy that we were beautifying his room. He wanted to put the nails into the wall himself. I let him, which was good for him. And if the nails bent or didn't go in properly I helped, so that dad could still enjoy the success. I never would have dreamed that dad would be happy the way he was today."

27/09/2015

"Everything still "normal". When I walked into the unit several patients were building things with blocks again. I must say that, going by what I saw, dad is still the most intelligent by far. He constructs all manner of things with full concentration and even in matching colors, while the others mostly don't know what to do with the blocks at all. They all like them, but kind of just shift them around on the table. While we were having coffee dad had to go toilet. A caregiver led him to his room, since he wouldn't be able to find it himself. I had to laugh, as while he was gone I had to guard his plate from the other patients. Once they want something, they can be quite quick. Anyway, I rescued dad's cake…"

28/09/2015

"My visit with dad was "normal". It seems he is retreating further and further into his world, but obviously feels comfortable with the environment. Sometimes my arrival even disturbs him, especially when he is busy with the building blocks. Today it looked like he was just staring in front of him. But then I saw he was sorting the wooden blocks by the shape of their grain. He was so preoccupied that all I could do was just sit with him, especially since he again mumbled

184

and spoke at such low volume. But as I always say, every day is different. Even when I left, he barely seemed to notice."

6/10/2015

"Today I brought along some photos from the holiday in Spain we spent with our neighbors. Dad immediately recognized it. He seems to live predominantly in the past, is always happy to see photos, and can even point at people by name. That way we always have something to talk about for a few minutes."

17/10/2015

"Dad was in a good mood today and kept watching the peacock that sometimes wanders around outside. We had to laugh when he asked whether I would come back tomorrow, because when I said yes, he said: But make sure you bring Rosy! And I replied that it looked like Rosy was more important to him than me. That made him laugh as well. When afternoon tea was served, dad was so engrossed in watching the peacock that he dunked Rosy's dog treat into his coffee, much to the delight of everyone around. Dad got a fresh coffee."

24/10/1015

"Dad was very tired today and had to lie down 45 minutes after I got there. Apparently, he didn't sleep well the night before. I wanted to bring him to bed, but couldn't manage alone. Dad is not able to lie down properly and lifting him is too hard for me. So one of the staff came and we both straightened dad out in bed. He was already half asleep."

*Mum' visits with dad continued along the same lines for the next few weeks. Sometimes he was too tired and just wanted to sleep, other times he enjoyed and acknowledged her visits, was happy to see her and interact for maybe half hour or so and other times he was completely lost in his delusions. Most messages from mum, other than those perhaps referring to special events at the rest home, which were always enjoyed by the residents, simply stated the day had been "ok".*

14/11/2015

"Today's visit was a little difficult. Dad recognized neither me, nor Rosy. He told me he didn't know who we were. So we just sat together and tried to make the best of the situation. Back home I had a whiskey, but even that didn't help much today. Tomorrow is another day. Even though dad doesn't recognize me, I can somehow still "access" him on some level and can sometimes help him in certain situations. That is of comfort to me."

16/11/2015

"After he allegedly recognized me yesterday, today I was a stranger again. He spoke of a wedding, but didn't know whom he was going to marry. When I asked whether he meant me, he said "NO". There was live music at the unit and so at least he had some distraction. Anyway, today he was planning a wedding…"

20/11/2015

"I am writing this mail with a heavy heart. I wanted not to, but it is better you know before you get here for Christmas. For a little while now dad has become somewhat violent when he doesn't want something/doesn't agree with something. 3 days ago he injured a caregiver on her wrist (she was still in pain yesterday) and late afternoon yesterday it took all their strength to hold Norbert and calm him down. I got a call after the doctor had a look at dad and they asked that I sign a "restrain order" for dad. When dad was very aggressive a few days ago and injured the caregiver it took several of them to hold him. I am very worried that he is now too unpredictable and could possibly hurt other people, but as the doctor says, it's also for dad's protection since he easily loses his balance and when he gets enraged there is a risk that he falls and hurts himself as well. I received the call tonight and they asked for my temporary permission to restrain Norbert. I gave it and drove to the unit. I don't want to write about how I felt… These restraining belts are similar to safety belts in a car; the ones you use for small children. In the event they place dad into a large comfy chair and "tie him down". Such a seizure, which it is apparently called, utterly exhausts him and he quickly falls into a deep sleep. The belts are left on only for 30 minutes. When he wakes up, they are taken off. Then dad obviously

186

doesn't know anymore what happened, which makes him very confused. They say without my permission they cannot use these belts, but how else could they calm down someone who develops such enormous strength when agitated. Dad also now gets some medication, which reduces aggression. My question today was how long dad will be able to stay in this unit. They told me that should these aggressions get worse, there would be another assessment based on which dad might need to be transferred to Waikanae where the terminally ill patients are placed. Because dad can't walk too well anymore and needs help from a caregiver I asked whether dad could get a Zimmer frame. Unfortunately, that is not possible as he may use it to attack others (as he did in Rawhiti when he attacked them with his chair). It's just too dangerous. The staff is truly very caring, lovely, and helpful, but at some point, they have to protect themselves and other patients. I am very sorry to write such a letter. But I didn't want to leave it until you get here."

21/11/2015

"I signed the form today, which was a little bit easier than I thought. Dad was not in a good mood at all and when he doesn't want something to happen or doesn't understand something…In any case, I saw how he got angry from one second to the next. Luckily, I was able to distract him, but witnessing his outburst made signing the papers easier. I agree with your observation about the cyclical nature of dad's outbursts. The only explanation I have is that he can only hold it together for so long. It was the same after a he had been in Rawhiti for a few weeks, and now after a few weeks here. Keeping him sedated is already being done to some extent, but laws are stringent and they are careful about how much and what they administer. I often wonder now whether it would not be better to just "switch off" his brain with medication or whether to have him live with these depressions and seizures (if you want to call that living). I don't think our conscience would allow us to make that decision – it would be horrific. I can only get a glimpse here and there, into what is going on in dad's mind, when he talks about stuff. He is still afraid of others, including us, wanting to harm him. And when he is like that, only a lot of patience and love will enable me to get near him.

187

My visit was "Ok". Why dad is deteriorating so rapidly, nobody knows."

23/11/2015

"On my way to the ward today the manager came and told me that they indeed have arranged for another assessment. Dad's aggressions are becoming more and more frequent and dad develops such strength that it takes 3 caregivers to hold him. In the long run this is becoming very difficult for all involved. I told her that you and Sharon are arriving on 16 December and that you would want to be there if and when dad gets transferred to another unit for what will be the 'final stage'. She promised things would be manageable until you get here."

25/11/2015

"For now dad will stay at Langdale! We had our meeting with the doctor and the head nurse, who had done a very thorough assessment and reviewed all records. The caregivers were also asked whether they thought it was possible to keep dad there and they agreed to it. Dad's aggressions apparently stem from certain physical difficulties: the constant falls, the sudden bouts of sleepiness, the fear, the helplessness etc. Of course they try to address all that with meds, but these don't take away that dad feels helpless and over-challenged, which can in turn make him more aggressive. This morning for example he fell in his room. He hurt his lower lip and even his leg. The concern at the moment is that staff might not be able to give him the undivided attention he might need. At the other facility, the caregiver-patient-ratio is better, which could help him cope a lot better. They will continue to deliberate and let us know in about two weeks. Unfortunately there was an "accident" towards the end of the meeting, which will unfortunately means that Rosy can no longer come along for future visits. One of the bigger patients collided with another, who fell backwards and hit her head on a trolley full of towels. One of the caregivers cried out loud and rushed to help her. At that moment Rosy got loose and nipped the caregiver's leg; quite forcefully, too. Of course I apologized profusely, but it just means Rosy can't come along anymore."

27/11/2015

"Went to visit dad and found him in a comfy chair, fast asleep. He almost had another fall, but they caught him and placed him in the chair. I asked whether I should stay, but they said they wanted him to get as much sleep as possible."

01//12/2015

"I think we may have to prepare ourselves for dad's transfer out of this unit. The nurse told me, that dad's illness is progressing rapidly. Tomorrow the doctor will talk to me and give me more details. We all know dad's health is deteriorating rapidly, but hearing it is very painful. But I guess it is better we are prepared than just getting hit with it out of nowhere."

02/12/2015

"The meeting went very well and they are really trying hard to keep dad there for as long as possible. It looks like he now has a urinary tract infection, which may be the reason for his change in behavior. It is being treated and perhaps once it's gone his aggressions will also get less. We agreed that I make some badges in German language; everyday words to help dad understand. Things like "nurse", so the caregivers can wear them and dad might be able to identify them accordingly. They will also call each morning as soon as he wakes so I can help translate. They have to take his blood pressure in different body positions, i.e. lying down, half-upright, standing etc. so they get a better idea why dad keeps falling over. They will also try to motivate him to do some light gardening together with one of the staff, even just for 10 minutes. I will also bring along photo albums again and maybe some CDs or DVD's. They said we should try to provide stimuli as much as possible. When I got there this afternoon dad was asleep. The caregivers told me he had had another fall, but had since been sleeping soundly."

9/12/2015

"I took a lot of photos from the 1960s with me today. Photos of his colleagues, sports events, and parties. It is incredible how much dad can remember from these days (even though he no longer remembers our wedding)."

*A few days later Sharon and I arrived to spend Christmas with mum and dad. There had been some debate among us whether we should have dad at home for the occasion and the rest home even opined it might be possible. In the end though and as much as it pained me to be the voice of reason, we decided against it. Dad's behavior had become unpredictable, his falls a daily occurrence, and if it came to an incident while he was at home, none of us would be equipped to deal with it. And even if we were, it would create a memory that would threaten to erase all Christmases prior. I must say that when we visited dad again for the first time in months after our last stay in New Zealand, we were quite shocked at the change we saw. Mum had written about her visits on a daily basis, but I guess she clung to whatever good she could find in the situation to be able to cope, and had left out how bad it really was. Dad was no longer coherent in any way, shape or form. He slept. A lot. And he got tired within minutes of having to pay attention to visitors. He easily got irritated, "walked" off in the middle of "conversations" and ordinarily simple things like getting showered, dressed, or undressed often became major missions involving multiple caregivers.*

*It was also a difficult time in the sense that mum, having been the "principal protector of all things dad" for so long, was extremely sensitive towards anything to do with his care; often to the point where all I could do was to take a deep breath and step outside as not to blow my top. She hung on to dad; dad who didn't exist anymore the way she thought she could still detect in him. And it was hard watching it get worse. Luckily, mum agreed that we could instead celebrate Christmas with dad at the unit. She had decorated his room, had brought his favorite musical Christmas item (a singing reindeer) and we brought along platters of dad's favorite foods which we spread out on Christmas patterned tablecloth. Whereas the year prior he had still been at home and despite his delusions and some "hiccups" along the way had still enjoyed his Christmas dinner, I am not sure whether he was still able to attribute much meaning to the occasion this year. We helped him eat his food and spent an hour and half with him, mostly trying to get his attention and get a little bit of a festive spirit going. It had been a long-standing tradition to read the bible on Christmas Eve. Dad would read about the birth of Jesus, there would be a brief prayer and then it was time to open presents and eat. This year I was supposed to take over the tradition, but I just couldn't. It still hurts me that I was unable to, but there were too many memories attached*

190

which made the situation even more unbearable. Still, we had a good little "celebration, but dad showed no sign of emotion when we left for home.

The visits with dad always followed the same routine: We would arrive, mum would try to feed dad whatever goodies she had brought with her (whether or not dad ate whatever mum brought along had become her personal gage for whether it was a good day or not such a good day; food was one of the few things that still allowed for a familiar connection). Then she tidied up his closet and his dresser, tried to have afternoon tea with dad and get some sort of conversation going, which usually revolved around dad retelling his latest hallucinations or just picking at the carpet or any other items with some sort of pattern. In between there were seconds of semi-lucidity, where he would say something that fit into the conversation or recognize an event or person from photos mum would bring along. Each one of us had our own way of coping, so no matter how painful it was to watch at times we just followed mum's schedule while there. We flew out again in the second week of January. There was little else we could do.

14/01/2016

"Dad and I looked at old photos of dad's side of the family and a lot of others. It passes the time and after close to an hour dad tires and I can bring him to his room and say good-bye. I try to do something different every day, anything that might peak his interest. And sometimes, like with the old photos of his first communion in 1948, bits and pieces of his memory return and he starts talking. Whether what he says is all real or correct, who cares. The main thing is his mind is busy."

24/01/2016

"The visit with dad was great. First, they all played all manner of games with the inflatable ball I had bought. If it's about sport, dad is always keen and even likes to take charge. He lasted over 20 minutes, non-stop, but then he had to sit down. But I could tell he had a lot of fun. It is clearly evident that dad loves being involved in physical stuff – not going for walks – he never really enjoyed that, but all kinds of games. After "sports" we again looked at old photo albums and he still paid attention. I think he just needs to be motivated and his mind stimulated constantly. I'll think about a few things. And dad's enthusiasm for ball games is infectious: the other patients join in and so the all form a little game group, laugh and enjoy their time. The caregivers also have a lot of fun and play along with them."

*I mentioned before how we all had our own ways of coping. This message was a classic example of mum's coping mechanism. Looking at it from afar, these messages would seem very positive and the situation in the unit full of activity and fun, with dad in the middle of it. Sadly though, this was more mum's coping mechanism talking than a reflection of reality. Mum would take the tiniest glimpse of hope, of positivity, and superimpose it on everything, make it larger than life, and then focus on it to the point where it would block out everything else, including reality. I am not writing this to be critical of her approach. After all, how could I be, when she devoted all her time, her life to getting dad "through this"? How else was she going to keep on going from day to day? No, I am writing about it because it took some time for me to realize that that's what it was: not actual improvement in dad's condition – for which I would have given my right arm, or both arms, or whatever - but a reflection on how her mind was attempting to deal with, and to some extend ward off, the inevitable for as long as possible.*

*It had originally confused me how things could be so swell one day and then so abysmal the next. It wasn't until our Christmas visit that I saw what was really happening. So much she had written about and said on the pone finally fell into place as not being actual and unmoderated "updates", but rather events seen through the filter of her trying to cope, up to and including probably subconscious denial. If there had ever been an important distinction, not just for my own sanity but for assessing dad's condition and making decisions in relation to his care, then this was it. For anyone dealing with a loved one afflicted by dementia and relying on another family member's reports, I believe this is a crucial point to remember: You need to make your own assessment of the situation during a visit. Everything else you hear may or may not be a true reflection.*

26/01/2016

"When I got there dad was not in a good way. He hallucinated and saw worms everywhere. He even took is afternoon nap on the floor. After a few minutes I asked him whether he needed to go toilet and the caregivers helped him. Afterwards he was completely different and we enjoyed our time together. Dad was again in a good mood."

28/01/2016

"My visit with dad was ok. Nothing worth mentioning, which is good. Apparently this morning he kept asking whether Gisela was visiting today – this routine seems to have taken hold in his mind. I brought him cherries and he was over the moon."

6/02/2016

"Just to let you know dad is Ok at the moment. There was entertainment at the unit again. Our friends from Singapore are here for a visit and dad danced with Kay and then me. He was totally happy."

12/02/2016

"A little problematic with dad today. As is the case sometimes, he was very confused, didn't recognize me, was very tired, fell asleep at the table. I got him a cup of coffee and later a cold Yogurt and he came to somewhat. But as you have seen as well, there are good days and bad. It always changes."

15/02/2016

"It's quite funny: Dad seems to have honed in on my visits around 2pm (but he can't actually tell time). So for a few days now he has been refusing lunch, but the staff put it aside for him. He always says he will wait until I get there. Then I accompany him to his room, get his food, which they reheat and sit down with him. That way I can also assist him when he needs help with it. He likes sitting with me very much. Who knows, maybe he remembers the way it used to be. The caregivers already laugh when he refuses to eat without me. After lunch we usually go to the lounge for a coffee, which he also likes, just as he enjoys the cup of coffee together."

17/02/2016

"The visit was Ok. Dad sleeps a lot at the moment, is very quiet, but not really depressed. The caregivers tell me he is usually in good spirits and is eating well. That is of some comfort."

19/02/2016

"The visit was nice today. They again had musical entertainment and dad danced. It seems aid him, because he seems to "wake up" when he does and even becomes "talkative"."

21/02/2016

"So far, so good today. Yesterday dad apparently had a little disagreement with another patient. I got a call, because procedure is to advise me. Thank God, it wasn't too bad and the head nurse said that Norbert was provoked, just defended himself and was not at fault. I guess it happens sometimes, since some of the patients are quite aggressive and unpredictable, while dad is consistently more of a quiet person."

23/02/2016

"The visit was a little difficult at first, because dad hallucinated and didn't want to come out from behind the door. He couldn't walk properly anymore at that moment and then slept for half an hour. After that he didn't remember anything form before and was in good spirits, we could talk and I gave him your regards and hugs. So in the end it was still a good visit."

24/02/2016

"Today I was even allowed to cut dad's beard. I didn't do a bad job, even if may say so myself. I cut back especially the part around the mouth, just like he used to have it (I looked at photos beforehand). Dad loves it and when he looked in the mirror even told me where to correct a bit here and there. He was fully into it."

25/02/2016

"The caregivers were rather busy this afternoon, because two female patients became very aggressive and tried to punch each other. The third lady, since the staff were busy, tried to steal the plates with

194

afternoon tea. Thankfully, I saw it and darted over to the kitchen area. She was very placid when I explained to her that the cakes would attract flies if she tried to remove the cling film (of course there were no flies). She smiled at me and thanked me and I was able to take her back to her chair. Dad remained unfazed throughout the whole thing and so were the other patients. Just a lot of kafuffle. But dad was in good spirits and so all turned out well."

03/03/2016

"Today dad didn't know anything at all actually; not even who I am. And so we just sat together, like two strangers. But dad talked a lot and ate his afternoon cake and sandwich, which he enjoyed. You know, I can handle these mood swings very well now."

# Chapter 11 - Waking Sleep

04/03/2016

"Dad's, what the caregivers call "sleeping sessions", are increasing. When I arrived, he sat on the small sofa in the corridor and was fast asleep. A nurse and I helped him into bed and he barely woke up before falling back asleep. Yet, he kept talking about his meetings and contracts with various people. He was dreaming very lucidly and I was able to understand him clearly. That lasted for around 20 minutes, and then he slept on without further dreams. We just sat in his room together."

10/03/2016

"Not so good with dad today. He was very confused and only wanted to sleep. I wasn't even allowed to help him lie down properly or put a pillow under his head. I stayed for 90 minutes, then told staff I was leaving and that he was still asleep. Let's see how it goes tomorrow. Today he was beyond reach."

11/03/2016

"Another difficult one today. First he was in deep sleep and didn't know who I was, but was somewhat ok after he woke. What is making conversations difficult is the extremely low volume with which he speaks. I researched online and found out that there is a special speech therapy for these illnesses. So today I asked the management and found out that it is available for dad at no cost. They will initiate sessions on Monday. If I hadn't researched, nobody would have thought to help Norbert in this way. That puzzles me a bit. Ah well, at least something is happening now. It is very frustrating for dad that nobody understands him, which I think is only natural."

12/03/2016

"Dad's health has worsened a little bit. One of the patients who used to play piano has been diagnosed with Lewy Body in addition to Parkinson's. As his wife told me, it took around 12 ½ years for the illness to develop to this point. For dad it has only taken 2 ½ years. This illness has really hit dad incredibly hard. All of the other patients' family members I spoke to said that the symptoms developed over many, many years. There isn't a single one where it was as hard and fast as with dad. Today was better than yesterday. Dad spoke clearly; his "stories" of course, but we were able to deal with it well."

14/03/2016

"A good day with dad. When I left, he said: "I enjoyed today, it was very nice." His mood was great, his eyes were clear and we played Jenga. He was very patient and we played almost an hour.

17/03/2016

"Dad was Ok. I wanted to shave him after afternoon tea, which he also wanted, but then he had to go toilet and sometimes it takes forever for him to get ready again, let alone permit someone to help him. Today it took over one hour. So I postponed shaving until tomorrow."

18/03/2016

"Entertainment again today. Dad enjoyed and smiled from ear to ear. He doesn't mind being the only one with me or one of the car givers on the "dancefloor". Dad used to enjoy dancing for hours at a time, and that drive remains, even though his legs desert him. Never mind, the main thing is he has fun, which he does."

31/03/2016

"I waited over an hour for a doctor's visit that had been announced, only to find out the doctor had left without seeing Norbert. I maintained my composure because of dad but have since contacted Dr. Stephenson. He will again accept dad as his patient, so we will change doctors. I tidied up dad's cupboards and by now he is missing two winter pajamas, 5 socks and his morning gown. I told the staff and I hope they take it serious. I will need to inspect his things daily from now on. It's incredible what I find in dad's cupboard each day. I mean, dad is the same as the others: he doesn't know his room anymore and just goes anywhere he thinks is his, lies down and sleeps."

4/04/2016

"A long meeting with the doctor this morning. Dad's meds will be further reduced. He no longer needs the pills against anxiety and depression, or at least not for now. He has taken these meds from the beginning. Physically dad is truly Ok, if only his brain played along. But that, it doesn't, as we know. Dad was fine this morning as well, even spoke English with the doctor, much to everyone's surprise. I also mentioned physical exercise and might ask TJ if he can come once a week to maybe just do a 30 or 40 minute session with dad."

12/04/2016

"We had an appointment with the speech therapist. A young, attractive lady which dad liked immediately. She tried to talk to dad and dad tried his best to answer. She was incredibly patient. She asked dad his name and he said "Robert". He also no longer knew where we are from or where he was born. There is nothing left of all that. The assessment took around 45 minutes, but even though he tried to speak up, he couldn't. His vocal chords are healthy but his brain somehow blocks his speech. She brought along a small device, about the size of a mobile phone, with a cable and earpiece and microphone. It has a speaker so when he lowers his voice I can hear him more clearly. We tried it and it was great. But after she left he didn't want to use the device anymore. Now after two days dad still doesn't want to use it. Aw well, I don't want to torture him with it. We will manage somehow. I will return the device. It was worth a try."


24/04/2016

198

"Dad now more and more often refuses his meds, but for some odd reason accepts them from me. Yesterday as well, he just didn't want to take the pill to moderate his behavior. And you know dad: if he doesn't want something he is very stubborn. So when I got there they asked if I could try and indeed he took it from me without complaint. So I have asked them to call me if there is an issue. The meds are very important for dad and I don't mind driving over for a quick visit to give them to him."

26/04/2016

"Dad slept in his chair the whole time. In between, the doctor came and examined him as dad can hardly walk now. He opined dad might have developed arthritis, which is affecting his whole body. He will do some bloods just to be sure, since he suspects something else, but said he would discuss once results are in. Dad is now getting a lot of pain medication, because arthritis is very painful, as you might know. For days now, he has been sitting or lying down in the reclining armchair. We now agreed that I would have his Lazyboy chair transferred from our place so Norbert has his own recliner."

*On 20 April 2016 I received a message from my son TJ to call him urgently. Mum was unable to write about the day they had had at the unit. Something had happened. We spoke on the phone for a while. What he and mum had witnessed in terms of dad's illness took "bad" to a new level. I could hear that this would stay with TJ for a long, long time. Luckily, mum was able to write about the incident a couple of weeks later and so I will give her account of what happened, instead of summarizing the phone conversation of that day:*

"I have asked the doctor to give some kind of medication to dad which takes the fears away that dominate his thoughts in these moments and whereby he feels someone, some enemy, is physically attacking him. The reason for my request lies in what happened last week:

Dad had been sleeping, but had become incontinent (both front and rear). He didn't know what had happened and tried to get undressed, which didn't work. His whole room got soiled in the process. A caregiver wanted to assist him to go and shower. They got as far as the corridor but then dad had one of his sleep attacks and, in slow motion, lay down on the floor. Nothing works in those instances and he is almost like in a coma. So they wrapped him in blankets right where way he was to keep him warm and put his head on pillow. After a few minutes dad woke – the caregiver stayed with him. He wanted to get dad back up and into the shower but dad hallucinated that the caregiver wanted to kill him and turned aggressive. They tried to gently persuade dad but nothing worked. They called me as well to come and speak with dad, but he was so wild and full of fear that he didn't recognize me either. They had to hold me back so that nothing would happen to me. It took three caregivers and the nurse, to keep him in the shower room. But he still wouldn't calm down. Meanwhile they brought meds for sedation, which he didn't want to take. And yet, when I gave them to him, he took them. It took around 15 minutes for him to become calmer. But to be honest, I was at the end of my strength and drove home. I mention it so you understand why I asked the doctor for some kind of medication that will take away these bouts of aggression. Dad was like a wild animal in a cage. Unfortunately giving dad additional medication may impact on the effectiveness of others he is already taking, so might not be possible. We know that this illness is not curable and there isn't enough research, so everything they prescribe is more or less on a trial and error basis. They will increase his anxiety meds, but have already foreshadowed that this will increase his sleeping bouts and he will sleep even more during the day. It is a hard balance between keeping dad this way and allowing him to have these terrible fits. They have one medication, which they can drip onto his tongue during incidents like this, and although it may not be possible for staff do administer it, at least I can try. I just want dad to live in peace as much as possible. He is suffering enough already."


03/05/2016

"The first half hour was good. We looked at a book about the painter Holbein and dad was quite interested. Then suddenly he became restless and wanted to go somewhere, probably the toilet, I thought.

But he wanted to go by himself, which is no longer possible of course. So I guided him, even though he didn't want to be touched. After a few steps, we were in the corridor, he was at the end of his strength, and I was barely able to support him. So I called out for help and the caregivers came running with a chair. But dad was stubborn and only with gentle force were we able to get him to his room, the caregivers with chair in tow. Once there he didn't want to go toilet anymore and instead sat down on his bed. When they tried to explain that they would need to clean him, he became very aggressive. I saw for the first time what strength he summoned as he squeezed the female caregiver's wrists. I told him he was hurting her, but he got so irate that I had to remove his fingers by force. We let him sit on the bed and I stayed with him, so the caregivers could actually look after others as well. He was half asleep and wanted to take off his shoes and track pants. I was able to reach him finally and he told me that he had a lot of pain in his upper legs and that he felt so cold. So I got the nurse and it turned out his knees were swollen. He got pain meds and some cream on his legs. The swelling probably stems from his many falls, after which he often crawls around on the rough carpet in his room (you know how stubborn he can be if he doesn't want anyone to help him)."

04/05/2016

"I managed to get dad to sit down in a wheelchair. If I can get him used to it, then I can at least wheel him around the garden and extend his daily radius a little."

11/05/2016

"I have taken the small tables out of dad's room and returned them home. He doesn't use them and even tries to sit on them. Plus that way, the caregivers have more room to move about the hoist they now use to lift him off the floor and back into bed. It's quite a big machine, but very practical. It consists of 4 belts, which are passed through under dad and with which he is lifted very gently and slowly. He barely wakes up during the movement. I am glad they have things like this."

13/05/2016

"Dad now lies down wherever and whenever and sleeps. At least they are not sleep fits per se, so he doesn't just fall over. When I got there today, he was lying outside in the garden. They had put warm blankets on him and had put a pillow under his head. Later we woke him and had coffee. But today he didn't really want to see me, at least in the beginning."

19/05/2016

"Today was one of those which showed that dad's health has further declined. I read up on this illness on the web and learn a lot. But when what I read actually happens to dad it hurts very much. Well, it's another day tomorrow. There no longer seems to be any consistency between days though."

28/05/2016

"After a week of being relatively Ok and having afternoon tea together each day, today dad didn't want to know me, was grumpy and tired. So we brought him back to his room and stayed for an hour. But he only woke up briefly and didn't even want to be touched. Who knows what was going on in his brain?! I think the time has come for what can best be described as some form of good-bye. We have to accept that without the Centralin he won't be able to live well at all, but that because of it he sleeps an inordinate amount (daytime, nighttime). It is not easy to come to terms with it and it will take a while until I can get used to his condition. But in the end, which is better: his horrible fits or sleeping? I don't think I even have to answer that.

## Chapter 12 - Lewy Ping Pong

29/05/2016

"There is not much we can do for dad. I render assistance when needed, but these calls are rare now. Because of the meds, dad is far-removed from everything. And to be honest, even if you decided to come, you would only be able to stand it for a little while. It's not only that dad doesn't know us, it's also the smell that hangs over everything, including form the other patients, which one has to get used to as well. I think maybe one, one and a half hours is as long as one can stand it."

06/06/2016 (Dad's Birthday)

"When we got there, dad was very confused yet happy to see us. We brought his chair into the lounge and unwrapped the sweets and the shirt I had got him. Dad tried everything, but then got tired and fell asleep. Then your call came through. I heard the telephone ring and knew it was you, so woke dad and told him you were calling. It was unbelievable: he was wide-awake immediately (which rarely happens), spoke clearly and in a loud voice (which also almost never happens) and was totally happy. From that moment on his birthday had started. He sat with all the other patients and their visitors. Everyone sang Happy Birthday and he just kept smiling. He said thank you and even wanted to hold a speech, but although that proved too difficult in the end, it showed us how happy he was. Then there was a beautiful birthday cake with candles, which he blew out. Dad ate 3 (!) pieces of cake. Then there were Lamingtons and ginger cake and pasty slices and even sandwiches. Dad ate another vanilla slice, but then he had to give up. But later he still ate some of the sweets. And because it was Queen's Birthday as well, everyone sang God Save the Queen. Dad participated in everything. We were amazed. – So all in all it was a great birthday, which started with your call."

07/06/2016

"First dad slept quite long, but then he got lunch (he didn't want it at lunchtime) and so we sat in his room. Norbert enjoyed Spaghetti with sauce and sausages and even some sandwiches, plus a couple of pieces of ginger cake afterwards. He was in good spirits and even smiled at me. So it was a good visit today."

20/06/2016

"Dad was not in such a good mood today. He had some lucid moments during which he became fully aware of what was happening to him. These were some very hard minutes for both of us. I was glad that this kind of consciousness doesn't last long and we ended up spending a good hour together in which dad felt better. I shaved him and put lotion on his face, he ate some kiwi fruits and mandarins. He seemed to like being pampered and looking well groomed."

27/06/2017

"The visit with dad was more or less for nothing today. Dad sat with another patient on the little sofa in the corridor and both were fast asleep. I couldn't wake him up. So I sat there for a while and waited. Dad barely managed to open his eyes and didn't want to go for his coffee either. In addition he said he had a meeting with the government before he went back to sleep."

05/07/2016

"Today we went for an outing with the unit's minibus. It was a wonderful day. The manager took Norbert and another patient, Brian and me for a drive out. We drove all over Elizabeth Park, the sun was shining, no wind. Norbert was excited and recognized several places. Whenever there was a nice view, we stopped so Norbert and Brian could get a good look around. Unfortunately, we couldn't let them out of the bus – they didn't want to either actually – because it is just too difficult getting the patients in and out, especially putting on the seat belt. But both were completely happy."

17/07/2016

"We have had many good days with dad, so it was no surprise that today things were different again. Dad slept almost the entire time (almost 1 ½ hours). He was very confused. I fed him afternoon tea. This state may last a few days then it will get better again. But I prefer him sleeping to him getting aggressive."

20/07/2016

"I think dad's confusion has increased yet again. We have an appointment with Dr. Lehman, the unit doctor on Monday. Let's see what he says…"

*In July Sharon and I visited mum and dad again. This time we could only afford to come for two weeks, but it was a worthwhile visit as it once again went some way towards confirming my previous observations about dad, how he continued to deteriorate, and how mum would interpret things as part of her coping mechanism. It was a stressful two weeks full of "hard" visits with dad, "hard" conversations at home and a lot of tension as we were all stressed, with no way to take time out to digest the daily madness that life had become back home.*

17/08/2016

"So far so good. I would write if something serious were to happen. But at the moment dad is just very stubborn. So today he neither wanted a shower nor get dressed. They leave him be when he's like that. There's nothing they could do anyway and one day without shower isn't going to kill anyone. His beard is too long but even that I wasn't allowed to go near. His most-used word is "NO!" So I didn't shave him."

23/08/2016

"Dad was Ok. I brought some ice cream, which he ate straight away, and three pieces of cake and two sandwiches. At the moment he seems to like just about everything and the caregivers spoil him accordingly."

01/09/2016

"Dad was Ok again. His vocabulary, be it English or German is getting less and less. It is becoming very difficult to guess what he is saying. But his appetite for food is still there – at least something that brings him joy."

02/09/2016

"A great day with dad. I was able to speak with him "normally", at least a little. But he didn't want lunch. Instead he had a double portion of afternoon tea, cakes and sandwiches. I brought him some chocolate kisses. So at least he was full. When I arrived, he showed me a small wound on the back of his hand, but couldn't explain what had caused it. It's not a big wound, but not small either. Even the staff was puzzled. But they dressed it and afterwards everyone, including dad watched the movie "Shrek". He liked it."

04/09/2016

"Dad liked the new track pants I bought for him and opined they are comfy. And the truffles I brought disappeared in seconds. You wouldn't have believed it: as if he had been starving. But he was happy. Later this was followed by two big pieces of cake, 2 sandwiches and potato chips. Suddenly dad said his arm was broken. Because dad can't remember all the words, we tried to determine what he meant. There was no visible trauma, but the nurse will keep an eye on him and advise the doctor tomorrow. It could even be that it's just his brain that tells dad there is something wrong with his arm and that he then feels actual pain. One of the staff also opined it might be his shoulder. It is so difficult to determine whether dad actually suffers from an injury or if all stems from his mind. But we have to take it serious in any case. I am glad I visit every day and can be of some help. Tomorrow for example, I want to try and get him to wear incontinence "nappies". These are better than the inlays or pads, which often move around, and dad complains about. I'll try it for a week and see how it goes."

06/09/2016

"Unfortunately I was told today that dad can no longer participate in the weekly field trips. The risk is too great because of his mood swings. I already worried about it, but to hear it and to know he can't go anymore is very painful. Whenever he feels the slightest bit of stress, he gets angry and becomes completely uncooperative. And when he is like that he develops such strength that the staff are powerless. At least he smiled at me when I arrived and said: When I see you come in it's like the holidays each time – it was very emotional."

29/09/206

"I was with him for an hour today, but he either slept or liked the caregivers better than me. I wasn't allowed to do or touch anything. Even the grapes I had brought along he only accepted from the caregivers. I am not disappointed or sad, since his behavior matches exactly what can be expected. I think his illness changed him again a little bit. But as long as he remains friendly and smiles at the staff I am happy, because then we don't have to worry about aggression."

06/10/2016

"Dad had another one of his sleeping fits and he lay next to his bed. They had covered him as usual. We couldn't wake him. The staff got the hoist and lifted him back into bed. He woke up in the process because of back pain. I got him the breakfast he had missed, but he didn't want to be fed by me. I then had a chat with the doctor and the nurse. He will make an appointment with the neurologist. They will decide whether dad can stay, since his mental condition has been rapidly deteriorating as of recent. Meds will be adjusted accordingly and they will wait a few weeks to see if that changes anything. Unfortunately dad is aggressive every day now and sometimes needs several caregivers at once to "help" him. It is becoming difficult to manage. But I think they are trying everything they can to keep him there. You can imagine I am not feeling all that well today."

## Chapter 13 - Dusk

08/10/2016

"We will have to come to terms with the fact that dad has taken another huge step downwards. He often (including today) does not recognize food on his plate or on the table anymore. They try everything to feed him, but he is very stubborn and doesn't allow it. Instead actually eating or drinking, he now eats "imaginary" food, meaning he pretends to take a grape, puts the imaginary grape in his mouth, chews it and swallows. It's the same with drinks. And because he refuses help, they now try to give him high energy shakes and smoothies to give him what he needs so he doesn't develop deficiencies. Since he still likes sweet things, he seems to accept these shakes. But if he tries to drink or eat by himself it ends in a mess. When I arrived today they were cleaning his room for the third time already. He is not easy to handle at the moment. He doesn't understand why he needs to be cleaned or why he should sit down or whatever. I had a long talk with the head nurse. I don't think it will be long before dad will be admitted to the other unit for the "last stage". Please be assured though: You shouldn't think about flying here. There is nothing you can change and dad doesn't even know what is happening around him."

15/10/2016

"Dad was first confused and then slept most of the time. His illness appears to be progressing rapidly at the moment. Even the caregivers say so. He hardly gets out of bed and is being fed because he has sudden spasms in his arm and so the food and drink often goes flying. But he also often doesn't know what to do with food anymore. This may be temporary, but I don't think it is. His morning aggressions are still there. I think they exhaust him to the point where he then just sleeps."

*It was time to book another flight, this time for the following month. I managed to put some contract work on hold until December so I could see for myself what was going on with dad. I knew from past developments that there was always a lot more than what mum's messages let on…*

24/10/2016

"It was the same with dad today as it has been for the last 10 days. He sleeps, is quite often agitated, and sometimes needs two caregivers to calm him down. Usually they give him a few drops of the emergency medicine when he starts acting up, which lets him calm down completely within minutes. Yet sometimes he refuses to take it and we have to try all manner of tricks, for example today we put some cake on a spoon with the medication, put it up to his mouth and with a lot of sweet-talking he opened it just long enough for us to pour it in, followed by the cake. Sometimes we also mix it with yogurt. He just has to take them as otherwise he would lose control completely. After some minutes I can then even touch him and he speaks a few words."

31/10/2016

"This morning wasn't all that nice for the staff, Dad didn't understand why he should shower or wash. So they cleaned him in bed, since he also didn't want to get up. When I got there at 2pm, they had at least managed to get him out of bed and I was able to persuade him to be wheeled into the lounge. He refused lunch but then ate double portions of cake and sandwiches. We have another doctor's appointment on Thursday and they will see how they can sedate him."

02/11/2016

"Dad's health is rapidly declining. From today on I will change my visiting time to 11.30am. It's often the time when dad wakes up. Lunch is at 12 and I want to help him eat. Dad struggles with it, and it has happened on occasion that he didn't know how to swallow anymore (it looks like his brain has closed another door). It can therefore sometimes take very long for him to complete a meal. Other times he is better and it works. But those days have become rarer. He somehow still seems to have an inner connection to me (something I am so glad about). The caregivers tell me that he often says my name. Maybe I can help somehow with dad's nutrition. The staff is incredible as always. The look after him with angelic patience. They are truly God sent."

3/11/2016

*There are no written accounts of what happened that day, as mum was emotionally unable to write about it. But I was unfortunate enough to witness a similar event during my visit in late November, but apparently even what I saw did not come near what mum had to witness that day:*

When I arrived at the rest home, there seemed to be some sort of commotion in the corridor leading to dad's ward. Caregivers ran back and forth carrying towels and a chair. As I turned the corner, I could see two of them standing in front of the bathroom, almost backing away. They seemed relieved to see me. I looked inside the bathroom and there was dad, naked and clinging to a soiled towel. His eyes were those of a madman and his small hunched figure was readying for a fight. In the corner was a bucket with more soiled towels, already soaking. The room smelled of feces and it was clear he was having one of his episodes. He had fought off the caregivers. Quite incredible, when considering that this was a man, who could no longer walk or often even stand unaided. Yet miraculously he allowed me into the bathroom. I held him by the arm, the stench becoming almost too much to bear. I tried to persuade him to come with me. Fixated on the caregivers, he refused. I tried to get him to put on a morning robe and he slowly obliged. Talking to him in German, ever so calmly and patiently, I managed to coax him out of the bathroom and into his room across the hallway. The caregivers were clearly relieved. Once in the room he told me the "whole story" about this being a conspiracy and them wanting to kill him and he didn't know what all this was about. I simply agreed with everything he said, managed to wipe him down a bit with a towel, and then helped him put on at least a pair of incontinence diapers. I then managed to sit him down and, slowly having taken off his morning robe, managed to put a singlet over his head and arms. He sat there for a while, just staring ahead. He calmed down. One of the caregivers came in and helped with the rest. There was no more resistance. Nobody knew what had prompted the incident. It was the lowest point I had ever seen dad at and not one I care to remember, except for the purpose of this book."

*That day mum got there a similar incident happened. But let's just say the one she witnessed was even worse…walls soiled and dad fighting off caregivers with a chair; a man who less than 3 years earlier was still actively engaged in so many things…Rotarian of the year, cycling, reading, tennis and gardening to the point of exhaustion. It's something that's easy to forget when you get stuck in a room with Lewy for a while. I think writer Mark Lawrence said it best when he said:*

*"Memory is all we are. Moments and feelings, captured in amber, strung on filaments of reason. Take a man's memories and you take all of him. Chip away a memory at a time and you destroy him as surely as if you hammered nail after nail through his skull."*

05/11/2016

"Today I brought along some ice cream and creamy rice as well (something which dad always liked). He first enjoyed a big portion of ice cream, and then had fruit and a little bit of lunch. It was Ok today, in as far as it still can be called that. But I was with him between 2pm and 3pm which is the best time for him. A little later and things get worse again."

*I arrived the evening of 8 November 2016 and visited dad the very next day. As always, mum's descriptions of the situation had been heavily moderated to keep me from worrying too much. But the person I saw that day bore little resemblance to dad the way we had seen him but a few months before. We walked into his room and found him lying on the floor, his upper body half propped up against the wardrobe door. He was lying on his side and under his elbow was a puddle of dried blood. We tried to get him to sit up to see what was wrong, but it was difficult. He was seemingly asleep, yet managed to mumble. This was now almost a perpetual state for much of the day: His eyes were closed, his arms were moving as if pulling invisible leavers or strings, his pupils would move rapidly under his eyelids, yet he was completely removed and unreachable. Eventually we managed to get him up enough to see his arm. He must have scraped along the wardrobe hinges while falling, which resulted in a deep scratch along his forearm. We called the caregivers and they got the hoist. He moaned and groaned as he was lifted up and back into bed as if every muscle and bone in his back were causing terrible pain. Reading between the lines of mum's mails, this was what I had been afraid of seeing upon arrival. And my fears had become true. I continued to visit him, sometimes with mum and sometimes alone. They were incredibly challenging and*

211

*extremely sad visits, but amongst it all there were moments so precious I wouldn't want to have missed them under the circumstances. Bastard Lewy was now actively at work, dismantling every aspect of the father I had known and with clinical precision at that. Like a swarm of safari ants stripping a victim of literally everything by way of a million bites with tiny, but powerful jaws, Lewy was hard at it to make sure dad became more and more unrecognizable compared to who he had been but a few months before, let alone a year ago.*

21/11/2016

"I just got back from the unit. Dad was in bed and hallucinated, but it must have been about something nice as he smiled a lot in his sleep. He ate the ice cream with his eyes closed along with some fruit salad. Then he was too tired and went back into a deep sleep."

22/11/2016

"The same as yesterday. Dad seemed awake but had his eyes closed and moved about his arms, but there was no connection. He didn't want his ice cream. I stayed for an hour but he didn't even react when I said good bye. His was totally involved in his world. I watched him move his arms about, play around with his cushions and talking to someone whom he obviously saw in the room. It must have been someone nice since dad smiled a lot. But as I said, even when I tried to talk to him, there was no reaction."

24/11/2016

"Dad will stay in Langdale! As we suspected he will be transferred into the hospital wing. The rooms are identical, but the toilet is much bigger and has a proper shower in the ensuite. I already know the staff and the lounge is also almost identical. The staff will help with the move and hang up the pictures in the new room etc. This will be next week. It's not a locked unit since patients there are no longer able to run away. We had the meeting in dad's room and he even contributed a few sentences. Dad is now getting a self-adjusting air mattress and will be moved into a different position every 2 hours, so he won't get any skin problems from being in bed all the time."

25/11/2016

"It is a great relief that dad doesn't have to move to a different place anymore now. My visit was the same as every other day: He was sleeping, then half-awake for a few minutes and held my hands. He doesn't want to be touched otherwise. Clinical manager Miriam said today that I should try to make the best of the time that remains…"

26/11/2016

"Well, as I wrote already, dad's health has again deteriorated. I am quite emotionally exhausted, could hardly sleep. That is why I remembered the promise you made me give you to decorate the house for Christmas despite everything. So I put up the Christmas tree and then mopped the house at 4am."

27/11/2016

"TJ hadn't seen dad since October and was shocked as well. But at least dad was awake for the first time in days (well, what we call "awake") and we took turns in the exercises you did with dad when you were here: stand at the foot of the bed, reach over and take his hands and pull up his upper body. Dad truly enjoyed it and smiled quite a lot, didn't want to stop. Of course we didn't go overboard. Because of the exercise dad was again tired and we said our good byes."

28/11/2016

"Dad has been refusing anything with any kind of solids in it. Even yogurt with peaches. He spits out the small pieces. They are changing his meds. He will no longer need to take the anti-aggression pills and they only keep some emergency stuff for any incidents. I went back to see him this evening. He didn't want anything at all. For lunch they had made him a shake with mushed banana which he was able to swallow, but that was it."

1/12/2016

"Dad was moved into his new room in the hospital wing today. They moved him using the hoist. When I arrived today, he saw me straight away and smiled. He drank some juice (they have these special cups so he doesn't choke) and had almost finished his Spaghetti."

2/12/2016

"The caregivers do everything they can to nurse dad back to health. This afternoon he got a choice: two energy shakes, eggs and mashed potato, fruit plate, vanilla pudding, pureed vegetables or the ice cream I had brought with me. He had the drinks, ate half the hot meal, and then gave preference to the ice cream over the pudding. If the patients don't want one thing, they are always given an alternative. The caregivers said it would be good if he gained some weight, which I agree with and which is also why they are trying so hard. They told me this morning for the first time dad wanted to get up by himself. They encouraged him and are also doing exercises with him. After the meal, he was of course very tired again and I went home. Dad still sleeps a lot, but that is normal. I am happy how he made the adjustment to the hospital wing."


3/12/2016

Dad had a good day today. Imagine, he wanted to and with our help managed to get up! He stood for quite a while, which was quite strenuous for him. But all we had to do was watch out that he didn't fall over. He was virtually standing on his own. He was awake and talked a little bit, but unfortunately, we couldn't understand what he was saying. But he looked out of the big window towards the small children's playground in the middle of the atrium. We stayed with him until, tired from standing he fell asleep,"

5/12/2016

"The visit at the home was like the other day. Dad likes the drinks, which are thickened with some special powder, because pure juice lets him choke and cough. He also ate a little custard but he disliked the main course (mashed potato and a creamy sauce). I stayed for one hour - he slept after his lunch and I waited for him to wake up again, but that was not to be."

6/12/2016

"I am glad that today I can report something nice: Dad got up by himself for the first time and walked with the help of two caregivers. You should have seen his face: he was so proud of himself and everyone congratulated him. After lunch he again got up and wanted to walk again. Imagine, he wanted to be helped to the toilet. Of course they had to change him then, since his "walking" isn't at normal speed – but for dad to get up by himself, that hasn't happened in the longest time. Afterwards he was knackered of course and very tired. But so see the happiness in dad's face was wonderful. I wish you could have been there. Unfortunately, I didn't have my camera with me, otherwise I would have taken a photo. Everybody at the home says transferring dad was the right decision. It's not as busy as at the other wing – all the other patients are also very ill and dad likes the peace and quiet. Of course I am aware that his health improvement is only temporary, but it makes me appreciate these moments even more."

8/12/2016

"The visit with dad was somewhat Ok, even though dad was very confused and barely ate. But that's how it is with him these days: one memorable day and then one to forget. I am learning to take each one as it comes. It would be too exhausting otherwise."

9/12/2016

"The visit was the same. Dad's mind has slipped away even further; something I had already expected after he had a few good days. I had made him some applesauce, but his taste seems to have changed. I try something different every day and in addition take along the ready-made chocolate mousse (he hated it when he was healthy, but now loves it), since the mashed up food at the home seems too hard to swallow. In addition, they could put a bit more effort into presentation. I complained yesterday. The meal looked like....well, it was brown. I tried it and it was not very good. Let's see if my complaint worked. I won't let it rest otherwise. It could also be that dad barely tastes whatever he eats. But the brown stuff yesterday...even *he* refused. At least today it was brown again, but tasted better."

11/12/2016

"Dad had a little bit of lunch (scrambled eggs and mashed potato) and something to drink. But he didn't want the ice cream anymore. Then he slept and I stayed with him for a while, before I drove home."

12/12/2016

"When I go there today dad was in his armchair and they were they were wheeling him into the lounge – today was barber day and dad got a haircut; quite short but it looks good. Dad was a little better today. He ate well and we talked as in as much as that is possible, but he smiled here and there. He ate two small pots of chocolate pudding, his lunch and drank almost two cups of juice. I asked the caregivers whether he spends all his time in the chair. I am worried about his back. But they allayed my fears and said they make him get up in the afternoon and help him walk a few steps. I am relieved that we had one of the better days today."

13/12/2016

"Dad ate chocolate pudding but refused the meal. Never mind. I stayed with him for a while after he went back to sleep. He only sleeps very lightly and sometimes hears what I say. You wouldn't believe it, but while dreaming dad very clearly spoke a few sentences in German. This illness is a mystery. Normally he can't speak properly at all anymore. There is probably no explanation for what happened today…"

15/12/2016

"Dad was Ok. He ate his spaghetti and some ice cream and then slept. But the mental decline has progressed to a point now that it is very, very sad to see him like this. I inquired about the hip protector today and they will measure Norbert so they get the right size. They say dad might only be a medium now, down from XL just a few months before. No wonder given the small portions he eats."

16/12/2016

"They had a little family Christmas celebration at the home today. There was an entertainer who sang Christmas songs. Dad had a good day and we communicated the best way still possible. Dad, very quietly, tried to sing along in his own way. But the fact that he tried really touched me deeply. It was quite an emotional visit for me. Then he was very tired again. I stayed for a while and then said good bye for the day."

19/12/2016

"When I got there his eyes were open, but he just stared skywards and I couldn't get through to him; neither could the caregivers. He wanted neither food, nor drink. Later he "returned" for a few seconds, but then slept again. The caregivers told me he had a tiny bit of food this morning, but they are not allowed to give opinions about his illness. Only the nurses are permitted to do that, but even they seem quite guarded. I mean, I can see for myself what is happening and when I ask them, they confirm my fears. Dad's brain continues to deteriorate. But I still stay with him around one and a half hours."

21/12/2016

"It pains me that we are not to give anything to dad for Christmas this year. But I will try to maybe make some kind of salmon mousse, mixed with some cream cheese. Maybe you have an idea how to season it. I spoke with caregiver Xalvador and he too said we could try it. I just don't know how to incorporate the bread. Of course white bread would be best. But how do I mash it, the whole thing I mean: the salmon *and* the bread? Maybe even add a little lemon?"

23/12/2016

"I spoke with the two nurses. They want to only use the sedation if absolutely necessary, so that dad can be "with us" a little more. He still shows aggression, but he can't act on it anymore. He just doesn't have the strength. Only his hands remain strong and he can fight with hands and feet when he doesn't want to be washed. Tomorrow I will see for the first time how long it takes for dad to perhaps change now that he doesn't get these pills anymore."

25/12/2016 – Christmas

"The visit with dad was better today, as I had expected. We did some gentle arm and leg exercises, which he seemed to like. Then he slept for a bit. When he woke, he said something I didn't understand, but he repeated it several times while I watched his mouth very closely. I asked: "TJ?" He smiled and nodded. He was full of joy to have seen his grandson yesterday. I will write to TJ and tell him about it. Maybe he will visit his grandad again soon. Sometimes it's is nothing short of astonishing how dad reacts. The salmon mousse I made for dad didn't turn out well. It was too salty and so I had to leave it behind."

# Part III - 5 Days in January

The last three and a half years had been full of emotional ups and downs with mum's daily messages swinging back and forth between hope and despair, between ever-rarer glimpses of dad the way he once was, followed by inevitable further decline, usually within less than 24 hours later. The prospect of reading mum's mails about dad's condition, especially during the last year increasingly filled me with dread and much of life itself was now dominated by the kind of "news" I would receive from her on any given day. As dad's condition worsened, we were on edge on a 24-hour basis, constantly weighing up the need to be with him against the need to maintain our jobs and thus our own lives and future. For almost 18 months we had been living, if that is what you want to call it, suspended in an alternate universe of conflicted emotions, the impossibility of reason when it came to dad's illness and the ever-present uncertainty by which it was chiefly marked. Holidays, previously cherished as family occasions often despite and across geographical distances, had lost much of their meaning in the process and the joy of celebrating family tradition that had previously been the backdrop to so many visits, had long been replaced by the necessity to react to critical developments in dad's deteriorating health. Emotional sanity had long departed and life shrunk down to weekly "go or no go" decisions in the face of dad's worsening struggle. I had visited dad in November, staying as long as I could until late in the month. At that point, dad was sleeping most of the time, some days up to 22 hours. It was hard to tell whether it was the effect of medication or just his brain shutting down, but what had started as virtual bouts of narcolepsy had turned into a semi-permanent state. Walking, by then was practically out of the question and by late November even when aided, taking a few steps had become impossible. On rare occasions, he would try to stand on shaky legs, but this usually proved so exhausting that within a few minutes he would collapse and return to his trancelike state. He wasn't always sleeping though. Sometimes he would just lie there, eyes closed and unreachable. On good days he would squeeze our hand and what could barely pass for a smile would momentarily cause the corners of his mouth to lift, the rest of his face stoically frozen and his eyes shut. On the rarest of days, he would wake long enough to look at us and interact for a few minutes. These were the most precious moments we were still granted with him and yet the memory remains etched into my brain accompanied by the feeling of complete despondency. His eyes, once bright, sparkly, and full of the cheekiness he had been known for all his life, had recessed into his skull, become narrow and pale, almost glassy. The look on his face, whenever he saw us was one of urgency, pure helplessness and confusion, as if reaching through a thick fog towards something desperately needed and yet so elusive. His lips would quiver in an attempt to mutter barely audible words, but each time his brain would ultimately betray him and it was occasionally that the single words he managed to articulate had any comprehensible meaning.

There was one such instance, I will remember for as long as I live: The only way to get dad out of bed and help him maintain some kind of social connection with the world around him, was to use an electric hoist to lift him into a reclining armchair. The latter could then be wheeled into the common room where patients would spend their days, take their meals, listen to music, and watch the surrounding meadows through the large room's panoramic windows. There, staff could also time things a little better in regards to feeding dad, which was of course only possible during the brief periods where he was wake and mentally present enough to take in what more often than not by now was only liquidized food.

It was the last day of my visit before having to fly back to take care of some residual work before the Christmas holidays. Last days were always the hardest. No, they were the worst. I had flown in and out for visits every few months since dad's illness first assaulted him in 2013. Each time he was worse, each time I didn't and couldn't know when I would be back and each time there was a real chance that our good-bye would be the last. I had thus come to despise them to the point, where during one visit in early 2016 I even couldn't bring myself to go on that last day. Instead I sat at mum's and dad's place and cried; a decision I thoroughly regretted almost immediately and for which I secretly berated myself the days and weeks following and until I saw dad again a few months later.

On that day, 20 November 2016, I once again fought the emotions that had been building in the knowledge that the moment would arrive yet again, but with it this time an increased awareness that things were nearing the last stages and a high probability existed that I would not see dad alive again. Following the death of loved ones people often say one should focus on life and the fact that it will go on for those left behind; sometimes adding that the knowledge the person is now in a better place should give comfort. But how do you deal with the fact that you are saying good-bye to someone who is still living, in the knowledge that chances are, this will be the last time you see them? How do you focus on "life going on" when at this point, your whole universe is in limbo and when all life has done is to go from one grinding halt to another for several years in a row?

On the single occasion where I had lacked the courage to see dad on the last day of my visit, I had ultimately resorted to justifying my choice by telling myself that he didn't recognize me anymore and that he would neither notice nor remember my presence or absence from one day to another. Naturally, this explanation although true on most days, did not account for exceptions to this unfortunate rule and in my focus on emotional self-preservation I had failed to recognize how precious and ultimately soothing these could be as enduring memories of an otherwise dark and desolate human chapter.

It was only during my next visit a couple of months later, for which both my wife and I were lucky enough to be able to travel together, that I realized the above more than ever. Mid-2016 a few months before losing the ability to walk, dad was still able to sit for a while, walk unaided within the patients' lounge or in his room and would at times even dance a few slow steps during the home's musical entertainment afternoons. He would still sit with us and although he would mostly stare straight ahead or focus on the floor, also say simple words, occasionally react to light-hearted comments and enjoy being fed a piece of cake or, his favorite, good quality ice cream. Sometimes he would get restless and once helped to his feet would simply walk away with no particular direction, or stand and hold on to a door or window frame and just stare into space, his eyes focused on something only he could see. This was one of those days and after around 45 minutes, which at that point still marked the limit of his ability to stay awake or remain "somewhat present", it was time to once again say farewell. Oddly enough, upon our arrival and many times after, he had immediately recognized my wife and so we both told him that we loved him, hugged him and with a thumbs-up from the caregivers, began to make our way out. Mum was always keen to maintain her visit routine, sometimes much to our dismay as her self-imposed time restrictions seemed to limit opportunities for happy moments, which dad's illness would only permit completely at random and not in line with her or any other fixed schedule. I now understand that this was her way to establish some kind of normality in a life that had become all *but* normal, but at the time, it pained us to see her subject herself to these self-imposed and self-enforced time constraints. So as usual, and like on so many occasions before, mum led the way out. She seldom looked back these days, unlike when dad still walked with us and even sometimes lamented that he could no longer accompany us outside. As always during the last visit, I lagged behind that day, forever torn between the impossibility of staying, the sense of duty to just be with dad and the reality that in less than 12 hours I would once again be in a taxi to the airport. Dad had been sitting in his light brown recliner facing the French doors to the path that led through a small garden area where the caregivers and patients well enough to help, maintained a number of flowerbeds. As usual, he had just been staring ahead, barely recognizing and much less acknowledging our imminent departure. But just as I walked away he pushed himself up and, holding on to the window frame suppressed the door handle. The others were too far ahead into the corridor for me to call out to them to wait. The caregivers and I exchanged glances and shrugged our shoulders. There was no telling what he would do from one moment to the next, but getting up like this was certainly unusual. He was determined to go outside and so I held onto him and guided him through the door and along the path. He seemed determined to go *somewhere*. Based on experience these episodes of temporary obsession with a singular goal could last a while, so not wanting him to fall I slowly walked along, propping him up as best as I could, while the caregivers were finishing up with another patient. We walked the 20 or so meters to the other side of the garden where the path ended at another pair of French doors leading to one of the two accommodation wings of the rest home. It was sunny but cold and breezy and I worried dad could catch pneumonia wearing just a T-shirt, o tried to hurry along as best as I could. We got to the door. It was locked. Dad tried the handle, again and again, his face without expression. "It's locked dad, I think it can only be opened from the other side", I tried to explain, knowing full well that he was likely to neither listen to nor comprehend what I was saying. "Let's go back dad, what do you think?", I gently tried to maneuver his body in the opposite direction, all the while worried that he may not last the distance and like so many times before fall flat forward as his legs would gave way. To my surprise, he reluctantly shuffled back with me, ever so slowly, his feed never leaving the ground and him just gazing downwards. What had happened to my father, the man who all his life had taken pride in his athletic ability and never shied away from a challenge?! Although I *knew* the hunched figure I supported next to me now, shuffling across the concrete on unsteady feet was but what his illness had made him, it was impossible to reconcile the two images. I can still feel the warmth of his body as my arm locked in under his and I spoke to him quietly, telling him that I loved him and that Sharon and I would come back soon; all the while looking for any sign of recognition. Amazingly, we made it back to the doors to the common room, where the caregivers were standing at the ready. Dad pressed the handle and opened the door, but refused to go inside. I joked with him about how he was kind to let me go first and stepped through, but as I turned to help him in, I found him ever so slowly, like in slow motion closing the door again from the outside. At that moment, he looked up and our eyes met for the first time since we had arrived that day. His facial expression suddenly changed completely. He looked awake and serious as he concentrated, all the absent-mindedness lifted and replaced by clarity. And then it happened: He reached out, touched my arm, looked deep into my eyes and said with confidence and finality: "I wish you both the best of luck." A smile briefly flickered across his face and then the moment was gone. He closed the door, turned away, the caregivers taking over as I, speechless, and in shock stepped back. This was not *a* good-bye. For him, this was *the* good-bye to Sharon and me. The last clear and conscious statement I would ever hear him utter towards me and forever engraved in my memory. It was hard to hold back tears upon leaving at the best of times, but that day it was simply futile.

Fast forward a few months and here I was again in November 2016. The visit had been emotionally draining and at times quite traumatic. With Dad's decline accelerating more than ever, even short periods like a week or two often saw considerable change for the worse. At this stage, you learn to cling to moments, no longer hours or half hours, but now minutes or even seconds during which he would open his eyes, show signs that he recognized us, and Lewy Body allowed him a break from the mental and physical purgatory he spent most of his time in. One of those moments was when on what we had come to label as a "good day", he opened his eyes and stretched out his arms to me standing at the foot end of his hospital bed. I took his hands in mine and pulled his upper body towards me, lifting him up in a sit-up kind of fashion. He held on tight and smiled as we, completely out of the blue, started a little tug-of-war. Both mum and I spurred him on, commending him on his strength and joking about how he had kept quiet about his energy reserves. And indeed, he put all his remaining strength into trying to pull me over the headboard, grinning broadly as I pretended to struggle. We went back and forth, repeating the process several times and with each attempt, his face lit up more and more. Mum and I laughed and joked with him, full of joy and thankfulness for the reprieve the three of us had been granted. As expected, it was short-lived and after a few minutes dad fell asleep again, exhausted from what was more exercise than he had probably had in months. But it was a day that sustained us for weeks to come and to some extent still does even today, as one of the last few cherished instances of real interaction with dad.

224

But, much like so many times since the events of 2013 the day came again to say good-bye, albeit this time in the sad knowledge that dad's rapid deterioration would undoubtedly have me to return sooner rather than later and that the next trip would be the last of its kind. By now dad had lost the ability to articulate a good-bye message like the one during Sharon's and my visit a mere few months earlier. He rarely interacted, his hallucinatory state had become semi-permanent, and he rarely spoke anything discernible. Much of his time was spent lying in bed with his eyes closed, his hands manipulating imaginary items, as if pulling levers suspended in mid-air. Other times he would try to get up but then fall onto the carpet in his room, before entering into that same state right where he had fallen. Whenever he was hoisted into his recliner, he would pick up imaginary food items and pretend-eat or -drink, while ignoring actual food or drink offered to him. He would lean to the side and over the armrest and then stare at the pattern of the carpet, sometimes bending forward in an attempt to pick up imaginary objects from the floor. By all accounts the brief moments he was 'with us', let alone awake had now become far and few between. On the last day before leaving again this had been no different. He had been hoisted into his recliner and was sitting in the common room facing the window towards the green meadows of the farm next door, where geese and ducks mingled and a breeze was blowing through the tall poplars lining the train track some distance away. He had been sleeping in his chair for much of the time and not even a spoon of his favorite ice cream touching his lips had managed to bring him back that day. After sitting with him for a good while, we resigned ourselves to the fact that this was not going to be one of those rare "good days" we never gave up hoped for. With afternoon tea for the residents almost ready, we decided that it would be best to leave and the caregivers thus moved dad's recliner a little out of the way where he could continue sleeping quietly. And yet again, that's when it happened: As always I was walking behind mum and was just about to leave the common room. I stopped at the door and turned to look at dad one last time, fully expecting him to be in the same position he had been in all that time. Instead, there he was semi-upright, eyes wide open, a slight smile cast across his face and waving good-bye to me with one hand. Although he was unable to physically speak, his eyes spoke volumes. He seemed strangely content at this moment, almost resigned to his situation, yet not sad. Instead, he looked at me with that I can only describe as love, as if giving me permission to leave, almost like saying "it's ok" and "I love you". It was the very last time dad ever consciously communicated with me. It was also a moment that I feel brought closure to the two of us. A moment that across the room brought peace and sent a message louder and stronger than any words he could have formed. He was letting me go. Letting me go to do what I needed to do and for him to go through what was in store for him; what had started just over 3 years ago and which would eventually take 5 days in January.

I somehow knew the time for that last trip was near, that last and inevitable journey for dad. Christmas had been a mixed affair. Between monitoring email updates from mum, the rush to conclude contracts before the holidays and the fact that Sharon and I would not be able to see family that year, the holiday season had lost much of its meaning. Sharon did her best to keep the spirit alive, buying a Christmas tree and decorating it for our Christmas Eve together. Having traveled back and forth to see dad several times and knowing that "the call" would eventually come probably sooner rather than later, we simply couldn't afford yet another trip "just for Christmas". We were lucky enough to be able to afford all the travel so far and I often cringe at how these aspects in other circumstances impact loving family members who may want to do the same, but are less fortunate financially. I was an emotional wreck now and each time I received another mail about dad's rapidly declining health, space contracted and time stood still to the point where "normal" life as we had once known it had long taken its leave. Days were deemed "good" or "bad" based on the updates we received from mum. "No change" was a good day. It's hard to understand for people who haven't lived through it how sometimes the minutiae of mum's descriptions could make a difference one way or another. Dad took some liquids today; it was a good day. He ate a spoonful of ice cream; it was a good day. He woke for a few minutes and looked at mum; it was a good day. It was the little things that kept us going. And it was the little things that reduced us to tears, that kept us on

226

edge and which had me refreshing my phone's email every few minutes…

Unfortunately, since August and more so since November bad news had become the norm and the struggle between life's demands and my loyalty to dad whom I loved so dearly took its daily toll. I had angry outbursts at the slightest things, I broke down in tears watching the silliest movies, I hated myself when I laughed and most of all I was angry at God, for robbing me of these years with dad; these years we had both fought so hard for. You can read blogs about emotional responses in grief and they will tell you that my reactions weren't out of the ordinary and in fact quite normal. But you know what? When you're living it, that commentary just comes across as condescending. Dare those people tell me this was "normal"? What the fuck did they know?! I was angry most of the time, I drank a lot to numb anything and everything and to be able to function as a "normal" person and husband as much as was possible. Sharon was and is amazingly understanding and I feel blessed and humbled that she has actually been by my side these years despite my obvious shortfalls and usually bad stress reactions. She never once criticized me for any of my probably sometimes irrationally emotional blowouts during that time. Her tolerance knew no bounds. I guess my point here is that no matter what support you may or may not have, no matter how big or small your family or your bank account, you go through this alone; perhaps surrounded by people and people who mean well at that, but *inside* you go through it alone. So the next time you are with someone who is going through the same thing, the last thing you probably want to tell them is that it's "normal" to feel the way they feel, whatever it is.

Christmas went by. Mum had always been the one that kept the traditions alive, who maintained what our family simply "did" at Christmas, who rallied the troops, no matter how small in number. But this was a war of attrition and over the last couple of years, these things had whittled down to the lowest denominator possible under the circumstances, to the point where this year her efforts to just find *some* way, *any* way to still have a Christmas with dad, were excruciating to watch from a distance.

Only a couple of years earlier, when dad had been allowed to go back home a short while following his brief but traumatizing stint in the psychogeriatric wing of Penikoru hospital, Christmas, with the exception of dad's erratic behavior and the need to constantly keep an eye on him, for the outside observer would have seemed almost normal. I cooked, mum fretted over decorations and setting the table, my son was sitting at the kitchen counter and observing the goings-on as he usually does. There was a small tree in the corner near the TV, along with the singing Santa dad had always chuckled at each time it broke out in song. Bing Crosby and Dean Martin were providing the tunes and the smell of lit candles and cloves and other Christmassy things wafted through the air. It was almost "normal", except for us keeping constant watch on dad since his mind would tell him to wander off at random; sometimes just into the garden, but worst case, as at happened many times before, somewhere into the neighborhood or beyond, prompting a collective search on foot and by car. Dad had sometimes shown resolve and energy during his "escapes" which were nothing short of mind-boggling. That Christmas he was sort of "ok" on that front, but when we set up the food – buffet style was what we had always liked, as meals in typical European fashion usually lasted for hours – and tried to get dad to come and sit at the table, he broke down in tears. He was inconsolable. Something had obviously upset him. I walked with him as he left the room and headed straight for their bedroom. He ended up standing in the middle of the bedroom, utterly distraught, crying, and rummaging through his wallet. "What is the matter dad", I asked confused, "Don't you want to sit with us and have Christmas dinner?" He looked around as if he was searching for something, his fingers clumsily examining his wallet. "How am I going to pay for this", he finally said through his tears, "I don't have any money and all this is expensive." I tried to console him by saying it had all been taken care of and that he could rest assured that there was no bill at the end. It took a few attempts until he yielded and actually believed me. You see, that is the strange part: he and mum had been together long before I ever arrived on the scene and he and I had gone through so much. Yet when it came to these situations, he always believed *me*. He always listened to *me*. It's something that to this day I don't quite understand and have trouble reconciling. All I can think of is that he really did see something in me, that he was proud of me and that he even trusted me to make the right decisions. Nowadays I still wish every day that I could tell him this and how in everything I do in life I try to make him proud….alas most revelations come long after the fact, and unfortunately often far too late. In the end, we sat down for dinner that year as we had always done when we were together as a family and we helped dad with the food, laughed, and enjoyed the sense of normality that for an all too brief a moment had returned to our lives.

This year there would be no such thing. In fact, the whole world it seemed, had been turned upside down and much of what may have passed as tradition one way or another would have to be foregone. Mum though, ever-determined and tireless in her efforts to give dad the best experience possible, still kept going. She brought Christmas decorations to the rest home, along with dad's beloved singing Santa and Reindeer and with dad now mostly unable to eat solids even blended some smoked salmon and cream cheese for him. Dad used to love seafood and whenever it was on offer he would happily leave everything else and eat platefuls of the stuff; an affinity that carried over to me and which resulted in many a happy meal for the two of us as mum never liked anything that tasted remotely "fishy".

The year before, we were still able to sit with dad in his room at the rest home. Having prepared cold platters and all kinds of things that for us simply belonged to family Christmas, we had had at least a good hour of quality time with dad, who was if not "with us" in that sense, at least awake and receptive to being fed. Food had always been important in our family. I don't know if it's a European thing, but much of what we or anybody else did in our social circle always revolved around home-cooked meals, buffets, barbecues and restaurant visits. Food stood for everything that was good and much time was spent talking about it, commenting on it and reminiscing about it. Food is what brought people together. Food was life. Even when dad's illness progressively ravaged his mind and body, dismantling his capacities one by one until there was virtually nothing left of who he had been less than 30 months prior, it was that relationship with food, which was the last thing to go. His taste had changed and he subsequently rejected many things he had loved prior to falling ill, but his love for chocolate and ice cream stayed with him.

Towards the last month of 2016 mum increasingly lamented his rejection of food as his hallucinations took over and he often wasn't able to discern anymore between real and imaginary items. Then, in December, things took another turn for the worse when dad intermittently "forgot" how to swallow; his brain now even shutting down reflexes and the last of his motor functions. As many times before, once we got over the initial shock of this new development, we tried to cope with it, forever in the hope that with every step down the ladder of Lewy Body there would eventually come a plateau or as crazy as it may sound in retrospect, maybe even a small improvement. It was a journey of negotiating with this bastard of a disease for an ounce of hope in a losing battle. Mum hung on from day to day, the qualifiers for what constituted an "ok day with dad" now reduced to whether he would eat a small cup of mousse, opened his eyes or showed some sign of recognition at key words. The dismay we had all initially felt at the first signs of dad's illness seemed trivial compared to where we were now. Even today, I still can't bring myself to think about what might have gone on inside of dad's mind all this time. The thought of him feeling trapped, panicked, and alone in this body and mind that were slowly but steadily eroded by this dastardly illness, is just too much to bear.

I had stayed in constant contact with mum over the holidays. Her visits with dad over Christmas had been somewhat "Ok" in the sense that not much had changed for a week or so. The aggressive episodes he had had until but a couple of months prior had since been replaced with extended periods of sleep to the extent that catching him awake during a visit was now a matter of pure luck. Then, shortly after Boxing Day, mum told me about a new and worrying development. Dad was now having intermittent seizures, uncontrollable muscle contractions that caused him a lot of pain and distress. I guess we knew things were now entering what so many call "the last phase", but as with everything Lewy Body, nobody was or is ever going to be able to give any reasonably accurate estimate. LBD is a cruel and unpredictable dictator and works as it wants to work, taking its time however long it wants, before it suddenly delivers another blow. And in as much as you get to know this fact over time, there is no getting used to it. Although there was no doubt that dad would probably not survive for more than two to three months, even the doctors admitted there was no telling how long this state would persist. I was thus again wrestling with myself whether to travel or not and I made mum promise me to be brutally honest and not spare any details, so that we could make the decision at the "right" time.

Then, on 29 December 2016, the following mail arrived:

*"Dear Rob & Sharon,*

*I wish I could write a message just like the ones from the last few days, namely that everything was "Ok" when I visited dad.*

*Sadly, nothing is "Ok" anymore.*

*Since yesterday dad is virtually unable to swallow anymore, or only with extreme difficulty. They position him so that juice or other liquids can run down his throat [instead of having to swallow]. The muscles have ceased. In addition, his involuntary movements have increased considerably. They are often painful for dad, but he can't swallow any medication. They are now looking at injecting painkillers. Also, his inner organs don't work the way they are supposed to anymore. Consequently he doesn't "know" when he has to go toilet and consequently can't initiate bowel movements. As a result he is constantly constipated which is causing him additional discomfort. Miriam the clinical manager said today that they were taking it "day by day".*

*Believe me, it is incredibly hard for me to write this mail. So see dad suffer like this...and there is so little that can be done to help him.*

*Immediately after my visit, I went to the store and bought a stick blender so they can mix the juice powder for dad properly.*

*I will now start visiting him in the mornings and late afternoons, so I can spend as much time with him as possible...*

*I know, dear Rob, it will be hard for you and Sharon as well to read this message. I wish I could be with you right now."*

Mum has always had a talent to deliver bad news in the softest possible way, which sometimes made it difficult to fully assess the situation. This one though spoke volumes between the lines. There was no mistaking it for anything else: things weren't good. And yet things hadn't been good for so long that it was hard to maintain any perspective on reality whatsoever. Now rereading these exchanges I often wonder, whether in hindsight I made the right decisions, whether I should have done this or that differently, spent more time, traveled sooner, never left at all... But those thoughts are not helpful and as emotionally draining as they are now academic. Hindsight may be perfect, but is not always useful. A Burmese colleague of mine calls it "past future tense", an American friend titled it "post-dicting", what whatever you want to call it, questioning the past with the benefit of hindsight unless for the purpose of learning and advancement, is seldom fair or healthy.

I needed to know what was going on. After so many emergency trips, so many "bad news" messages and with no idea about what lay ahead at any stage of this miserable journey, I had lost all ability to judge what the "right thing" was anymore. I suspected this would be it, but I guess there is often a bigger gap between gut feeling and conscious realization than we tend to acknowledge, especially when the realization is tied to something we dread. In this instance though, there were volumes between the lines of her message and it was all that was needed for me to make the decision to travel. Her message the very next day confirmed I had read correctly.

*"Dear Rob,*

*I just got back from the market and turned on the computer. I cried when I read your message. I tend to cry a lot anyway at the moment no matter how much I try to hold it together and put on a brave face towards others.*

*You asked me to tell you honestly how I feel about the situation: Of course I don't know either how long dad still has to suffer. But going by his facial expression things do not look good. I have the feeling dad will not be with us much longer. Maybe he would recognize you one more time, who knows…*

*I took two sleeping pills last night and so I was able to sleep for a few hours. But of course this is now the hardest time we have to go through. That's also why I won't even drink any alcohol, since firstly I don't know when a call comes [from the rest home] and secondly I want to spend whatever time I have with dad without any impairments.*

*Believe me, I wrestled with myself whether to ask you to come. But on the other hand this is such a personal decision that only you can make for yourself.*

*I better close now. I am also depleted – from all the emotions: glad that you are coming, unspeakably distraught about dad – to the point were I am shaking. Would it also be possible for Sharon to come?*

*Lots of love, and thank you for your mail from last night.*

*Your Mum"*

Now, when you live and are running a business in a country like Myanmar, things are never as straight forward as they are elsewhere and I can honestly say that the urgency of travel brought home the fact more than ever. We had always been able to manage our commitments and make arrangements for regular visits throughout dad's illness since, apart from one or two prior occasions there was always some leeway around time frames and thus plans could usually be made days if not at least a couple of weeks prior. This was different. In retrospect I guess we should have been better prepared. But this type of preparedness would also have required acknowledgement of the fact that, to put it bluntly, dad was effectively dying; something neither my heart nor my mind were ready to concede, let alone contemplate. Death had always had an uncertainty attached to it and certainly not a specific date – nobody, not even the doctors had been able to give any estimation; not with an illness that took a different path for every patient. The fact had been a soothing truth, as it went some way to push the thought of dad ever getting to this point out to some vague and distant point in the future. I had therefore relegated it to a far corner of my mind, where it menacingly lurked from day to day, but was somewhat confined by the uncertainty. Now everything came to a peak. The world slowed down. Sharon and I were caught in a flurry of preparations and yet it was as if we were walking through molasses. Sharon will tell you that I have always been a stickler for planning when it comes to travel, perhaps even excessively so sometimes and yet the task suddenly seemed almost insurmountable. I think packing my black suit jacket – the only suit jacket I owned thanks to years of humanitarian work – was the hardest. I berated myself for packing it, hated myself for packing it, as if packing it would seal dad's fate, would replace a long-held question mark with a full stop. After all, he was still alive! Dare you pack clothes for his funeral? What kind of human being are you?! Emotions overtook what we deep down knew was reality and in between the tears and the anguish I held on to that glimmer of hope that maybe this wasn't *it* after all; that just like other times before, he somehow plateaued, that maybe weeks would turn into months…and maybe even another year.

I vaguely remember zipping up my suitcase and glancing at the Christmas tree that still stood in the corner of the living room, its electric lights maintaining their monotone flicker: incongruous, surreal. We quickly decided that I was to go ahead and "assess the situation" while Sharon would begin putting contracts on hold and wait for news. We had to – or so we thought - prepare for a long haul and I had promised mum I would be there as long as it was necessary. After her latest messages, my concern increasingly shifted back and forth between dad and her. I knew he had all the care he needed, but she was struggling to cope. I remember saying good-bye to Sharon, hugging her before heading off into the unknown. I don't recall the flight or anything else really until mum and I entered dad's room at the rest home a day later. It was already evening and ordinarily I would have waited until the next day before I would visit, as not to disturb dad's sleep. But in recent weeks he had spent most of the day and night either sleeping or far removed from the world around him, eyes closed and unreachable, plus there was no way I could have slept anyway.

234

The room smelled of something. Even now, I can't put my finger on it; a mix of medication, of cleaning agent and of something else; not death, no, but bad nonetheless. One look at dad and my worst fears were confirmed. I had seen him but 6 weeks earlier and despite his condition, his weight loss and overall declining health his appearance had still approximated dad the way I had always known him, or at least the way he had been for the last 12 to 18 months prior. The tiny body I now saw lying there under the blankets, his skin stretched tightly across his emaciated face, his mouth wide open as if gasping for air, was not what I had expected. Dad's skin was flushed and glowing almost feverishly, his hands cramped up and holding on to the blanket under which I could make out his legs, stiff and reduced to sticks since I had last seen him. I felt pushed against the wall, my first instinct to run, run and keep running away from what I was seeing. Thankfully mum, never faltering in how she cared for dad in the most loving way, took the first step for me, leaning in close to dad, holding his hand and whispering softly that I had arrived to see him. On many previous occasions, this had been enough to elicit some kind of response, no matter what his condition. But not this time. Not anymore.

I held his hand, stroked it for a few moments, and let him know that I was there; there to stay. Dad and I had never really been the "touchy" types and generally when he was still healthy we would hug twice each time I visited: on arrival and departure. That's how things were, that was normal. I had often told him that I loved him, something that on account of his upbringing had been a hard thing to get out of him even for mum during their early years. He had always said it in return; a little rushed perhaps and not as loud, but he had always said it to me nonetheless. Now holding dad's hand was all that was left to do. There would be no more replies to my "I love you's". We stayed only a few minutes that night, listening to his breathing and watching him, lovingly and in disbelief.

That was Monday.

# Day 1

The previous night, still in shock after what I had seen, I had contacted Sharon and asked her to book the first available flight. As much as I had not wanted to have to say it, but this was the time for us all to come together. I am still glad I made the decision to contact her straight away and while impressions were raw and unfiltered. So often in life we let the part of us that hopes, that little eternal optimist that resides in all of us, come out and paint our perspective rosier than it actually is. We just have to give it enough time. When it comes to avoiding the unimaginable, even a weak 'maybe' is sometimes all that it takes to delay what we otherwise already know needs to be done. I had allowed this so many times over the past 3 years, but now time for optimism had run out. Even that little voice inside my mind that had normally sprinkled specks of doubt over every decision had fallen silent. We were now talking weeks, if not days.

Tuesday morning we made our way back to the rest home around 10.30am. I was raring to go earlier, but doing so as mum rightfully pointed out would have put us on a collision course with the nurses' schedule. Dad would "wake" – or whatever "wake" stood for these days – around nine or so and it normally took a while to get him ready and presentable. The home had 12, sometimes 14 other patients and a nursing staff of 4 on most shifts. This required a high degree of coordination and made mornings a labor intensive and stressful time for all involved, as each patient had his or her own needs and symptomatic quirks, including "toilet accidents", fits, outbursts and various other behaviors that would ensure no two days were ever the same for the wholly dedicated staff. I must admit I made the morning trip with some apprehension; torn between wanting to see dad and yet still reeling from the impressions of the evening prior. Part of me just wanted to crawl under a rock. I parked mum's little car as we had always done - same spot, creatures of habit – and mum, as usual started to walk towards the entrance. Mum had had her hips replaced a few years earlier and would frequently complain that she couldn't keep up with my fast pace whenever we were out. This was the only occasion were the opposite was true.

Mum was on mission. This was her daily routine. She had seen the decline and although she was just as distraught and shaken, her love for dad, her dogged determination to do anything and everything for the man she had devoted her life to, no, who *was* her life, gave her an unprecedented level of energy. As she marched towards the entrance, I found myself lagging behind. I was a kid again. As much as I tried to pull myself together, I was a whisker away from falling apart. The more I tried, the worse it got. I took a deep breath. We entered the small foyer that opened into the spacious common room, where patients would spend much of their waking hours. This was the "hospital" wing of the rest home and several of the faces were familiar from the time when dad was still in the "regular" care ward. I say familiar, because their decline, too, had taken its toll and with many now, the resemblance to their former self was merely fleeting. We turned to look into the lounge room, more as a matter of routine from a time when dad had still spent a few hours each day sitting in his recliner and interacting in some way or fashion, before his trance like state had mostly confined him to his room, and ultimately his bed.

Much to our surprise though, dad was there! They had managed to dress him and he was sitting in his dark orange armchair, semi reclined with the caregivers trying to feed him. I know I have said this a few times now: how each new shock was always the worst. And yet, that is probably the most notable aspect of bastard Lewy. You see a loved one decline to a point you have never seen before, and each time the distress, the shock, the sadness, helplessness, and sheer horror that stir are unprecedented and worse than at any other time before. There is no "getting used to it". Bastard Lewy makes sure of that. The person sitting there in the recliner was only marginally recognizable, even compared to the night before. Dad was wearing a blue, white and yellow striped polo shirt and a pair of Khaki pants. He had always been an XL, or during the "good years" of the 1970s and in between his many yoyo diets, perhaps even a little bigger. Now his clothes looked as if they had been draped over a clothes rack, several sizes too big and just loosely hanging off him. His head was resting back against the headrest of the recliner, his eyes fixed skyward somewhere towards the ceiling above him. His arms and

237

legs moved in some sort of repetitive wave-like motion, which instantly reminded me of Parkinson's patients I had seen in documentaries. The worst part though, was his facial expression. His weight loss had caused his skin to pull tight across his face, giving it a skull-like appearance. His lips had retreated and his mouth appeared disproportionately large, now permanently revealing his teeth, freezing it in a sickly grin. It is hard to describe the feeling of love, compassion and repulsion that all came over me at the same time – a complete paradox of emotions, which in lieu of any other phrase that comes to mind and even at the risk of sounding pathetic, tore at the very strings of my soul.

The person whom I looked up to most in my life, whose love had not only persevered even at times when the agony and sorrow I had caused him would have given more than enough cause to abandon me, who had subsequently opened a door for a relationship that was so close on a level that is hard to describe even today, was now chillingly but a faint shadow of himself. And I could do absolutely nothing; nothing to ease his suffering, nothing to stop it, nothing to help; nothing but watch, be there and witness. I walked up to him and held his hand as I leaned over to make sure he could see me properly in his reclined position. The mask that his face had become remained frozen for a moment, but then suddenly there was a flicker in his eyes, the corners of his mouth began to quiver and the shaking of his body increased. He knew I was there. At that point I had to let mum take over for a moment. We had always said that dad shouldn't see us cry, that he should feel our love and our hope for him, not our despair. I stepped out into the little foyer, breathed deep, and tried to regain my composure while mum tended to dad in her usual quietly loving fashion. She had mastered the art – and it is undoubtedly an art – to control herself completely during her visits and only allow herself to break down once she closed the door behind her at home. It is a strength, I am sad to say, I do not possess. After a few minutes I returned, my nerves having settled after the renewed shock. Mum had described in her daily messages how dad had eaten less and less in the past few weeks and the fact was now more than obvious. The last time I had seen him he already barely touched his meals, but luckily had still retained a fondness for all things sweet. It's weird how

238

Lew Body affects anything and everything that has to do with the senses as well. And so Dad's taste had undergone significant changes, especially in the last year or so. He had always liked sweet stuff, but much like myself had always been a bit of a "snob" when it came to quality. He loved homemade baked goods, good chocolate and premium ice cream, but would just as easily not eat them if they weren't right. He loved sour tastes, like lemon and only just ripe plums and abhorred things that were overly sweet. This was completely different now to a point where it had become a case of the sweeter the better. Cakes, served at the rest home daily during afternoon tea, were the cheap ones with thick layers of sugary frosting and artificial jams, the kind dad had always frowned upon back when he was still well. Now he would eat them by the plateful; well, at least he would back when he was still able to. Now his "food" intake had been reduced to one or two tiny containers of chocolate-flavored mousse and the occasional shake made from geriatric dietary supplement powder, both spoon-fed, ever slower and slower as time went on. In very German tradition, we had always been a family of "foodies" and we could spend hours and hours talking about where to buy it, then cooking it, eating it and talking at length about what we had just eaten. Food meant well-being, food was happiness, food was celebration, food was something to be looked forward to from breakfast to supper, 7 days a week. And so naturally, much as it had always been tradition in our family, mum initially gaged dad's condition, in fact determined whether he had a "good" day or a "bad" by how much he ate and now, as that was no longer possible, whether he ate at all. In the earlier stages of his illness, during his first stints in the psycho-geriatric assessment unit and then during the brief period where we thought it was still possible for him to remain in an open rest home, it had always been about brightening dad's day with something he enjoyed; something that reminded him of the past or simply something that tasted great and constituted a change from what was served at the facility. His joy eating these things became mum's joy. His smile became mum's smile. An empty plate or bowl meant it was a good day for both. But as with everything when it comes to bastard Lewy, there is only retreat from his assault, constant readjustment and witling things

239

down to the lowest still remaining options; hope, since it dies last, being the final bastion. Although a foodie myself, I had never understood mum's obsession to get food into dad just for the sake of it and even when it was obvious that he was either uninterested or unable to eat. It was her mission, her way of assuring herself that she was living up to her pledge never to give up on him and in the process look for a glimmer of acknowledgement or joy, even. It was a pledge that mum took serious, not out of a forced sense of duty, but pure love and devotion; a pledge that came naturally, with the territory of a marriage that had now prevailed for over 50 years and during which the line between the two as individuals had all but evaporated, fused them into the inseparable unit they were today. There were times when I wanted to shake mum and yell at her, whenever she would yet again try to virtually force dad to eat something. I guess we looked at things from different perspectives, but I am still convinced that some of this was much more than a coping mechanism on her part and instead an obsessive-compulsive outcrop, a symptom of the trauma she had sustained and was still subjected to on a daily basis. But what was I supposed to do? It was another conundrum I found myself caught up in; one of so many during that time. Initially there were a few times when I got angry with her and insisted she stop trying to shove things in his mouth, to the point where I visited dad by myself here and there so I wouldn't have to witness mum's daily food routine. Then she would tell me that I didn't know what it was like, because I hadn't been there and that she knew what to do and what was right; something in as much as it was factually correct hurt me immensely. I wrestled each and every day with the decision to completely give up our business and the life we had worked so hard for, to be with dad. And each time when I visited, the realization came that there was little I could do to help; in fact in most cases my presence, I felt, was disrupting routines and kept mum's life from resembling some form of normality in as much as that was even possible. Even mum would tell me so time and time again. And yet in these instances when we argued, she would always say the one thing that would end up hurting me the most: "You don't understand. You haven't *been* here."

Her approach to caring for dad thus at times took us on a collision course, fueled by the stress and sorrow, the hopelessness we both felt and which in as much as it can unite people, can be a powerful force of division as we come to the realization that in the end we are all alone in our pain; a pain which is as different for each one of us as it is all consuming. Now, as mum opened the little cooler bag with the daily "goodies", the one she had prepared each and every day ever since dad's condition had progressed to where he could no longer stay at home, unwrapping the spoon and placing the napkins and the chocolate mousse on the window sill next to his chair, it became more and more evident that the "good" days had come to an end. I could see dad struggle. Not struggle with any particular "thing", but struggle with staying alive. His body no longer obeyed whatever rudimentary signals his brain was still able to send, he was unable to communicate whatever conscious thoughts or feeling remained, let alone articulate anything beyond moans and grunts, uttered on the back of muscle pain and what would have been extreme soreness from lack of movement and confinement to his bed and armchair. I watched with horror that day as first mum and then the caregivers tried to feed him. She placed a small teaspoon full onto his lips. Dad continued shaking and making strange sounds, that seemed to emanate not from his clenched teeth, but from somewhere deep within him. She moved the spoon across his receded lips, something that even at a later stage had always elicited a response and usually caused dad to open his mouth. Nothing. After a few attempts, mum managed to get some of the mousse past dad's chattering teeth and into his mouth. She calmly and quietly encouraged him, all the while trying to keep the mousse from running out of his mouth. Dad could no longer swallow by himself and so every bit that when down his throat was a game of chance between esophagus and windpipe. Dad sputtered and tried to cough. His body still allowed the reflex but no longer all the associated actions. Mousse sprayed. Unable to get rid of the irritation in his lungs, his rasping breath turned into loud an unbearable gargle and a tormented moan. In an out of body experience, I could almost see that last flicker of hope evaporate and leave. I had never seen mum turn away, but now it was her time to spend a few moments alone in the quiet foyer. Next up was the dietary supplement shake, usually mixed to a smooth pulp just thick enough to drip into his mouth and not to run straight down the wrong tube from there. I was at the verge of exploding. What was happening was clearly uncomfortable for dad and he had no intention or capacity, or whatever you might have wanted to call it, to eat. And yet they kept trying to get this vile stuff into him. I felt at yelling at everyone. "Can't you see what you are doing to him? Can't you see what is happening?" But I also remembered what mum had said: I hadn't *been* there. So I probably knew nothing. And so I bit my lips. I now wonder whether the caregivers tried so valiantly for dad, or actually for mum, knowing that he eating would get her, too, through another day. But I guess that's a moot point now. I might as well have yelled, because it didn't take long for things to go horribly wrong. Dad began to convulse, a singular gag reflex finally taking over and fighting against his rigid body. He was in agony and moaned loudly between gargling coughs. I never knew that a human being could make such sounds. The caregivers aided him by bringing up the back of the recliner and leaning him forward, usually the best way to clear whatever had found its way into his lungs. What happened next was as disturbing as it was revealing about where things stood. Having been leaned forward and supported, dad's upper body tilted to one side, his head drooping forward almost like someone trying to throw up over the railing of a ship. A thick gooey white stream of what had once been a nutrient shake, now mixed with all manner of fluid virtually "fell" from his mouth in one large gush; so much in fact that given what he had "eaten" so far, it represented the entire intake of several days. Virtually none of it had found its way into his stomach and instead had slowly begun to suffocate him. He kept convulsing and twitching and moaning and only after a few minutes of clearing out his mouth with swabs and patting him on the back to loosen whatever else remained trapped, was he able to be reclined again and almost immediately went into a deep sleep. The caregivers brought him back to his room, while mum and I spent a few moments digesting what we kind of knew we had just witnessed: The last attempt at trying to save dad. We quickly made the decision that from now on at least one of us would be by his side. It is hard to convey the gravity of this and what making the decision meant. We didn't have to say it, we didn't have to talk about it, but we knew that it was the quiet admission that now it wouldn't be long, that of all the things that had been taken from dad and from us by bastard Lewy, everything which had succumbed to him along the way, hope indeed had just died last. I could see mum was neither in a frame of mind nor probably willing to leave dad's side at that point and so I "volunteered" to go get a few essentials so that we could stay with him. The caregivers were incredibly understanding, but since this was a dementia care hospital wing and not a hospice, probably also felt a little out of their depth. This was far from business as usual, even for them.  On one side I welcomed the opportunity to get outside, sit still at the driver's seat of mum's car for a moment and watch the trees sway back and forth in a gusty early summer wind. Although so much of it had been done already, crying still provided a brief vent for the pressure that had nowhere else to go. I went to the shops and bought a bunch of stuff to bring back. The hospital food was always on offer, but since it was made for the patients, it was usually soft and although tasty, far from what would have passed for a meal in our family. And if it was one thing I knew would at least momentarily pull things together, it was something that mum liked to eat. Next up was a pit stop at home. Mum's and dad's dog had become a little paranoid over the years and wasn't all that good by herself, so a quick chat to the next-door neighbors, a handing over of the house keys and before long I found myself driving back to the rest home. I can still see snapshots before my mind's eye of this but not of other emergency trips during that week. It is the one I can most vividly remember. I think it was the feeling of absurdity that I had as I was standing in line, waiting to pay for a few sandwiches at the bakery. I was waiting in line to buy something to eat. I was wasting time dad didn't have, buying something he could no longer enjoy with us, just so *we* could eat. Life seemed farcical; to be agonizing over chicken or ham, while life was slowly, painfully slipping away from dad! I felt awful. When I came back to dad's ward, he had been changed and readied for bed, which at that stage really had nothing to do with the time of day, but was all about comfort and dignity.

He was resting; his upper body slightly elevated in his hospital bed, which a few weeks earlier had been fitted with an inflatable mattress that automatically changed pressure between its various compartments to keep dad from developing sores from the 22-hour periods he now spent in bed virtually motionless. His breathing was calm now, not raspy and forced. The gargling noise had disappeared and only once in a while he would try to cough briefly without opening his eyes and then return to what looked like a deep sleep. Mum was sitting there, oblivious to the world as her gaze never so much as moved from dad, as if willing him to go back even perhaps just to how he had been a mere few weeks prior, and desperately trying to pull him out of this state with nothing but her love for him. I put the bags in the corner and we sat there quietly for a moment, just being with dad and listening to his breathing. It wasn't long before a knock on the door was followed by one of the care givers poking his head in to see if we needed anything and how dad was doing. Time had very much become irrelevant and I don't even know how long we had been there. The kind caregiver, Xalvador, a young man from the Philippines like so many others of his team was one of the most compassionate and patient people I had ever met. I don't think I ever saw him get upset with anything or anyone; not when patients struck out at him in uncontrollable fits, not when they soiled themselves, dropped their food, went off on wild rants or just held onto him rambling incoherently for what seemed like hours at a time. He always smiled; he never wavered in his resolve to treat people with the utmost dignity and love, even. I often wonder what his life looked like after the long shifts at the facility; whether he broke down sometimes or how he coped with working in a place where people never recovered, never got better and their various conditions took them apart, dismantled them until they returned to an infantile stage before inevitably dying from health complications. I have worked with former SEAL team members, have met hardened veterans and active fighters all over the world with enough guts and testosterone to bottle, and sell it, and yet this small statured guy in his turquois scrubs had more strength than all of them combined. He showed up every day, wearing his smile as if nothing had ever happened no matter what the previous day had looked like. It seemed as though

244

the harder things got, the softer he tread, the kinder he became, his confidence and professionalism never compromised by things which would have tested even Mother Theresa! He and dad had already formed a special bond very early in the piece when dad was admitted to the closed dementia ward before being moved to the hospital wing. This was when dad could still speak. His mind was already all over the place, but he still had memories and the capacity to articulate them, and Xalvador, despite his busy schedule never missed an opportunity to listen when dad had one of his "better" days, during which a mishmash of themes comprised of memories and hallucinations sometimes poured out of him without so much as a breather. The rest home made a point of keeping its patients entertained and so regular concerts and special activities were organized for all manner of calendar events. 4th of July? American Theme. St. Patrick's Day? Irish theme. Olympics? Sports theme. And so on it went. It was during the last occasion that dad was able to attend, a cultural day where each patient and their families displayed something of their culture and different country-specific songs were played, that a very special photo was taken of Xalvador with dad outside beneath a birch or some other tree with the blue sky above, dad in full Bavarian garb; Lederhosen, felt hat, red socks and hiking boots, as he had always loved to wear on hikes and in his role as German representative during Rotary Club Octoberfest. You can clearly see their connection in the photo and how Xalvador always managed to engage his patients at, not his, but *their* level, paying careful attention to them and valuing even what he was able to learn from them, no matter how advanced their condition. I looked at him as he now poked his head through the door seeing if everything was Ok, and I could see a look in his face I hadn't seen before. I may not have known him all that well, but what I saw was definitely out of the ordinary; a tug of war between compassion and duty, of wanting to help but unable to do so, knowing where things were headed; the only safe haven the routine, the facility's daily schedule, which forced staff to disengage and simply "take care of business" sometimes, lest probably they all would have lost their mind in the process.

"Do you think Norbert will want dinner?" he asked hesitantly, almost apologetically. I looked back and forth between dad and Xalvador several times. I did not know the answer to this simple question. I started to panic. I looked at mum, she looked at me, then back at dad and Xalvador. How do you answer such a question under these circumstances? The room began to spin, I felt that whatever answer I could give, they all seemed wrong. Should I say yes and then we would try to feed him, probably resulting in an episode like earlier that day? Should I say no and effectively deny dad food? *Deny. Dad. Food?* After a few moments mum thankfully made the only possible decision and asked to hold his meal so perhaps he could have it later. It was an easy lie we could tell ourselves in order to get around the obvious: that he wasn't going to eat anything. Not now. Not later. And possibly never. Never again. Xalvador looked visibly relieved and quietly closed the door. Mum sat in a chair next to dad. I sat in his recliner watching them. Mum whispered to him in soft tones, holding his hand and here and there kissing him on the forehead as she had always done all my life whenever one of us was sick. They had gone through so much together, survived the war, found each other and overcame all the adversity thrown at them by my disapproving grandparents, had worked out the "kinks" that had plagued their upbringing and had then made it in life. They had grown together in every way imaginable, and fought for it to stay that way a few times when things had gotten rough. They were the proof that love, that lasting relationships like theirs weren't just fate or happened because they were meant to. They had to be fought for, inch by inch, shaped and molded to become what they both wanted. Life had been good to both over the years and until that fateful day in August 2013, when it all began to go pear-shaped. It was hard to reconcile that what I saw in front of me would be the end of their life together after all they had worked for, sacrificed, and overcome. Life isn't fair as they say, but that is just the tip of the iceberg. Life at that moment was nothing but a sadistic, malevolent, or at best uncaring accident of a thing we all stumble around in, completely subjected to its whimsical and random acts of cruelty. To date I had left God out of that equation and tried to remain strong in my faith. And so at that moment I prayed something I had never prayed for before: I prayed to God to please, please, please release dad from his suffering without more pain and agony. Although mum and I had had several

246

conversations around prayers like this and how we wished dad didn't suffer the way he did, praying such things also evoked enormous amounts of guilt. After all, all of us – or at least those who believe in God as the divine, all powerful all loving authority above all – pray to, either now or at least one day in future, have our prayers answered. Now imagine if the one prayer, the one thing you ask God for, the one occasion where he grants you that wish, is the one where you asked for your loved one to pass on?! That would be a tough nut to crack and chew on, my friend. And it was exactly that sentiment which mum and I had discussed. She carried a guilt on her shoulders, that what she had quietly prayed for would at some point be granted. She had hated herself for making the wish on dad's behalf for quite a while now. Of course that feeling of guilt wasn't rational, she knew that. But what did it matter? You can't help these things by rationalizing when looking into the helpless eyes of the one you have loved for over five decades! All I know is that I grew increasingly angry at how things were going. I hated watching dad suffer, but there was much more to it. If this was what the God I was praying to was capable of in spite of all the pleading, then what hope was there? But these were quiet doubts that started creeping in at that moment, almost instantly dismissed against my upbringing as a catholic, a branch of Christianity in which punishment and self-flagellation was part of the lifelong deal as human beings. We were sinners and thus suffering was what we were supposed to do. It was part of the deal. I remember stepping out several times, just standing in the hallway and looking out through a nearby glass emergency exit door at a big tree as it stood there solidly, with just its branches swaying back and forth in the wind. I focused on that tree until I thought my eyes would pop out, just to keep from going crazy. The sun was slowly fading and the outside lights came on, creating blotches of greenery wherever they shone, while the rest of the farm-like surrounds blended together in uniform shades of black and grey.

Throughout the night, dad would briefly wake up. His eyes would open but his pupils remained fixed. Nurses came and went, taking his temperature, making sure he was turned here and there to keep him comfortable. Mum and I would drift in and out, never fully awake and only occasionally asleep for a few minutes. Mum didn't want to move from her chair next to dad and I let her, although I was worried about her a lot. Occasionally I would stretch and walk up and down the now quiet corridor or spread myself out in the lounge room, while the night staff went about their routine. Sometime after midnight mum finally examined the bag of sandwiches and other foods I had brought hours earlier. I was worried about spoilage, but at that point, we were beyond caring. Watching mum eat gave me some hope that she would actually get through this. Dad rarely moved. His breathing ranged from deep sleep to shallow and we continued to watch his chest rise and fall throughout the night.

## Day 2

The next morning came without any change and before long we could hear the early shift of caregivers arrive, chatting to each other as they passed our window and the facility woke up to its normal routine of readying the other patients for their day. Outside the first rays of sunshine made an appearance, casting out the greys of dawn. But here in the room, together with dad we were in a bubble, somewhere in the no man's land between life and the death. Waiting for the unspeakable. Nothing outside or around us, not even time, mattered anymore.

The nurse came and took dad's blood pressure, then his temperature. It was up. Did he have anything to eat? No, he didn't, we replied. A short while later another one of the nurses, it was Xalvador's day off, came by with a breakfast tray. We had left the door open, to let in the noise of the everyday goings-on of the rest home; noises that with them carried life and people and chatter and all the things that had been sucked out of the room we were in. Good morning dad! How are you today? It's morning! Did you sleep well? Both nurses and we tried to act as normal as we could, tried to get dad to wake up and perhaps even react. Dad's breathing changed, indicating that he was no longer in deep sleep. His eyes opened slightly, but remained half closed. Mum got herself into a position where he could see her and she held his hand. She whispered something to him and each time she finished whatever she said, his hand would squeeze hers. She was overjoyed. The two of them "joked around" for a bit. Mum making funny remarks about the scare he gave us and dad squeezing her hand each time she asked a funny question. It was probably the last time they were able to interact this way: mum gazing into his eyes, he looking at her with all the focus he could still muster, his mouth forming something that might have been a smile and each of her reassurances giving him so much needed energy and comfort. It was such a precious moment that I actually got out my phone camera and captured it. I had been documenting dad's illness so that one day I could tell his story and yet when it came to this last stretch, there was somehow something so inappropriate about it, that I had felt increasingly uneasy. I am glad I caught these moments though and for anyone going through the same thing I can only say: "It may be hard but make sure you have your camera handy. It may well be the last time you get to see your loved one resembling something of their former self; you know: that inner light that shines through whatever the outer 'shell' may look like at the time." I, too, got a turn to sit with dad for a moment or two and we looked into each other's eyes. I was not as skilled in all this as mum was, in fact I felt quite inept. Instead I tried to keep from breaking down, told him I was happy that he woke up and was with us this morning, asked him about what we should do today and all manner of other clumsy and meaningless questions I could think of, just to say something at all. His mouth, as was the case most of the time now, was agape and his breath raspy. But he kept his eyes fixed on me as if to say: "I'm still here. I am holding on. I am still with you." The nurses came with perfect timing, for his daily routine; not just a chance for mum and I to step outside for a moment, but also to gage the staff's opinion about how things were from a professional perspective. The clinical manager, a kind and compassionate countrywoman of Xalvador's, came along and inquired about how we were holding up. The nurses had been somewhat coy in responding to especially mum's many questions. I could see they were hesitant to tell her what we all kind of knew and thus the phrase "day to day" became the new timeframe for their prognosis. Luckily it was Wednesday, when a doctor's visit had been scheduled and so we waited for the check-up, anxious and tired, while sitting with dad and listening to his breathing, getting excited when he opened his eyes and equally worried whenever more of the gargling sounds would emanate from his chest. I called my son, who was working in Wellington and told him that we were "on watch". I don't think I got out the full sentence, but he knew why I was calling. He was on the next train over. After what seemed like an eternity, I think it was sometime mid-morning, the doctor arrived. A casual, lanky, semi-grey haired geriatric specialist in his mid-forties. He checked dad over, on one occasion having to lean him forward in his hospital bed, resulting in dad moaning from the strain of movement. Not just physical movement we assumed, but also from constipation, as his internal organs no longer functioned the way they used to and effectively had stopped processing a few days prior, whatever he was

250

given. We waited outside. In retrospect, I actually don't know what to make of his diagnosis that followed. For some reason he, too, shied away from stating simple hard truths and instead just listed a number of issues he had identified. Yes, dad had a temperature, yes his breathing was wheezy and erratic and no, he hadn't eaten since yesterday, nor taken water. I think it was at that point that a simple and no matter how hard-to-stomach "he is dying" would have set us free, would have given us what we were desperately grappling for in that state between defeat and desperate hope. Why did the doctor have to beat around the bush like this?! To be honest, I still don't know why. There was one thing he said though, which had been on our mind and which had been foreshadowed as a precursor to death in many Lewy Body patients by the sources both mum and I had scoured on the internet over the months: Dad had pneumonia. If you ever read up on the last stages of the disease, you will see this go through the cases like a red thread. Inability to swallow, then aspiration, the pneumonia and that's it. Incidentally, in our darkest hours, of which there had been so many these last couple of years, we often said that some kind of quick and severe infection would probably be the only thing to save dad from an agonizing death. And yet, as it turned out it didn't. Instead it slowly eroded, slowly and agonizingly killed what was left of him while we got to watch. The doctor's prognosis was vague as usual. Dad might go on like this for a day, perhaps even a week or more. That was, until the doctor inquired about dad's food and water intake. We answered honestly that he hadn't had anything, hadn't been able to have anything since the day before. I am not sure whether mum noticed it, but that's when I saw a change in the doctor's facial expression. Should we continue trying to give something to him, should we continue to try and at least give dad water? Our questions no doubt sounded desperate. It is in those situations that you long for anything anyone qualified can say that either takes some of the burden away or that gives you an insight you didn't have before or that simply confirms in no uncertain terms either what you hope for, or fear. Yet his answer gave us nothing of the sort. "You can try and give him something if he is receptive, but at this point it is unsure whether it will be of benefit." I'm sorry, but what the fuck kind of answer was that?! Guilt

251

ping-pong, is that what we were playing here?! You have a bunch of people on their last tether, agonizing over what to do, or not to do with their loved one who is in agony, who is in deep, deep trouble here. And you, as a medical professional dare sit on the fence? "Coulda", "woulda", "shoulda", "if's", "maybe's" and so on? I don't think I was angry at that moment, no. I felt helpless. I just wanted the doctor to go away. What use are you when all you do is come in, take dad's temperature, say he's got pneumonia and then leave us with a whole bunch of ambiguities?!

I think as I write this I am even more angry now than I have ever been at such unwillingness to be open and frank, at the refusal to for once consider the notion that a family might actually be comforted by the professional assessment that this *is* the end. Hard truths outrank easy lies any day of the week! But maybe that was just his style, or he hadn't had the experience yet. Or maybe he was a good doctor, but just not that good at giving out "the news". Who knows. I guess it never mattered. In any case, thanks to endless hours spent on the internet about symptoms, cycle of the illness and "what to expect" during the end phases – although I am yet to read an account that is brutally honest to the last breath – we knew what the word pneumonia meant in this context. For most at dad's stage, there was no coming back from it. And yet, the doctor had left us with a great degree of ambiguity, of painful guesswork. What had he meant when he said "You can try if he is receptive?" What the hell does that even mean? Dad hadn't been "receptive" for quite some time, but he still ate occasionally and drank a cup of liquid here and there?! Should we force stuff in? At which point could it be considered "force", when you are dealing with a patient who can't swallow but might well want to eat or drink?! Should we just stop food? Or drink, too? What about other options? What. Should. We. Do.

The doctor left with a look of empathy and a smile, but in the end as quickly as he had breezed in. I know I may be harsh on the guy, but again I don't think he had been in that situation too many times before. And if he had, I'm sorry, but it didn't show. So mum and I and by then my son TJ returned to dad's bedside and continued our vigil. Lunch passed and then afternoon tea. Each time staff would pop in with a tray, offering to give something to dad or in fact, us. Neither he, nor we were "receptive" as the doctor had put it. Instead, dad just kept doing what he had been the last 24 hours. He wheezed, he occasionally opened his eyes, then fell back into his world and even snored during the night.

Now I know this may sound like bad humor. But when you are stressed like this and at emotional breaking point, anything, however small it may be will set you off in giggles. One of nature's quirks, I guess, to help you get through the unthinkable. TJ and I were awake; mum had nodded off in the recliner. After much debate, we had finally convinced her to get out of the uncomfortable dining room chair next to dad. She had been out like a light for a while. Dad kept making rattling noises as fluids again built up in his airways, but he was, as far as we could tell, mostly peaceful. TJ and I stayed awake for a while and just watched him, each alone in our thoughts. Then suddenly dad would startle us with a snort, followed by deep snoring noises. We nearly jumped out of our seats before realizing he was actually in deep sleep! I looked at dad in a mix of relief and grief and said: "Dad, really. You make us all come here, give us such a fright and make us sit here all night... just to listen to you snore?!" TJ and I couldn't help but crack up. It was the last funny moment I had with dad. And he wasn't even awake to witness it.

Another long night came and went. Dad had now been without food or water basically since Monday, as thanks to the episode on Tuesday, the little food he was able to take never reached its proper destination. His breathing became noisier towards early morning and he had to be turned frequently now so that the fluids that were building up again could somehow drain by way of gravity. The room began to look like a refugee camp by now. All of us in our chairs, twisted into uncomfortable positions, covered in blankets and surrounded by dad's things as well as our own, in addition to food and drinks. In the beginning, we didn't dare eat in the room. We felt terrible for dad not being able to take anything, not even fluids and felt it was disrespectful, even cruel if we ate in his presence. Whether given his state this was rational or not didn't really matter at that point. The doctor had not left us with a lot to go on. He had neither made a decision nor given any definitive advice on what to do in relation to dad's inability to take food or liquids. He did add that anything they would or could do, at this stage would only go towards marginally extending what little time was left. At the same time he prescribed antibiotics to fight the pneumonia and told us it would come down to whether these were successful or not. Afterwards we had felt stuck in a complete conundrum, confused and not knowing what to do. Nurses barely commented and the clinical manager, too, offered appreciated compassion, but little else for us to base any decisions on. Effectively we sat there, watching dad die, while technically we had the tools to at least prolong his life. We could ask or order for a drip, we could try to tube feed, we could do something, couldn't we?! Rationally viewed, the situation was much clearer though: He would no longer be able to take any water or food by mouth, he had had no movement in days, his arms and legs starting to look a pasty, unhealthy beige, he was hardly responsive and even if the antibiotics worked, he would never "get better" in the conventional sense. Opposite this was the emotional side, the love we felt for dad, the responsibility to do all we can for him, to help him, to get him back, no matter how unlikely or even impossible that may have seemed. And then there were the pangs of guilt. How dare you sit in front of your father, who has torn himself up all his life to give you everything, *everything* he could, provided for you, devoted all his energy to building the life you were privileged to live as a result, and you don't even try to save him! What kind of person are you? Go, do something! It was one of the longest and hardest nights of my life, not even to mention for dad and what must have gone on inside him as he lay there, helpless, caught up in that world, that prison that dementia built, and clinging on to the last fibers of a life that less than 3 year ago he had still loved so much.

# Day 3

Another sunrise came and with it first light cast an eerie glow over our little group in dad's room. Opening the window just a bit, we let in some welcome fresh air. The facility's HVAC system was working well and the temperature control was spot on, but with four people in a room that measured probably no more than 3x3.5 meters and much of it taken up by the enormous hospital bed dad was in, even the temperature adjusted air turned stale at times.

Another morning of daily clinic routines began. The noises from the rest of the ward all seemed exaggerated after a long night of listening to little else but dad's breathing, the occasional beep from the small compressor attached to the air mattress as it shifted pressure every hour or so, and the whispered, tired conversations when the uncomfortable chairs yet again prevented us from getting much needed sleep. Mum's looked defeated, her eyes and features sunken. I don't know how she managed to last, but she did. Pure love and willpower, I guess. The two most powerful forces in the known universe. Dad's face now had a reddish tint. He has a temperature, the nurse said after she had checked dad over, which was now done every few hours even during the night. His blood pressure, surprisingly, was steady, as were his pulse and heartrate. I say surprisingly, because extreme blood pressure fluctuations had been an integral symptom during the onset of his illness and consequently accompanied him throughout its course. They tried blood thinners, blockers, regulators and a host of other medications I wouldn't even know the name of; some to stabilize his mind, others to fight off the myriad of physical symptoms, which over time read like a "best of", or in this case "worst of" version, a ragtag assembly of bits and pieces normally inherent to other illnesses ranging from Alzheimer's, Parkinson's, multiple sclerosis, heart disease, osteoporosis, UTI and a raft of others. When they tried to move him, he seemed very stiff. His legs had lost almost all their muscle tissue and were now subject to involuntary spasms. Dad had been a rower, a tennis player, a hiker, a cyclist, a bowler and a keen gardener. His legs had always been strong and he had kept fit right until that fateful day in August. I owe much of my own physique to his genes in that regard. But now his body was losing weight even more rapidly and was stiffening in addition. He moaned loudly when they shifted his position or tried to turn him so the fluid could drain and he could breathe. He was visibly in a lot of pain, one of the few feelings his face was still able to clearly portray, which made it unbearable not just for him, but for those of us who were watching helplessly. I think that was the time when mum's will to fight for dad kicked back in. "Fighting for dad" had become her motto, her quasi battle cry when she thought some aspect or other of the care he received wasn't right, something he should be getting wasn't being delivered or when a doctor yet again tried to address one of dad's symptoms with a medication the side effects of which were likely to be worse than the temporary fix they were meant to provide. Admittedly sometimes mum went overboard. After all, when it came to dad's welfare, you couldn't keep her down. But once that train left the station it was also hard to stop and so at least looking from the outside in, I think there were a few occasions where she overshot the mark. But who could blame her? "Fighting for dad" was not only the las last thing left to do, it was also the only thing that could let her sleep at night, if at all, in the knowledge that she had done everything humanly and in some cases probably "superhumanly" possible. Who was I or anyone else to judge that?

Dad clearly got worse, his breathing now increasingly noisy. The gargle that had originally seemed to come from the back of his throat, was now deeper, more like a gurgle of liquid from deep within his lungs. The cycle was always the same: He would start wheezing. Then after a while there was a hiss as if air was passing through a narrow passage. Then a low and steady rumble or gurgle would follow, which slowly intensified until it sounded like someone blowing bubbles in a milkshake through a straw. Once it got to the point where it felt like one could almost see the bubbles, dad would convulse and moan and sputter while trying to cough. On the rarest of occasions, just when the event was at its worst, his brain would send one more saving signal to his throat and he would swallow. And each time he was able to, we breathed a collective sigh of relief. Mum would fetch the nurse, they would turn him and use swabs with little pieces of foam attached to them, to clear out any remaining sputum

256

from his mouth. Then there was peace again for a little while until the cycle kicked in again. This change was mum's cue to again spring into action. And at the same time in her doing so, I learned something about myself, which I still don't know how to feel about. Mum had been jumping up and calling nurses, getting assistance and summoning caregivers for all manner of things. After all, our job now was to be with dad and we spent every waking minute, which at this stage meant pretty much every minute, watching him closely for any change, whether for better or worse. When mum was watching dad and even when she wasn't her mind never stopped working on what else, no matter how small or big, could be done to make things better for him, to ease his suffering, to offer some comfort or relief. And so when it became apparent that the cycle of breathing, near suffocation and then sputtering and extremely painful coughing was the "new normal" that dad's body had established, she immediately decided to ask for the doctor, no, *demand* that he should come. I, on the other hand froze. The situation seemed so overwhelmingly surreal, so incomprehensibly horrible that all I could do was watch. I had reacted to bad situations as part of my job and competently so, yet here I froze. I had an anger inside me that mixed with anguish of a level I had never felt before in my life. And the force of that toxic mix had me pinned to the wall. I don't really know how to describe it, but it felt as if I just wanted to evaporate, spontaneously combust and disappear. I knew I had to be there, I knew this was dad. Dad! And yet I felt just as rigid, as paralyzed as he did in his hospital bed. I still berate myself on occasion for this. I say on occasion, because if you let these kinds of feelings in too much they will destroy you. And I have subsequently come closer to that point than I ever imagined possible. Guilt, if you let it, is like a cancer of the soul. I *still* try to shut it out. Psychologists call that compartmentalization, I guess: "An unconscious psychological defense mechanism used to avoid cognitive dissonance, or the mental discomfort and anxiety caused by a person's having conflicting values, cognitions, emotions, beliefs, etc. within themselves." But how else are you supposed to cope with something like that? I know mum would say that I shouldn't beat myself up, that there was nothing I could have done. But rational arguments seldom work when it comes to those little terms like "should have", "could have" and "if only", which are as persistent and relentless as they are dangerous. In any case, mum acted. The doctor returned. His diagnosis didn't change, but his prognosis did. We were now looking at days, if that.

Much to my surprise, he raised his eyebrows when he heard that dad still hadn't taken any food or water. It wasn't so much the question, it was *how* he had asked it that ended up adding a huge burden to an already growing pile of aspects I felt terribly guilty about. He didn't ask whether dad had had anything to drink or eat since his last visit the day prior. He asked whether "*we* had given him anything"! To him both questions probably would have meant the same thing, but to me this sounded like an indictment. *WE* hadn't given dad any food or drink. *WE* were withholding it from him. It was *US* who were responsible for the way he was right now and where he was heading.

In a situation otherwise devoid of any silver linings, you hang on to every word of someone you believe may be able to offer help, or at least an answer to the myriad of questions that keep rushing through your mind. And so every bit of what is being said counts. Every. Word. Counts. "Had we given him anything?" was the opposite of helpful, was the opposite of an answer. To me it implied we had not done something we should have; in fact, that we had failed dad. Mum explained that he had been neither really awake nor responsive since Wednesday morning and that he simply wasn't able to take anything by mouth. Thankfully she also asked whether we should keep trying. The doctor checked dad over and concluded we should only do so if dad showed will or readiness to take anything. "Will" or "readiness", what a cruel joke. Dad had lost conscious will weeks ago and readiness to do anything at least 4 to 5 days prior. Everything had become a guessing game based on clues like his moans, how much his teeth chattered, small movements of the lips and other mostly rather subtle hints. We had been watching dad for 48 hours now and there were simply no clues to indicate that his present state would change for the better at any stage. Mum was increasingly getting upset with the lack of medical help dad was getting and I started sinking deeper into a state of shock and apathy.

Sharon arrived and, after a long flight came straight to the ward. She hadn't seen dad since last August. You could tell by her face, that the change dad had undergone was not just drastic, but utterly frightful. I was enormously grateful that she had been able to get there so fast; not an easy feat given our running obligations in Yangon and the need to secure connecting flights from there. We spent a while in the corridor outside dad's room, hugging and crying. This was worlds apart from what we had thought we were flying into. I stood at the glass door again for a while, after Sharon had gone back in to see dad. I stared at that tree outside for the longest of times, watching it just stand there, solid and glorious, rooted firmly and unshakably. I had had several "sessions" like this with the tree in the past few days and as odd as it may sound, it gave me comfort; not the lasting kind, but at least a point to focus on and anchor myself in, in the storm that was raging around me, unhinging my life with every moment that passed. After a while, I returned to the room. Mum and Sharon were now sitting on either side of dad. His breathing was less noisy, but decidedly more labored. His eyes had opened somewhat, perhaps halfway, following Sharon's arrival. Despite his almost complete memory loss during the later stages of his illness, he never forgot Sharon. Even when Sharon couldn't be physically present and it was just me flying in to visit he would sometimes look up at me and say "Africa", referring to both Sharon and our home in Kenya. And every time she did manage to accompany me, he would greet her with a big smile and wide eyes which were always a sign of remembering and recognition. I would like to say there was some reaction even this time round, but to be truthful whatever it was may have been purely coincidental and although soothing to imagine it, there was little to justify that assessment. Dad's eyes now remained closed most of the time. When he did open them, it was barely halfway and his blue eyes stared blankly in the direction his head was facing. His breathing became more and more labored; he spent much time on his back, his mouth agape, giving him an almost corpse-like appearance. We kept watching him intently throughout the night, calling the nurses when we thought it necessary, dabbing his forehead with a damp cloth and moistening his lips with one of the sponge swabs to keep them from drying out in the HVAC adjusted air. The day, like many before it, had been an emotional one, with the occasional small argument erupting between me and mum over our different approaches. I know now that I should have just let her be, but it was just as painful to watch her trying to keep dad from losing a fight he could not possibly win, while watching dad's life ebb away with each agonizing hour and day. Walks up and down the corridor had become the only activity still possible under the circumstances, apart from the occasional dash to the store.

Dad had now had his last drink of water on Monday and his last few precious calories on Tuesday morning, although not much of what was put in his mouth actually made its way in the right direction. Thus as Thursday night rolled around he had gone without food or water for 72 hours. Since his mouth stayed open most of the time and he was unable to drink, his tongue had begun to turn a different color. At first first pinkish, then darkish blue and ultimately grey and white, it started to shrink and recede. Finally and no doubt thanks to mum's insistence, things had started moving later in the day and efforts were made to ease his agony and make things just that little bit easier, although the very word in this context is a complete euphemism. Dad was given an oxygen mask so he could perhaps breathe easier when his breathing became labored and he was given pain and fever medication via suppositories to deal with his elevated temperature. An alarming development however was that his face started swelling up as well as his neck, to the point where his eyelids resembled something of a boxer's after a long and brutal fight. There was even bruising and bluish blotches did appear her and there. I have only been around a few people at their moment of death in my life, most notably my grandmother, dad's mum. Going by what I was seeing it was hard to conceive how dad could still be alive. In addition to the swelling, his face was pale, his skin clammy and almost translucent, his mouth just an open hole with a dried up tongue, from which deathly rasps of labored breath escaped in uneven intervals. And thus we watched his chest rise and fall, rise and fall, rise and fall, as intently as we could, in full expectation of the final moments being right around the corner. But yet the night went by, just like the night before it, without so much of an indication of what would happen or where things were headed other than the inevitable we were all only too aware of.

## Day 4

Dad had made it through another night, which was as unexpected given the changes we could see in him throughout it as much as it was confusing in many ways since we had been certain just hours before that this would be our last night together. His eyes remained closed and it had been hard to tell whether he was awake or sleeping. Dawn came and went as we continued our vigil, watching his chest move up and down, watching him labor and agonize with each breath, listening to the horrific sounds that emanated from his chest; sounds so alien that I can still hear them today. I had never known that the human respiratory system can produce such noises. And to be honest I wish had never heard them. Luckily, by the early hours of the morning, and thanks to constant repositioning, the swelling around his face reduced. His eyes went all the way from puffy to sunken, now with dark rings around them. The skin around his cheekbones, mouth, and forehead once again went as tight as a drum's. Because of his fever, we had to keep dad wrapped in a sheet as not make the pneumonia worse. It was impossible to tell whether he felt hot or cold since his skin felt clammy to the touch regardless of temperature and he virtually no longer responded to external stimuli. I say 'virtually' because there were a few exceptions still, despite his appearance. Mum sat next to him throughout the previous nights and continued to do so even now that we were on day 4. She would lean over and rest her forehead on his, whispering to him and telling him that she loved him and that things would be "ok"; after all, we were a family and all of us were there with him. It was on those occasions that his hand would ever so slightly press hers, an incredible sign that somewhere across that vast barrier of torment, fever and the fog of dementia, dad really was still there. Somehow mum's voice, her touch and if I dare to speculate as much, our collective presence brought him back for a very few moments, if only enough to gently squeeze her hand, without any other sign of recognition or physical movement. At first I was skeptical as we had seen his arms and legs spasm for days, but unlike those involuntary movements, these were singular and deliberate squeezes and even if they weren't, I wasn't about to say anything that could take away from the momentary happiness mum felt when "her Norbert" fleetingly returned to her through this simple gesture. Thanks to the fever suppositories dad was given every 6 hours, his temperature had remained elevated but what undoubtedly would otherwise have been a high fever, was been kept at bay. We counted the hours minute by minute, torn between our prayers for dad to be released from his suffering and guilt for wishing so, when all we really wanted was things to be the way they used to be, back when bastard Lewy hadn't yet made his unholy entrance into our lives.

Dad's breath continued to fill the room with that awful gurgle, a terrible sound which in retrospect can probably be likened to the noise a coffee machine - one of those filter ones - makes when it pushes the last remaining water through its mineral deposit-congested pipes. But this was a human being these sounds escaped from with each labored breath, which together with the dimmed night lights saturated the small room in a palpable aura of imminent death. There were times when I was so focused on dad that I caught myself unable to breathe as I watched his chest rise and fall. His tongue by now had turned into a desiccated lump, curled back in his mouth and no longer moving, the cavity that used to be his mouth completely dry despite our best attempts at keeping it moistened via little sponge swabs and cloths. I again secretly prayed for his release throughout the night. I had gone through several religious phases in my life and, having been brought up catholic, sort of took the long way round to finding God again after that, via brief excursions into Buddhism and even a closer look at Islam. It wasn't until maybe four or five years earlier when I had started working for a faith based organization, that I thought I could see the power of God at work in their midst and the unity and energy their belief supplied immediately drew me in. Catholicism to me was, for the better part a religious branch tainted with centuries of exploitation, of convincing people that they deserved to be punished, that we were all born sinners and essentially done for if they didn't constantly repent. It had turned me off religion for the longest of times until I made this new discovery, namely that being Christian was something to be celebrated along with Christ's love for all mankind. It had been a complete turning point and since then I had made significant changes in my life, both in terms of what I did and how, as well as

263

how I interacted and prayed. Lots of good things had happened, along with some great challenges and defeats, but I had felt that somehow God always had my back throughout and my faith had given me an enormous amount of strength to carry on even when the chips were down. It was thus with great faith and devotion that I pleaded with God throughout the night, as I had done the nights before, so that he would grant dad the release he so much deserved. This man had done so much good in his life, had devoted himself to the wellbeing of his family, had lived to ensure fairness and justice for others (I don't think I have mentioned this, but dad used to also be on the district labor board, negotiating with employers and resolving grievances), along with always and without fault looking for ways that those around him, be it family, friends, colleagues, club members and even strangers, were looked after to the best level he could achieve. He already had endured more than anyone ever should through these last three years. He did not deserve this. He was entitled to go without this pain and suffering. Yet God did not listen. I wracked my brain to rationalize why God would do such a thing to dad and by virtue of the fact, to us. I had heard someone say once that not all burdens we are given are actually meant for us. That the message some burdens carry is actually intended for someone else; kind of that sometimes we become collateral damage as we think something has been given to or placed upon us, when in fact the "learning point" or revelation is intended for someone else. At that point, that sentiment, if not a most convenient way of deflecting existential questions around it, almost seemed to make sense. But what revelation to anyone could be worth such suffering? Why would anyone, let alone the all-knowing, supreme, and all-loving God make dad suffer, just to give someone else a brainwave? The concept, the more I thought about it, seemed more and more preposterous. Not only that, but it pointed towards a God, who obviously wasn't as empathetic, as all-loving as scripture made Him out to be. And yet, as I sat there watching dad and waiting for a sign that he might be awake or at least not completely unresponsive, I decided that this was no time for doubt, but that perhaps this was a time to pull together all the faith that I could muster, dig deep and pray as fervently as anyone had ever done. All that was left from an athletic physique and an active mind was this bundle before me, wrapped in a white sheet, sunken and its form barely filling up the single bed, with dad's emaciated features sticking out from the cocoon, facing skywards with his mouth agape and his spirit somehow refusing to let go of this life.

## Midnight

As a new day arrived, little had changed.

Dad, unable to eat or drink and largely unresponsive had now been without food or water for 4 days; longer than we, or even the doctor thought possible at that stage. A terrible record for dad and one I wished every minute we sat there, we could have somehow helped him avoid. His bowels had stopped doing their job and reduced circulation to his legs and arms had turned them a waxy white. Now completely unable to move, he was in pain pretty much all of the time. Although he had had his eyes mostly closed the day and night before, he now started opening them just a tiny bit here and there, struggling to lift his eyelids each time as if they weighed several tons. The past few days we had always been happy to see him open his eyes, which of course had always been a sign of him being awake and perhaps even "with us" for a few moments. But now, looking at what gazed back at us, it was different. Before his illness and even still in the early stages, his eyes had always sparkled with life and when he laughed they almost danced above his broad grin. Dad's laugh was always hearty and he could sometimes find himself in stitches over the silliest things. His jokes were sometimes pretty silly I have to admit, probably like most dad jokes are, but he could laugh at them with such energy that usually one couldn't resist the urge oneself. He loved to pull faces when someone would try to take a photograph of him and then laugh and laugh, even at himself. His eyes always truly had been the proverbial window to a caring and joyous soul. American Comedian Michael Pritchard is credited with saying: "You don't stop laughing because you grow old. You grow old because you stop laughing." Dad had never grown old for exactly that reason. He loved to laugh; he was quietly passionate about things, meticulously dedicated to whatever he had set his mind to. Laughter, both his own and that of those around him were his fuel, his elixir, just like ceaseless project management was his engine. Without diving into a whole chapter of quotes, there is another one that reminds me of dad in this context. Actress and Comedian Amy Poehler once said: "There's power in looking silly and not caring that you do." I already mentioned that dad's love for dressing up goes all the way back to his youth. Costume parties were all the rave in the 1950s and photos of him as a Viking or even dressed up in his mother's get-up (may sound a bit creepy by today's standards, but it is a truly funny image) are cherished memories which echo these quotes most vividly. Dad was a practical joker and loved making people laugh, it was that simple. But all that had vanished now. His eyes now almost had a glaze over them as they stared straight ahead, dull and yet so full of agony. If the rest of his body mostly suffered in silence, then these eyes screamed the fact so loudly it was deafening. With his gaze fixed straight ahead, we would all take turns in positioning ourselves so that he could see our faces one after the other, as we talked to him and amongst ourselves, pretending things were "normal" for his sake, when they couldn't have been further from it. It took a lot of energy that increasingly came at a premium as hours and days wore on. Another evening came and now the four of us settled in around dad in the small room again and got as comfortable as we could for the night ahead, while the rest of the world carried on.

During the night, dad's breathing once again became noisy and labored. This time though it was different. Rattling breathing in was followed by moans of suffering while breathing out. It was agonizing to listen to and no doubt even more painful for dad. Thankfully a new night nurse had come on shift. An older guy, clearly experienced and with a lot of compassion. We once again asked out of desperation if there was nothing else we could do. Mum, having worked as part of an old age care team decades earlier knew a few options, but of course couldn't just get her hands on prescription-only medication. Thankfully, the kind nurse agreed to seek permission from the doctor to administer Morphine. Medical staff had likewise agonized for the past two days over whether to give some to dad, but each time they had had to weigh up the potentially fatal side effects of a slow-down in heartrate and breathing against the possibility of him getting through this infection and in fact recovering somewhat, no matter how remote the chances.

In retrospect it was properly one of those borderline cases, where the line between Hippocratic Oath and the harm it compels those who take it to prevent are at odds with each other; one where it purely comes down to the individual tending to a patient. Refrain from easing suffering to avoid potentially fatal side effects, despite miniscule chance of recovery from this secondary condition within an existing, already progressive, and ultimately fatal illness, or reduce pain through heavy medication and thus risk patient death; undoubtedly one of the more difficult decisions for a medical professional to make, but even more difficult for the family watching their loved one writhe, spasm and groan in agony, all the while with the prospect of having to endure unimaginable suffering for a yet to be determined timeframe and in the knowledge that death, regardless is the ultimate outcome within days. I am sure the doctors had the best for dad in mind when they mulled over the treatment decision. They too knew and said, although not in so many words, that any reasonable expectation of recovery was fading by the hour, if it had ever even existed. And so having checked dad over and seeking permission from the doctor, the night nurse finally returned and dad was given an in our eyes long overdue dose of morphine. In addition and much to our relief, he was also given decongestants and a muscle relaxant. I think seeing dad the way he and to a lesser extent, after 72 hours of vigil, *we* looked now was enough for everyone to realize that this indeed was no longer a fight for survival, it was an opportunity for dad to let go of life and for us to let go of dad in the most dignified fashion humanly and medically possible.

Mum hadn't left the ward in several days, using the facility's showers to freshen up and only occasionally dozing off for a few minutes whenever we managed, despite her protest, to order her into dad's former armchair. Sharon had come straight off a long haul flight and neither rested nor freshened up in two full days. We had been living off corner shop sandwiches and caffeine in the form of Coke or Coffee. TJ had come straight from work more than 36 hours ago and hadn't slept nor showered. I was much the same, although the trips to and from the shops, home and the hospital wing provided momentary and short-lived reprieve. We knew things could change rapidly from one minute to another and being away just at the moment we were all supposed to be with dad was unthinkable, no, unbearable and so every outside errand was conducted in a nervous

268

hurry. We hadn't even had time to withdraw money from our account in Myanmar and thanks to international banking sanctions, formally already removed, but informally still in force, there was no way for us to access funds. I had invoiced a client asking for payment into my NZ account, but clients being what they are, payment was late. Meanwhile rent in Nairobi was due and our Goddaughter in Kenya urgently needed the funds we had promised. Let's just say running to the bank and the shops, in as much as it had to be done, had me swear all the way and there were times when even just standing in a queue for probably less than 3 minutes, I felt like I was going to lose my mind. In retrospect it would have been better just to put life on hold outside dad's hospital room as much as it was inside already. But I guess we tend to burden ourselves with things at times, which in hindsight lose all their significance and meaning. Actually, that's probably true for most things in life. It certainly was for dad at that point. Dad's breathing calmed somewhat after the injections, although the rattling and gargling continued. But he no longer groaned with each breath and here and there it actually looked like he was sleeping.

As dawn gave way to full daylight and the facility sprung to life in its usual way of rattling trolleys and cheerful banter between nurses and patients as the latter were readied for breakfast, our room remained frozen in time, removed from the world around us. Mum still refused to go and get some rest, as did the rest of us. We knew death had its own timetable and would not care much about us, let alone where we were when it would come for dad. We had seen dad deteriorate, then stabilize, improve and get worse and then just get worse over the last 4 days, each day, each in our minds the last. We had come this far together, dad and us, it seemed unthinkable not to be there with him when that final moment came simply because we may have wanted to sleep in our own bed for a while or sit around at home. There would be enough time for that.

And yet, now after 4 days it also seemed as if dad and death were playing cat and mouse. His heart rate had remained surprisingly steady; his pulse was weak but stable as was his breathing: despite the pain and congestion, dad continued to labor, to power on through each breath. He had defied the doctor's prognosis and proven us wrong at every turn, just when we thought the moment of release had come. For all intents and purposes the fever medication and the morphine were having some effect, probably giving dad that little edge his body needed to keep going despite the inconceivable suffering. I would continue my daily trips back to mum's house to get supplies, make sure everything was Ok and brought bits and pieces that everyone had on their "wish list, usually just cold drinks or something to eat. I had brought in whiskey a couple of nights earlier and stocks were replenished. While it had seemed an odd thought to have a drink by dad's bedside, after the first 24 hours of staying awake and of living through the trauma that came with these last steps of his, of our journey together, a sip or two during the long nights had increasingly been appreciated by all. We still ate outside in the corridor mostly, but likewise increasingly as it became more and more evident that dad was indeed "not with us", we did sneak in a bite here or there; always mindful not to bring in anything "smelly", like fried food or hot meals, which were liable to stink up the room, something which naturally seemed despicably inappropriate given that dad had not eaten for several days. Every couple of hours nurses came, checked his pulse and checked his temperature. Then they would straighten his sheets, reposition him from one side to the other or onto his back, and elevate him into a reclined position whenever the congestion in his airways threatened to suffocate him. They did so with routine, but also with a compassion and even love for their patient, which I had never seen before. They had been on the journey with dad and us for the two years. They were there when he was first admitted to the closed non-hospital wing of the home. They had looked after him throughout, from the very beginning when he was confused but physically still able, had helped him dress and go to the toilet and when those things became more and more difficult, and had lived through some traumatic moments with him; even when he had used whatever strength he could muster to fight them off when they tried to coax him out of the shower. They had fed, cleaned and cared for him when he could no longer do anything but sit in whatever chair he had been lifted into. He was part of their family in a way, a family of broken human beings they so diligently and compassionately looked after day in day out and whose members never stayed long on account of their progressive conditions. But dad and the caregivers had developed a relationship that went beyond their jobs. Unlike many other patients, dad at least until the very late stages of his illness had always been placid, calm, friendly even and was generally not only easy to deal with but also, thanks to his background and wide range of former interests in history, travel and other activities, had managed to endeared himself to the staff. Then there was mum with her daily visits and chats to them which she never missed, just like she never missed the weekly entertainment sessions during which everyone gathered together in the main room. It is true that attitudes can rub off on each other and between mum, the caregivers and dad, something of a unit had formed over time, the fruits of which I could now clearly see in how much these professionals truly cared about dad and what was happening to him.

I had often times rolled my eyes when mum, as was her usual manner, yet again went to staff to make sure the tiniest pieces of information about dad were passed on; that things were done right by dad as she saw them, that dad got the best care possible and the caregivers had the tools they needed to provide it. "Fighting for dad" had become her obsession, virtually her raison d'être and she would sometimes take it to the extreme. I am sure initially she would have stepped on more than just a few toes whenever she "pointed staff in the right direction". But over time I also think they recognized it for what it was: her way of coping, her way of living up to the promise she had given over five decades ago at the altar and which she intended to keep, come hell or high water, until the end. And in the end I think this actually earned her huge respect as this kind of living commitment had been unprecedented in the home, where visitors, even spouses of patients would generally drop by once or maximum twice a week to check in on their own. Not only that, but staff had also come to see that in some way they weren't just taking care of dad, but that they were taking care of a unit. A unit, which consisted of two people whose bond of love was so unshakable, that they couldn't but be patient and equally caring whenever mum was in "fight for dad mode"; her nerves worn thin as a result of the

271

emotional and physical stress of her walk through these darkest of times, which seemed to extend before her like a never-ending tunnel, albeit one without a light at the end.

We were all in this waiting game together now. Dad, us and the staff.

I often wonder how much terminal patients, barely conscious and unresponsive, feed off the sentiments, the atmosphere created by the people around them, or whether it makes a difference at all. Of course there are clinical studies of people who were in a coma, had a near death experience or were unconscious for long periods of time in an ICU ward or similar, which all say people hear and take in what is happening around them. But you see, all these people had to come back first to make that statement. Obviously they weren't too far gone yet. After all they wouldn't have been able to provide the info otherwise. Where is the cut-off here? Is there some kind of no man's land between life and death or is it a clearly defined line: one minute you're unconscious, albeit alive and somehow to still able perceive things and the next you are dead; lights on, lights off? And where do patients with Lew Body, with severe Alzheimer or end stage Parkinson's stand in this equation? We know by the time they enter that last stage, their minds and their senses have been eroded to the point of even motor functions ceasing to work, not even to mention cognitive abilities. Add to this unconsciousness and the question arises whether the same principles apply; naturally one we will never get an answer to, since these patients don't "come back".

These preoccupied my mind a lot during these last days and especially each time the four of us, seated around dad's bed, were having conversations about various bits and pieces, but also about dad. Of course we refrained from talking about his condition or what we thought was happening, out of fear that he would actually hear us, a notion which at the same time also helped carry us through since it gave us hope that we were still able to communicate with him, even though he might no longer respond. The only thing I could do to try and find an answer, was to watch dad closely, which was essentially all we did, 24 hours a day. Yet unfortunately that answer would ultimately remain still out there as dad, like so many other victims of bastard Lewy would not come back to provide it.

Lunchtime arrived and as every day, staff offered us food, of which they had prepared extra servings just in case we wanted some. Just as every day, we declined. I think mum had some maybe the first day, when we were still somewhat hopeful that dad's ability to swallow might temporarily return; something that had happened before back in early December and thus probably given him some of the energy he had needed to make it through the holidays and ultimately this far. By now it was all about dad's breathing. If the typical respiratory rate for a resting person is $12 - 20$ per minute, we had now watched dad take somewhere between 80,000 and 130,000 breaths. 130,000 acts of intense labor, forcing air past a build-up of aspirated food, phlegm and obstructed airways. 130,000 chances for his system to give in and say: "no more". 130,000 acts of stubborn defiance and 130,000 miracles, each one watched intently by the people who loved him most, gathered around him in this capsule, far removed from the goings-on of the rest of the world. How many more would he need to take before God would act on our prayers? 20,000, 50,000, another 100,000? For the moment still, God was obviously busy elsewhere. All we could do was do what we had done within what had now become yet another "new normal", of which there had been so many over the past couple of years; yet none of them ever were "normal", not even by the furthest stretch of the imagination.

Afternoon tea came and the sugary treats dad had come to love so much this past year were offered and returned untouched. Much like dad himself, we were no longer "conscious" in the true sense of the word, except for our undivided focus on every nuance of his condition. I had quietly predicted that dad would not see the end of the day and knowing how emotional and chaotic things would get when the time came, I had taken mum outside into the corridor late that morning and we had had "the talk" about what arrangements needed to be made. I felt so awful talking about it, talking about funeral arrangements – there, I said it – *funeral arrangements,* when dad was lying in that bed just through that door and still clinging to life. I knew it was on mum's mind. She had said so during one of our long nighttime talks. And I also knew that it was a worry she didn't need right now. Much lesser things in the last few months had already had a tendency to quickly overwhelm her and send her mind spiraling. She would never have been able to make the calls that eventually needed to be made and quite frankly neither did I trust myself to do so after 'it' happened. So I sat in the small foyer and got out my phone and the yellow pages. My mind was mush. The reality that I was about to call someone and ask them to help me bury my father was probably, no, most definitely the most traumatic thing I could have ever imagined having to do and something I don't know I will ever get over. Just like mum, I had witnessed dad during one of his most severe fits of aggression. Smeared with and smelling of feces, clinging to a towel in one hand in an attempt to cover his naked shriveled body and threatening the caregivers with a chair in the other, he had stood in the shower room with a crazed, bewildered, utterly frightened and totally forlorn look on his face, as his hallucinations told him he was fighting for his life. I had helped dad change his adult diapers, made sure he was ok on and off the toilet, seen him bleeding on the floor having scraped himself during a fall following one of his sudden sleep onsets. I had seen dad at his most vulnerable, at his most desperate, at points so low that if he had been able to witness himself, he would not have wanted to live. When for the first time you stand in front of your father, him wearing nothing but a singlet, leaning on you and waiting for you to help him put on his diaper, you can literally hear something break within yourself. Something that cannot be mended. In as much as it is an act of caring, it is against the laws of nature. I know thousands upon thousands of sons and daughters around the world have to do this not just once, but on a daily basis for years and years, without so much as a chance for getting outside help. But the fact at that moment had nothing to do with how it makes you feel and what it stands for: a complete role reversal I don't think anybody is ever ready for. I certainly wasn't. Not so quickly and not in this way.

But sitting there, phone in hand, having to make the call for funeral arrangements took things to a whole different level. This was something I could have never imagined. Not in my worst nightmares. I had somehow always thought that one day I would "get the call"

274

while travelling, much like you see it in the movies and like it had already happened to others I know. Or I would be there at the time visiting their place and we would get a call from the rest home one morning. But to be sitting there, dad barely alive in one of the adjacent rooms and taking on the task myself literally made my world implode. I never thought looking for a funeral home would be so confusing. Even in the relatively small city mum and dad live in, there are at least four or five of them. Some call themselves homes, others services or directors. What's the difference? Who knows, right? I didn't want a director, I wanted someone to take care of everything. But what was "everything"? Where would they take dad? What kind of service would we want? Would they need a deposit? How could I arrange that without having to leave dad's side? Was the initial "transport" arranged separately from the funeral service? Who could actually authorize these things? Wouldn't we need someone to come and give formal sign-off? What about church? Is that where they would take dad? Or would I need to arrange that separately? The list of questions whirling around in my head at the speed of light was endless and despite what mum and I had spoken about, together with my emotional state threw everything into complete disarray.

For most couples the talk about preferences 'in the event of' – unpleasantness aside – at some point raises its head and comes naturally, especially when they have been married for some time. Wishes are expressed in general terms, but few actually explore how these may be fulfilled, let alone identify someone with the capacity to do so within their own geographical area. "I want to be cremated" is easily uttered, but what is actually required to do get "it" done"? Most people can likewise easily identify clothes they wouldn't want to be buried in. But which ones would they actually want to wear on that occasion? The favorite moth-eaten sweater auntie Jane knitted? The pair of pants they seemed to wear in every photo across the decades? The shoes they had never liked because they weren't comfy so got worn only to special occasions? Hard choices to make, when you're no longer around to help! Many will, with just as much ease state certain want's and don't want's in relation to type of service, and maybe even in general terms location for burial or places they would like their ashes scattered. But few actually think through as to

275

*how* the living may actually accommodate them post-departure. It was no different here, except for the fact that I had never been privy to mum's and dad's conversations around the topic and all I had to go on were the few snippets mum had been able to pass on between the tears we shared just broaching the subject. And I wasn't about to go back and go through the jumbled checklist, which was quickly building in my head amongst the chaos. I dialed a number...and hung up before anyone could pick up the call. I didn't even know what to say. How do you start a conversation like this? This wasn't your average inquiry. This was a 911 call of sorts, but one where I didn't know what to expect. One where no patrol car would just be "dispatched" to investigate the issue and one where emotions fast and furiously overwhelmed the simple fact to be reported. I reread the small advert of the service provider...and changed my mind. Nothing in particular had thrown me off, but I wasn't just going to go with the first one without research. Which is another question not many consider beforehand: How do you decide? You can't exactly be "just browsing" and shop around for best fit, when you know nothing about this "business". Plus, how would you even state the very fact if you were, or did? Now, the computing power of the human mind, universally speaking and with the exception of certain political or religious extremists from either side of the spectrum, is quite marvelous and even with today's science, beyond human comprehension. But it only truly reveals its complexity under severe emotional and physical stress: I had always considered myself as someone very capable of making prudent decisions even in the most adverse scenarios. I had helped relocate staff from war zones under active aerial bombardment, had negotiated with hostile crowds while trying to get a fatally wounded local to hospital, I had talked panicked supervisors through escorting their colleagues to safety while terrorists where going through their building shooting people in the head. I was, for all intents and purposes, crisis hardened. This however, as I quickly discovered was well beyond my scope. These were no Russian bombs, no upset villagers, and no Islamic radicals wreaking mayhem. This was dad, whom I had bonded with in the closest and most connected way possible between a father and a son. The person without whom I would be neither who nor where I am today or any day for that matter. I typed web addresses into my phone; I flicked through the pages, examined services, only to get more and more confused. I dialed a few more numbers and hung up just as I had done a few minutes before. I lined up in my head what I would, what I needed to say. : "Hi, my name is Robert Landeck and...." was as far as I got. Try again. "Hi, my name is Robert Landeck. I just wanted to inquire about funeral services. My fath...." Better, but I still only got so far. I rehearsed a few more times and finally settled on the fact that I would have to wing much of the introduction. I also focused on that what I was doing was not because dad was dying. It was because he had expressed certain wishes in case he one day did and I was following up to make sure that happened. Only in a more time critical fashion, I guess. I went back to my phone's browser and noticed one funeral home come up in many links, in fact most of the links now that I was able to focus better. When supporting local business, I have always been a proponent of the underdog, the person or place most deserving of praise and dollars, but this was no search for most 'deserving'. The most *deserving* people were dad and mum, and in exactly that order at that moment. Reluctantly I dialed the 24-hour contact number provided in the online advertisement. Going through their landline and probably some receptionist just would have exceeded my emotional resolve and ability to talk about anyone at all beyond that first point of contact. I cannot tell you the amount of energy it took to listen to each ring as I tried to connect. Part of me was wishing for all this to just go past me and take its course without my involvement, while the rest of me just wanted to come back to mum and give her the peace of mind she deserved. But again, I hung up.

I paced around in a small circle, unable to think, unable to do anything but surrender to the rush of images that flickered through what I nowadays describe as my "head cinema". You don't control the film, let alone the reel. It plays what it wants to and you cannot stop it. And there is no exit.

I sat down and breathed. Time slowed. Back to the phone and continue reading up on the internet. Booking a hotel or choosing a restaurant that way is easy. Many people leave reviews and even photos. Lots of information to make an informed choice. Not so much with funeral homes, obviously. They all provided services which at best were memorable, but which in the end everyone would rather forget than write about in a public forum. There were some testimonials, yes, but anyone who knows anything about testimonials is that they are generally cherry-picked from feedback or even solicited from clients for advertising purposes. They meant nothing to me. Dad wasn't other people. He was dad and deserved to be treated the way he would have wanted.

It was no use. I had to make a choice. It felt like the walls of the small foyer, kept in soothing, non-committal tones of pastel blue and grey, with its quaint little two seater and a few forgotten magazines, the arrangement of dried flowers and the board with the homes latest announcements, were threatening to suffocate me. I stepped outside the main door into the chilly late morning breeze. Executive decision time. Leap of faith. I dialed the number of a funeral home which seemed to dominate all the web searches. If they had enough resources to develop such a virtual presence, then surely they were also capable in other ways.

My hands shook as I dialed. This is for you dad. This is for you mum.

A friendly voice answered the phone. Not at all how I had expected it, but oddly and yet comfortingly casual. "I would like to speak with someone regarding funeral arrangements…" I paused and swallowed hard,"…for        my        father…who…is….here……….at Langdale……dying." I think the lady at the other end could hear that I had just about offered all the information I could at that moment. She immediately thanked me for calling and informed that the director on duty was out to lunch but that she would get back to immediately. That was disappointing, but at the same time, I felt a wave of relief pass over me. I had tried. I would just need to wait for someone to call *us*. I had done my bit. And I wasn't about to call others and go through the same story, peddling the business of taking care of dad like someone looking for a shoe repair. I stared ahead, lost in thoughts, at the small garden in the atrium of the facility, its wings arranged in a rectangular fashion around the inside and connected by walkways. It was tranquil, pretty even with its native plants, flower beds and a couple of what appeared to be fruit trees. I let time and space dissolve for a moment and let the breeze blow away the cobwebs of the last few minutes.

I don't know how long I had been standing there like this, leaned against the wall, gazing, not thinking anything, just being. The ring of my phone snapped me back into reality. "Hello, is this Robert? A soft spoken voice inquired. "This is Deirdre from the funeral home. You had tried to contact me." I instantly dreaded having to repeat what had been hard enough to utter the first time round, but before I got a chance, she continued: "I hear your dad is at Langdale". I swallowed so hard I am sure it was audible across the line. "Don't worry Robert, when the time comes we will take care of everything", she said calmly. I did not know what so say. "We can talk about everything later. Just give me a call when the time comes and we will come to look after your dad. We are available 24 hours, so don't worry. We can discuss everything later. Just focus on your dad now", she said slowly and calmly and each of her words lifted a weight off my shoulders, one that moments before had threatened to crush me completely. I can't remember what I replied as tears once again took over. I was so thankful to this woman I had never met, nor knew anything about. So thankful she had taken this insurmountable burden and lifted it in one sentence. Yes, dad wanted to be cremated. No, we hadn't talked about when. No, mum did not want dad to be embalmed. Yes, it was thus Ok for them to take him to Wellington hospital morgue, the only place with refrigeration in the region. Yes, the extra costs would be OK. The call had lasted less than 2 minutes. I took mum out into the corridor and told her that everything was taken care of and it was all that she needed to hear. This was not a time for great detail. Deirdre had recommended that we put some thought into which clothes we would want dad to wear, which was something that needed to be taken care of, lest we wanted to rush back and forth between the facility and mum's place on the day. We cried some more, hugged, and the single hardest thing I had ever had to do in my life was done. Or so I thought.

In addition to the comfort of knowing everything was taken care of, Deirdre's request also gave mum something to focus on and think about; a morbid but probably timely distraction. Back in the room things had changed somewhat. Dad's breathing had become a lot more labored and also quicker. It sounded like his lungs were working as hard as they could, but at only at half their capacity. His shriveled tongue now looked almost artificial, eerily curled into a tiny ball and receding back into his mouth. His lips, likewise had receded even more and his now permanently exposed teeth seemed abnormally large compared to the rest of his skull-like features. He was hanging on. Only just.

A little while earlier something else had happened, something, which I hope I will never have to encounter again for as long as I live. Three years earlier I had deployed to the Philippines, to assist an emergency response in the wake of Typhoon Haiyan, a category 5 storm that had devastated wide swathes of the country's central and south central areas, its storm surges wreaking havoc among coastal and island communities. Our response headquarters were located in what was left of a former golf course and hotel and the initial mission had been one of assessment and, along with it, identification, and tagging of locations where bodies lay. Nearby our headquarters was the morgue, where officials worked feverishly to try and identify the many remains, which were placed in body bags, before being piled up, and spread out in its open compound for mass burial. The smell of decay, the smell of death, is not something you ever forget. Once you have smelled it, it is something you will always be able to identify, even among a thousand other smells. Overwhelmingly pungent, sweet, and sickly, it is beyond an olfactory sensation to the point where it permeates all faculties. That very smell had suddenly appeared in the room; first like whiff, easily shaken off and dismissed, but then stronger and stronger until it took over all the remaining air in the room. It stayed for a good while and both mum and I instantly knew what it was. She too, had been through enough in her life to have made its acquaintance. We looked at each other. We knew. Death had just formally announced its presence.

We thought we had readied ourselves for days and yet each time we noticed a change, we found out that there is no such thing as readiness. Each time we looked at each other, our anguish, and helplessness plainly obvious, as if asking each other: "Do you think this is "it"?" And each time we would hold dad's hand and whisper to him how much we loved him and that we would always be with him and that everything would be Ok. We could do little else, now that we knew that death was among us in that tiny room. When I now look through the photos of week, I notice how as it went on I took less and less. I guess it was hard enough taking them in the first place, but I did so because I did not want dad's suffering to be meaningless and so perhaps as to give others on a similar journey the opportunity we never had: to look ahead and know what's coming. It was like riding a rollercoaster in the dark: You knew you were going up when you were going up and knew you were going down when you did, but you never knew what twists and drops lay just around the corner. I was hoping that somehow, through these photos I would one day be able to provide a tiny "flashlight" so to speak, so that others may perhaps get a glimpse of the track in store for them. I had always hated photos of the sick and the dead, especially loved ones, for the simple reason that the last image is usually how we remember them, no matter what other memories we can conjure up. I had therefore truly struggled with the need to document against what doing so would mean for my own well-being for the rest of my life. But as I started taken photos of dad the moment bastard Lewy grabbed him, I could also see that the camera had an almost therapeutic effect. Looking through a lens created distance from a situation which I had not found and would probably never find a way to deal with. I took a lot of photos and videos over the three years of dad's struggle, but I still avoid looking at them unless I have to for whatever reason. I don't know if that makes sense at all, but at the same time just having them, knowing that dad's journey is there in images and videos gives me great comfort. I guess only through them can bastard Lewy be seen for what he is, as he sneaks around and robs and plunders bit by bit from one's humanity. They are the only proof of what he is capable of, as otherwise it would be easy to forget how long and terribly difficult that road of a thousand cuts had been.

That evening we had some more whiskey and I don't know how it started, but we began telling stories we remembered about dad. A lot of funny anecdotes were there and especially mum had a lot to add from the days even way before I was born. There was even some laughter, as strange as it may seem looking from the outside in. We joked with dad and included him as best as we could in the conversation. We figured that maybe somehow he could hear us and that by telling some good yarns of days gone by he might be able to feed off the positive energy, which God knows was sorely needed under the circumstances. Mum, much like other mums I suspect, has always had an uncanny talent of remembering the most embarrassing moments from one's childhood and regaling everyone with them, especially when you're present and sitting right there. Nothing like your mum telling everyone about that time when, as a toddler you took of all your clothes and ran through the entire neighborhood naked until someone brought you home. Meanwhile the almost 50 year old you is sitting there wanting the ground to open up and swallow you whole. For the first time ever though I didn't mind all this at all and in fact welcomed whatever memories came up during our lively conversation. We were the people closest to dad and together with him as the center we were the core, the fabric of this little family, and there was nothing that could have embarrassed at that moment. I learned a lot through these 5 days and especially that evening. For example how the human spirit will always find light, even in the darkest hours and how the very reason for darkness itself is that it is meant to be brushed away by light. It serves no other purpose, lest we let it. I also learned that even the most overwhelming pain and suffering cannot even so much as challenge the bonds of love in a close-knit family. I had always known we were close, but it was only through these dark days that I learned what "close" really meant.

We continued our conversation, talking to dad and listening mostly to mum's anecdotes until we ran out of steam and along with it, most of the whiskey. Had it not been for dad lying there the way he was and the stark and undeniable reality of the situation, one could have easily mistaken these few hours as a family gathering back at mum's and dad's house; like so many we had had over the years, where laughter was as ubiquitous as food and drink, and we would usually be busy with both for hours until we popped.

The rollercoaster continued through the night. Watching dad, nodding off here and there until limbs went numb or heads bobbed, as it was impossible to find anything that remotely resembled a sleeping position in the uncomfortable dining room chairs. Intermittently we would have hushed conversations or just look at each other, perfectly understanding what each of us was going through without having to say a word. Then one of us would leave the room and go out into the corridor to cry. In the beginning someone would always follow so they could provide comfort to whoever had again reached breaking point. But by now going for a cry had become routine, and I think we all recognized that to be alone and cry here and there was the only outlet possible for each of us to come to terms with the impossibility of the situation away from the crowded room.

I don't know if dad could have ever imagined where he and we were right now. I don't know if anyone of us ever could have either. But I do know that in lieu of a choice in matters of fate, the way we were standing by him, the way we stood together as family, is what he would have wanted. I don't know if us being around him in this way gave him comfort, but even if there was so much as the tiniest opening in the haze of dementia and the fog of his body preparing for death, then I am sure what he was able to perceive did give him peace on some level. It simply must be so, lest the very concept of a loving family loses all of its meaning.

But dad was a battler. He never knew when to stop. Whatever it was he set his mind on, he would not rest or stop until it was done, often to the point of physical exhaustion and driving mum to the brink of insanity. In retrospect I believe it was this trait, which sometimes bordered on the obsessive, which was ultimately so engrained in his being that giving up, even in this situation was not something his body could even so much as "contemplate".

His heart marched on, his lungs labored. The rest of him, and us, waited.

## The last Day

Midnight passed. Another day of dad beating the odds had ticked by minute by aching minute. He was now wearing the oxygen mask almost constantly, which over time caused bruising on the bridge of his nose from the plastic edges and red streaks on his face from the tight rubber bands along his cheeks. We had to adjust it frequently as sweat and condensation let the mask slide downwards, probably making it even more uncomfortable. While both we and the doctors had been convinced that dad would pass on either Thursday or Friday, that confidence based on symptoms and observations had since evaporated and been replaced by the realization that there simply was no telling;. Death, dad, God or whoever, would do things in his own time. It had also been several days since the rest of the group had had a chance to rest or freshen up properly. Attempts had been made by one or the other to hitch a ride with me during my daily supply runs, but each time sleep had proven elusive and the unease of not being with dad and the uncertainty of what would happen from hour to hour, had always gotten the better and cut time away extremely short. We had come to the point though, where a shower at home, maybe something to eat and just a breather had now become a necessity. Since I had had several of these mini breaks, thanks to the daily drives back and forth to get food, clothes, and other things needed, we decided in the early hours of the morning that I would stay and this time mum and Sharon would go instead. Mum first only did so under protest, but she also realized that trying to lie down, even for just an hour would be the best thing after over 100 hours sitting in the hospital chairs, if there was to be any hope of lasting for as long as we needed to. It was around 5am and the first light came across the rooftops of the atrium complex just as it had done each day prior. The window was slightly open and that first clear morning breeze gently made its way through the gap. Mum and Sharon had left and TJ had decided to stretch a bit in the common room and so I was alone with dad for a while; the first time since I had arrived almost 6 days ago.

I remember the complete peace: the day had not quite broken just yet, the air was fresh, and I could spend some me-time with dad. It felt like a privilege, like an invaluable gift. There is a music album, which has accompanied me pretty much since dad got sick and which still has significance as a result. "Ghosts on the canvas" was the last full-fledged album by Glen Campbell, the country singer who rose to fame with hits like Rhinestone Cowboy or Wichita Lineman. Campbell, too, suffered from dementia and wrote the album in 2011, when he was diagnosed with Alzheimer's disease; the very personal songs as a result carrying many of his reflections on life. In a way, Campbell's later deterioration almost mirrored dad's and it is best reflected in "I'm not gonna miss you", a song in which he foreshadows one of the most painful times for families of dementia sufferers to go through. It is hard to put in words the indelible trauma of a loved one eventually losing all their memory of the people dearest to them, including even their wife, their children, their grandchildren, brothers, and sisters. They all eventually become strangers in the person's eyes, and yet he or she remains completely oblivious to what is happening to them. I remember the first instance, in the very early stages of the acute onset of dad's illness. Sharon and I were still in Kenya, going about life as normally as it was possible under the specter of potential sudden news of further deterioration of dad's health, following his hospitalization only a few months earlier in August 2013. When I picked up the phone and heard mum's voice then, I could tell straight away that some was wrong. She sounded quite distraught and I immediately feared the worst. She was calling for help. Following the events in August, dad had increasingly become somewhat 'peculiar' in many ways, but most notably in how he had become suspicious of mum and others, his mind spinning all manner of conspiracy theories about people "being after him", wanting to disown or even hurt him. He still had long periods where he appeared normal, but then from one minute to the next he would fall into a semi-schizophrenic and completely delusional state of mind. This had slowly crept into his personality but was now rapidly gaining momentum. And it was about to get to a peak which fortunately, or unfortunately as it were, I would ultimately be there to witness. Likewise increasingly, his delusions and hallucinations were accompanied by aggression, even towards those closest to him. Not physical violence per se, but certainly a demeanor that was in such grotesque contrast to who he had been prior to August that it made mum fear for her own safety. "Dad is not listening to me", she tried to say as calmly as she could, "I don't know what to do, maybe you can help me Rob". She went on to explain that just like every year, they had to sign "proof of life" statements, confirming they were still alive, so that they would continue to receive their German pension. It was a routine affair, which they had gone through each year around the same time and which dad had overseen since they retired in the late 90s. But when it came to putting his signature on the form now, he refused. Not only that, but he kept saying that he wanted to talk to his wife first and not the person that was trying to get him to sign a form, which he was sure was designed to trick him and take away his house. Suffice it to say it was mum, his wife of almost 50 years, whom he completely failed to recognize. Instead mum had become a stranger, an impostor in fact, whom he kept referring to as "the other Gisela". This duality had slowly started to develop in his mind a few weeks earlier and initially had seemed almost comical, had it not been so tragic. He would ask where "Gisela" was, with mum trying to tell him that she was right there. "No, no, not you. The *other* Gisela", he would reply slightly annoyed that this *person* in front of him was obviously trying to the pull the wool over his eyes. This dual perception of the two "Gisela's" would eventually reach even more absurd levels, when he later started speculating that mum, the imposter, was having an affair with him, which the other, "real" Gisela - the imaginary one – should by no means find out about. In the beginning we were still trying to see some sense in the way he was starting to think and act, see a glimmer of reason in between all the dementia-driven delusions. We spent much time analyzing what dad could possibly mean by some of the things he said and the way he spoke about the world the way he now saw it. I cannot even describe the amount of energy this guessing, interpreting and trying to find some remnant of rational thinking takes out of those caring for a dementia sufferer, especially in the early stages, when the personality changes are so shocking that it is only natural to try and disassociate the person as he or she presents now, from the "real" one, which you have known all our lives. The sad truth is however, in as much as

287

these attempts are natural and may even be therapeutic in the beginning, they apply reason where there is none and create an enormous amount of grief in the process.

In purely physical illnesses, the before and after is easily discernable on account of physical symptoms. The person him or herself before and after onset remains largely the same, emotional scars notwithstanding. But when it comes to dementia, at least in the beginning there is little, if any physical change. The person appears outwardly "normal", the way they have always been. Not only that, but in between these bouts of "abnormal" behavior they can be completely lucid, free of delusions and fully 'awake to their surrounds', behaving much the same as they always have. I remember our attempts in the beginning to snap dad out of these moments, in retrospect futile endeavors of course, but in the situation the only natural response when we knew that our "real dad" was still somewhere in there, and thought that he could somehow be coaxed out if we only applied patience and perseverance. In this instance mum had exerted all her talents of gentle persuasion, trying to explain to dad who she was and why they needed his signature on the form. German authorities are not exactly known for lenience when it comes to deadlines or lack of thoroughness in regards to paperwork, hence getting both their signatures on the forms and the forms to Germany on time was crucial for their continued income, as once a pension was stopped it would take months and months and a lot of agony to move anyone in the vast Teutonic administration to initiate a resumption of payments. Dad however insisted that he wanted to speak with his wife, the real "Gisela" and that this was all a charade by the imposter, along with the rest of the "people", to disown him and throw him out on the street. Under "normal" circumstances, mum would have allowed his episode to conclude and wait for an opening, for a period when dad was less confused and more receptive. This had usually worked quite well. Now though dad had taken things to a new level. Not only did his mind spin the already mentioned conspiracy theories, he also wanted the imposter out of the house and threatened to either throw mum out himself or go to the Police and report the plot against him. Both prospects obviously caused mum a lot of stress and in the end she had completely run out of solutions. Calling me was her last resort.

She had decided to "play along" with him in an effort to get him to talk to me. I could hear her explaining to him that I was on the phone, asking him if he remembered who I was and telling him that I would explain things to him. "Of course!" I could hear him say with the same level of conviction, which no doubt he had displayed moments earlier when he had threatened to evict the "imposter" from his house.

"Hi dad, how are you doing?" I tried to sound as nonchalant as possible. "Well, good, yes", came his stern answer. "What's happening dad? I hear there is some kind of problem?" I thought it best to let him air his grievance first so that he could maybe feel I was on his side and not part of the conspiracy. I also did not yet know whether he really knew whom he was talking to. At the same time, I didn't want to ask him outright as not to put him on the spot and thus risk losing him, which was usually the case when his mind was backed into a corner.

"Ah, well, let me tell you, we have a right mess here…unbelievable….unbelievable what they are doing to us here." He was clearly agitated and distraught. "Tell me, dad, what's going on?" I asked him, trying to mimic his level of concern. "Well they…Ah, I can tell you…it's unbelievable….a disgrace….those scoundrels. The things they are trying to do to me", he continued, "and Gisela, well, she is not here. If *she* only knew what is going on here!" His delusion was obviously still in full swing. I could hear mum in the background trying to assert her presence, but to no avail. Dad was rambling on.

"Dad, it's me Robert, remember?" I tried to get him back. "Yes, yes. Well I can tell you, such a disgrace…" He went on. "Ok dad, listen to me for a moment. You think you can do that? Just listen to me for a moment. Please?" I interjected as slowly, as clearly and as calmly as possible. His rant stopped. Much to my surprise, I had his attention. "You know it's me, your son, right? And you know you can always trust me, right?" I faked confidence, but was really quite uncertain

289

what to expect in the way of an answer. "Yes, yes, *of course!*" He stated, as though I had just asked a completely rhetorical question. "Ok dad, I'm glad to hear that. You know you can trust me. I know this is all quite distressing and I understand how upset you must be." I wasn't about to argue with dementia. He tried to resume his lament, but I cut in: "Dad, wait. You trust me, right? So just listen for a second. It would be terrible if you lost all your money and everything else, right?" "Yes, terrible. They want to take everything" came his reply, indicating that he understood what I was saying; that in fact this was now an actual conversation. "I know things are very stressful for you in that mess over there, but we will get through this. I will help you." I could feel he was listening. I was now on his side. "We will talk with Gisela about it later, but for now I need you to do something for me, would that be Ok?" "Yes, Ok." His reply came, much to my surprise, I must admit. "I want to make sure nobody steals anything from you. It would be terrible if you lost your pension, lost all your money, wouldn't it? We don't want that to happen!" I reassured him. The worry about money was a common theme throughout most of his delusions and one of the few weaknesses in the wall that bastard Lewy had built around his mind to date. "You know those forms on the table? I need you to do me a huge favor. Do you think you could do me a huge favor so I can help you keep everything?" "Well, yes, I think so" he said, sounding somewhat calmer than before. Getting dad into "help mode" had always been a surefire way to get his mind to focus on what needed to be done. "OK dad, thank you. That's great. I need you to just sign those forms. You can trust me when I say that nobody, *nobody* will take anything away. And later I, we, can talk with Gisela about all of this. But for now I *need* you to sign. Is that Ok?" He agreed. I told him I would be there soon and that he could always rely on me. He thanked me and wished me well, just as he always did at the end of our conversations. Mum got back on the phone, her relief palpable. Dad signed the forms and soon after calmed down, with the delusion dissipating somewhat, albeit temporarily.

I learned an important lesson that day: In the game that Lewy plays, you can find yourself either the most trusted person or a complete stranger, a foe and thief even, depending on which way the cookie crumbles on any given day. But there was something else that the incident and many after it taught me: namely that dad and I had a bond which even Lewy couldn't break. A bond we had fought for and forged between a father and son; one of complete trust in being able to count on one another no matter what. Unconditionally. I had relied on dad more times than I could remember throughout my tumultuous life and he had come through for me each and every time, no matter how much sorrow I may have caused him in the process. Now it was my turn to repay him in some small way, if that was ever possible. This one Lewy wouldn't, couldn't win.

Now, sitting in the quiet room in the hospital ward of the dementia unit that had been dad's "home" for almost 18 months, watching as he lay there - Lewy having stripped just about everything from him that could be taken away - it was time to reflect, to just be with him as the son he had done so much for and who loved him more than he could have ever known even when he was still healthy. The nurses had turned dad onto his side now, facing towards the door and the chair I had been sitting in for much of the night. His eyes were half-open, his pupils contracted and glazed over, dully staring into nothingness, empty and completely bereft of the spirit that used to sparkle within them. They spoke of a body that was spent, of a mind that had been robbed, of a battle already lost. I positioned myself so my face was in the path of his gaze and turned on Glen Campbell. The music played gently at low volume. This was my last opportunity to spend time alone with dad and share some memorable moments before time ran out. The last opportunity to perhaps reach across the divide which bastard Lewy had created and which death would soon make permanent and enjoy something simple together, be quiet together and let dad know that I was with him and loved him more than ever. It was my last chance to thank him for being the dad that he was, let him know how much I admired him and how much he meant to me, tell him that everything would be Ok, that it was Ok to let go and that whatever happened he could rely on us being together. The music kept playing and we just kept looking into each other's eyes, I held his hand, the world around disappearing, as fate granted us one of the most precious moments we had ever spent together.

We stayed like this as long as the songs continued, suspended in time and far removed from the hospital bed and the room around it. We listened to the entire album, just being *with* each other in his bubble, its framerate reduced to super slow motion. Then, when the last song ended and the music faded, the walls of our little bubble evaporated and life around us slowly returned, the usually soundscape of trolleys being pushed on their way to patients' rooms, doors opening and closing and muffled morning conversations slowly penetrating the serenity that had allowed this very personal moment during the golden hour of dawn. I will never know if dad heard what I was saying, let alone understood. I can only hope that maybe on some small level, deep inside him, he could *feel* what I was trying to tell him, the love I felt for him and how much I thanked him for the life that he had given me.

Curiously, throughout these moments, his breathing had remained calm and not as labored as it had before. Perhaps though that was just my imagination, or simply due to the fact that he was lying on his side. Regardless, I will remain grateful for this time alone with dad for the rest of my life and the serenity of that hour will remain with me as one of the most treasured memories.

Soon everyone returned and our band of four sat again, watching dad has he fought on. Much as I had expected, mum had been unable to find rest at home and a quick shower and a change of clothes for everyone had been as good as it got that morning. Yet the brief reprieve, fresh air and short change of scenery (and clothes!) had helped to keep energy reserves, which were nearing zero level, from depleting completely. It had also given her an opportunity to pick out some clothes for dad. We had tried together a few days prior, but the thought of picking out the clothes dad would wear when he died, no matter how prudent an act under the circumstances, had seemed all too abhorrent and inappropriate.

The mornings at the hospital unit were always busy, which was a good thing as that kept our minds from wandering, especially now. Nurses would pop their heads in to say good morning and take a look at dad. They would talk to him just as they talked to any other person, cheerfully and compassionate, as they again checked his pulse and temperature. The caregivers' palpable positive energy was always infectious and they never let on for a minute that they were dealing with a dying patient; a demeanor which I still much admire and which went a long way towards pulling all of us from the tunnels of despair our minds were trapped in and back into reality and into the fact that life was still, well, full of life.

To be honest, in the beginning we had been somewhat taken aback by the happy and sometimes even jovial way the care givers addressed dad, who was clearly in a very bad way. It was simply not in our culture to display any behavior that wasn't "befitting" - in other words completely aligned with the socially accepted tone of a particular situation. Germans clearly delineate between and gage their conduct against the different social norms around life events and other occasions with inherent prerequisites for conduct. 'Sad' situations and tragedy demand somber seriousness and displays of deep sorrow, "happy" scenarios on the other hand a suitably celebratory demeanor. There was nothing in between, no grey area. This relative lightness of being that resided in this predominantly Filipino team of caregivers was something that to me had seemed situationally dissonant if not totally inappropriate. And yet over time as things got darker and darker for our small family, the more I found something uplifting in the cheerful "good mornings" and banter that sometimes accompanied their less than enviable daily tasks. Finding humor in tragedy is an odd concept until it's the only thing left to help you cope with the unthinkable. And dealing with the otherwise unfathomable was this team's and so many other's livelihood, their daily bread so to speak. I have often thought about the emotional scars that many caregivers will receive and carry with them throughout and beyond their professional careers. After all, who cares for the 'caregivers'? A special breed of people whom society relies on yet obviously cares so little about? For many they remain an almost invisible accessory doing a job, like a quasi-part of the furniture, of the services we expect to be provided in a "developed context". The human side of the "service", the emotional cost is often forgotten. What makes a caregiver get up in the morning and cheerfully deal with the human condition at its worst and so

293

physically repugnant that most of us, neither fit for the job, nor mentally capable of coping, would never, could ever even contemplate the profession? And yet here they were, doing just that: apparently cheerfully coping, conjuring up levels of compassion I had never seen, and dealing with the most challenging situations with such lightness, that it almost defied the reality of a situation in which they themselves, like many of us, might find eventually themselves in as they, too, aged over time.

Friedrich Nietzsche was the one who said, "I was in darkness, but I took three steps and I found myself in paradise. The first step was a good thought, the second, a good word; and the third, a good deed." He also said that"... if you gaze for long into an abyss, the abyss gazes also into you." Without getting too much into philosophy here, but I think perhaps their calling lay somewhere between these two statements; somewhere between the compulsion to daily gaze into the abyss and the emotional freedom, the "paradise" that came with breaking its ties. In any case, it was something that seemed to come with much greater ease to these people, who themselves had parents, grandparents, aunts, uncles, all elderly back home in the Philippines, in India, in Sri Lanka; kin who in many cases were in equal need of help, but economic constraints meant that the need to contribute financially and enable a level of health care for these loved ones back home, necessitated working abroad. Their ability to spend their days in a different country, caring for people afflicted by some of the worst conditions imaginable and doing so willingly and cheerfully, all the while living in the conundrum, the conflict between being needed by and missing their families back home and the need for generating an income to support them, makes them heroes in my view; heroes across continents.

It was the same that morning: Xalvador and the rest of the team all said hello, made sure dad was changed, repositioned and medicated and we were holding up, were offered coffee and generally looked after. Dad's breaths had become shorter in the course of the last 10 hours or so. The gargling noise had worsened and it sounded like his lungs were filling with fluids. Repositioning still gave some brief relief, but wasn't able to stem the build-up.

Quick, gasping breaths in, short forced breaths out. His system, his heart, and lungs were fighting. His eyes remained half-open and unblinking, his pupils dry and glazed over. His mouth despite our best attempts, kept drying out and his tongue was barely visible now; a small rubberized piece of flesh, uselessly, absurdly, defiantly staring back at us from the gaping hole his mouth had become. We watched him as again the hours went on, his body's "will" to survive beyond any possible, any reasonable comprehension. It actually got to a point where mum and I, where we all looked at each other and asked: "How is this possible? How can his body hold on like this?" And yet it did. His body held on: Short gasp in, forced and even shorter breath out, the only image even coming close to it a fish out of water, gasping, trying to force oxygen into a body that was losing its ability to accept any.

After what felt like hours, mum decided it was enough. It had already been unbearable to watch dad suffer like this, but what was happening now went beyond the even remotely tolerable. Mum was determined to find a nurse, just like she had done so many times over the last few days, to get dad another injection to ease his discomfort, relax his breathing or do whatever it took; just to do *something*, however little or perhaps even futile as it may be , as not doing *anything* was no longer an option. Doctors and nurses had strictly been sticking to timelines, allowing doses only in prescribed intervals of 4 or 6 hours. But this was no longer the time to stick to regimens designed for recovering patients. And for once, I not only completely agreed with mum, but was grateful for her dogged determination to "fight for dad", a determination which was only rivaled by the love that compelled her.

It was to be the last fight.

Mum marched out of the room with complete and single-minded focus, in search of a nurse, a doctor, the manager, anybody who could help. Dad gasped. There was a pause. He gasped again. I panicked.

"Dad, DAD!" I yelled, fearing the worst had come. In an instant my mind was torn between staying with him and running to get mum. Also in an instant, I knew she would need to be there.

I started yelling uncontrollably as I stormed out the door. Mum, MUM, come here, COME HERE, QUICKLY!" Even though this took less than a second, I can still see mum on her way to the nurses' station, marching as she always did when on a mission for dad. I saw her turn around and start running. I immediately darted back. Even today mum says she will never forget the sound of my cries that day, of utter panic and desperation. I jumped back into the room.

Dad gasped. Once. Twice. Nothing.

"Oh my God, NO. DAD!"

I placed my hand on his chest, wishing his breathing to kick in again, wanting it to resume.

He gasped one last time. Then no more. I stared at him, wanted his chest to rise.

"Dad, DAD, oh no. OH NO".

Dad was gone. It was 11.17am on the 7th of January.

A rivulet of white spittle, aspirated supplement drink and blood trickled from his mouth. TJ dashed to wipe away the sputum, in what seemed a desperate attempt to undo the irreversible. I was paralyzed. Mum arrived and knelt beside him, her eyes wide with fear, perplexed by the suddenness of what was happening.

Dad's face drained of color and turned a waxy yellow. Whatever life had remained in his eyes, disappeared.

The rest is a blur.

I can still hear mum saying "Don't cry, DON'T CRY. He should not hear you cry!" But it was too late. Agony and disbelief took over and blended into a stream of tears. The abyss opened by bastard Lewy swallowed me up.

But there was something else. Darting my eyes in disbelief between dad's face, now frozen in death, his hands and his body which no longer moved the way it had done involuntarily and almost constantly for so long, an anger started to rise with such irrepressible force that within minutes it became virtually all consuming.

One of the nurses came in, summoned by the cries of agony and the waling that echoed from our room. She quietly, somberly checked dad's pulse and briefly closed her eyes, formally acknowledging what was already evident.

Between the tunnel vision of the cries around me the tears and the insanity and complete chaos of the moment, another voice cried out from deep within the darkness that was rapidly enveloping my mind. I was still holding dad's hand, which grew colder by the moment, looking into his half open eyes, which only moments ago had still contained at least a speck of life and at his chest that was now no longer moving, flat, collapsed. Empty. Mum was in deep shock and breaking down, the armor she had worn for dad's sake breaking up and releasing all that pressure and sorrow it had contained like a pressure cooker of emotions. Everyone was holding on to dad in one last, futile attempt to keep him with us; not to let death take him this way.

It may sound paradoxical, but for all the prayers, for all the pleading with God over the last five days, for dad's release from his terrible prison, this had not been what we had so desperately prayed for. The voice inside me continued to grow as mum slowly, gently placed her hands over dad's eyes and closed them. Forever. She then calmly folded dad's hands and wrapped a wooden rosary attached to a small craved crucifix around them. Dad was resting now.

And yet, despite the quiet which suddenly descended among the sobbing and blowing of handkerchiefs, the voice was now screaming inside me, so loud that it was threatening to explode my head. I had to step outside and look at the tree if I were to remain sane.

Why God? Why did you do this to dad? Why did you allow this to happen this way? Did we not plead with you and pray? Did I, did not our family do our best these last years to do things right by you? Was what we asked really all that much for an all-loving, all powerful being like you? And if not for us, why would you do this to someone like dad? Someone who had walked his life straight, as a believing Catholic in the service of you and his family? Where. Was. Your. Mercy.

The crescendo in my head was briefly interrupted by mum, who had stepped outside without me even noticing. "Would you be able to call Joyce? I had said we would call her when… she said she would come and hold a prayer with us. For dad."

I snapped back into reality. Of course I would call her.

Joyce was a retired priest mum had come to confide in during several counselling sessions and whom she had befriended in the process. A small, wiry woman in appearance, I had come to know her for her sharp and uncompromising statements, which during the few times we had met, had always seemed to sit somewhere between the quirkily uncompassionate and the situationally inappropriate. But mum liked her and that was all that mattered.

I called her the day prior and she had given me some 'spiel' that this was not what was usually done, but that for mum and dad she would of course "do it", another one of those statements I neither cared for not needed to hear. Be that as it may, she arrived shortly after the call. Mum was still at or beyond breaking point. The rest of us were barely keeping it together, mostly for mum's sake. We were in the corridor, trying to breathe, while we gave mum some time by dad's side.

Joyce arrived. Few words were said. I pointed her in mum's direction. After a brief hug, she asked whether we would prefer her to "robe up" or pray in the attire she was wearing. I couldn't have given two shits about it, to be frank. By then the anger I felt towards God and the betrayal of all I had worked so hard for to have faith in, was like a bad taste in my mouth, waiting to be spewed forth towards anyone who so much as tried to perpetuate that "myth". I initially joined the little gathering, but when I saw that mum was well supported and as Joyce began her prayer, I stepped out again. I don't remember what was decided as to the "robing issue" either, since I had no interest in being present for this farcical ritual that was to follow, which no doubt would talk to God's love and mercy, neither of which had been part of this equation. Not for a long time.

Dad had suffered more than any human being should ever be subjected to and God had done nothing but vividly demonstrated at best a disinterest in what was happening. At worst, he had knowingly and thus intentionally put dad and us through it. The Greek philosopher Epicurus asked: "Is God willing to prevent evil, but not able? Then he is not omnipotent. Is he able, but not willing? Then he is malevolent. Is he both able and willing? Then whence cometh evil? Is he neither able nor willing? Then why call him God?" My sentiments at that time exactly! The brief ceremony ended. I waited in the corridor. Seated on the carpet with my back against the wall, once again seeking comfort and quiet in that tree outside the glass door. It still stood and its branches still swayed, the way they had been doing long before I ever looked at them and probably long after we would eventually all join dad.

There was one more, steep hill to climb for the day. I needed to call the funeral home before I could allow to let go. I found myself surprisingly calm this time. At least I know whom I was going to speak with and the last conversation less than 24 hours prior had proven almost soothing; had allowed a sharing of the load so to speak. I don't know exactly what I said. I think I managed the first few words, before emotions again got the better of me. It was enough though and Deirdre, in her quietly calm demeanor somehow managed to get out of me the rest of the information she needed.

Time to give mum some space to be alone with dad.

I had said my good byes for more than five days, in fact several times in the last six months alone, and even that morning. The rage I felt was still there, but simply started running out of fuel. It was burning itself out, only to be replaced with catatonic apathy. I sat on the ground and watched the tree, intermittently hugging Sharon and TJ as they too were trying to come to terms with what had just happened. Before long I could see the hearse make its way down the winding driveway through the meadows running along nearby State Highway 1 and watched as two men in suits unloaded a gurney.

Along this journey bastard Lewy had dictated for so long, this was yet another hard step to take; proof that nothing in the bastard's game ever gets easier, only harder and ever more painful. Even now in death. I quietly let mum know that the funeral directors had arrived to take dad. Although she knew that dad had passed on, I don't think the actual separation by death really set in until that moment. Mum and Lewy had wrestled over dad for so long, mum with each round forced to settle for whatever lowest denominator the illness permitted. She had unwaveringly clung to each remnant of dad the way she had known him, each small sign that he had not gone completely giving her a ray of hope and the energy to do it all over again the next day. And the next. And the next. And now all that was left to hold on to was his body that lay there, lifeless and finally free of struggle. After that there would be nothing tangible left. Just memories.

I think letting dad go this way, for mum was harder than watching him die.

We had laid out the clothes for him to wear and the funeral directors, together with the caregivers dressed dad while we waited outside. It was not something I think any of us should have witnessed. It seemed to take but a few short moments and when we re-entered the room dad wore the casual, comfortable and relaxed clothes we had been used to seeing him wear around the house. His head rested on a pillow, his chin slightly tucked in. I have heard people say that the dead look as though they are in deep sleep, resting. I have never been able to look at it that way. There is something grotesque about a dead body, something so unnatural that I have always found it hard to attach these sentiments.

I briefly said another good-bye, touching his hands, before I had to turn away again. It was not the last image I wanted in my head.

Mum and I stood side by side, here at the foot end of the bed that had been his prison for so long. Mum was at breaking point. I held her while trying to focus on the garden outside through the curtains gently moving in the cool breeze. I heard mum utter dad's name through her tears, her body shaking in the knowledge that the last time she could ever lay eyes on him had arrived. The last moment after over 60 years, after a lifetime that had fused together the very essence of their being in love and with such devotion that even now it is hard to grasp in all-too-inadequate human terms. She would never see him again. Not. Ever. She had been strong throughout; amazingly so, driven by the single-minded focus on making sure dad got the best care possible. Her mission had come to an abrupt end at 11.17 that morning, her raison d'être ripped away with nothing but a void to replace it.

The two funeral home staff gently moved dad onto the gurney. I admired them for their professionalism and imagined how stressful even for them these situations were. Surrounded by and under the watchful eye of grieving families they needed to make sure every movement, everything they did was done not only with precision and with a high degree of efficiency, but also in an utterly dignified manner. They gently pulled the white sheet over dad's face as they readied to move him to the hearse. We would not see him again.

Mum and I walked slowly behind the gurney. Eventually I stopped and mum continued. Seeing dad being taken away, seeing him leave like this was beyond my ability to cope. His body moved slightly as the gurney sled into the holding rails in the back of the vehicle and was pushed into its interior. The door closed, the men got in and the car ever so slowly drove back up the road winding through the meadows. We looked on until they disappeared from sight, each of us in a stupor, each mind in its own way traveling with dad on his journey along the gravel road we ourselves had traveled a thousand times, yet which had been denied to him for so long.

Bastard Lewy had won as he always does.

# Epilogue

It had been a long summer's day and not even the poplar trees that lined the wide river separating the city of Frankfurt from its suburb of Sachsenhausen had been able to provide enough shade to stem the heat radiating from the streets and sidewalks. For much of the way I had followed the flow of the river, with its expanse of dark waters lazily flowing along and showing off its effortlessness for all to see.

It had been a long time since I had been in this place, breathed its atmosphere that was filled with history so rich that it felt as if the very concept of time itself had sprung from here. The big old dome towered over the old quarter, which stood its own against the steel and glass of the monoliths of the city's financial center that rose from nearby downtown. I had crossed the Eiserner Steg, the iron boardwalk, its steel reaching across the Main, its riveted steel trusses destroyed several times throughout its history and rebuilt each time, arching across the two cities; a lasting symbol of human resilience.

Sweating and with aching feet I shuffled along the cobblestone streets of old Sachsenhausen, made famous by apple wine, pickled pork and Sauerkraut, all iconic cornerstones of the state's national cuisine. The narrow roads lined by houses several centuries old, all featuring the classic German half timbering facades, had long been turned into a pedestrian area and since most of the several hundred old houses had been turned into pubs at the same time, become one of the city's main tourist attractions.

I stopped at a familiar place, its name as peculiar as its former owner. "Heini Hinnerkopp" or "Hank Back-of-the-Head" was open as it always was each and every day, with folding chairs and wobbly garden tables dotted about its cobblestoned courtyard from which two oak trees sprung and provided much needed shade. The outside though frankly, was mainly for tourists. It was on the inside that one would find the "real" Sachsenhaeusers, the ones who had always lived there and made up much of Heini's regular clientele.

I was only visiting and yet, being back among these memories, I again felt like a local and decided to sit inside, where murals of traditional drinking scenes painted on faded stucco along with the pub's simple dark wood apple wine counter and minimalist furniture gave the place a distinctly old-school feel.

I sat down by myself on a long bench that ran against the wall near the entrance; a luxury only reserved for this time of day, as in the evenings every nook and cranny would be filled with thirsty diners, both local and international. A tall glass of cool apple wine soon appeared before me, poured from a light blue glazed clay jug, the traditional vessel the beverage was served in the state over.

I sat for a bit, taking in the atmosphere, sipping away at the refreshing liquid and feeling a slight buzz as it made its way to my head faster than I had thought it might. I stayed lost in my thoughts like that for a while until a tap on my shoulder snapped me back into reality.

"So, this is where we meet", said the young man standing next to me, clearly relishing the surprise which was must have been plainly written in my face. "Where did you come from?" I asked, which only served to make him grin even more mischievously.

"I have been sitting over there for some time, but you didn't realize I was there, so I just watched you for a while", he said, delighted in that he had succeeded in sneaking up on me.

He swung one leg over the bench on the other side of the table, sat down and looked at me in anticipation.

"How long has it been?" I wondered out loud. It had been quite some time; not since my previous visit which suddenly seemed like a long time ago, although I wasn't really sure.

"I don't know", he shrugged his shoulders, "how old are you now?" He ran his fingers through his short wavy hair. "Much older than you still", I laughed and marveled at the fact that he still looked the same.

He was in his late twenties, clean-shaven and as always dressed casually but neat, his eyes teaming with a desire to find out more about what had happened to me since we last spent some time together. His broad smile with perfect white teeth and the penetrating focus of his bright blue eyes, made him look like a Hollywood icon, like a young Paul Newman or something.

"I just turned 50, I said", running my fingers through my beard before stopping abruptly as I became self-conscious about how its scruffiness seemed out of place against the clean-cut and youthful appearance of the man across from me.

"You'll get over it", he said, nodding towards the grey rug that now covered my face.

"Still itches like hell", I added, while he ran *his* hand across his clean shaven face, looking for stubble. "I wonder if one day I will grow one as well." he asked out loud.

"OH yes", I said with a quiet chuckle, earning me skeptical look from my young companion.

His apple wine arrived. "Here's to you", he beat me to the toast. "No, to us and all the good things to come", I replied. He leaned forward, resting his elbows on the heavy wooden bench. "So, Robert, how have things been? What have you been up to?" His smile had always been one of honest empathy and genuine interest in others.

"It's been hard these past few years", I began to explain, "A lot of travel, work in different countries, war zones even, a lot of change, a lot of failure and lot of new beginnings. It hasn't been easy at all."

He followed every word closely, then leaned back and crossed his arms behind his head. He now smiled broadly. "Don't worry, *we'll* get there", he said with quiet confidence.

Now it was my turn to look at *him* quizzically.

"We will come up with a plan and it will be fine", he continued, explaining in a matter-of-fact manner "there is always a solution to everything, you just need to lay it all out and systematically tick off each item. You will see, we'll get there."

I was mystified, but let it be. He was a meticulous planner, even at his young age; better than I ever could be. And he was never shy taking others' issues and making them his own "projects" to solve.

"What are you up to these days?" I tried to change the subject, "Married yet?"

He smiled, a little sheepishly perhaps, as he wasn't one to brag or lay his life out in the open.

"Well, I have met someone, yes. She's very nice. We see each other every day. I pick her up from work and we go for walks. She's into sports as well and we actually both go to the same rowing club." His eyes lit up as he spoke about her, his affection shining through in as much as he tried to stay matter-of-factly.

"That *is* some good news", I complemented him. He had been very committed to his studies and had been so involved in his sport and his fraternity, that I had wondered if he would ever find the time for other pursuits.

"So have you met her folks yet?" I asked, egging him on to give me more.

"Her parents don't like me all that much, so I usually wait downstairs", he shrugged with a sad smile. "But it will be Ok. It's about her and me, nobody else. She's very special."

"I never thought I see the day! Congratulations!" I cheered.

"Thank you" he said, lowering his eyes, almost shy.

"You said you travel a lot?" It was his turn to change the subject.

"Yes, it's difficult to find the right place for a home. Both Sharon and I want to settle down, but it's hard to change from a career that consists of taking on overseas contracts. It's a real conundrum. What do you choose: the money or the happiness?"

306

He looked at me as if I was speaking in riddles.

"Happiness of course", he replied plainly, then adding with a good dose of pragmatism: "as long as you are still able to make plans for the future and look after Sharon, naturally."

That's exactly what I liked about him. He was young, but he knew what to do and how to do it; not because of wisdom or life experience, but because of an inherent sense of wrong and right and what each meant for achieving his goals and overcoming obstacles without harming others.

"You know, I would like to travel like you do one day", he looked across my shoulder as if imagining himself on a long journey. "I want to have a proper home, but I feel this urge for adventure. Maybe I'll get a chance one day to do what you do."

"Don't worry, you will", it was my turn to smile at him. "You will do things and go places you wouldn't even dream of right now, believe me. Yours is going to be a great life!"

"Is this the old man Robert speaking?" he laughed heartily. "Maybe you should come to the rowing club with the others later. You used to row, didn't you? We'll have a bit of a competition and it will make you feel young again!" he quipped, as always up for a challenge.

"I don't think I have ever been as fit as you, even at your least fit!" I hated to admit it, but he had always been crazy about sports and his twenty-something body would no doubt kick my butt up and down the Main River. "It's Ok", I just put up my hands in defeat instead. "I never stood a chance against your endurance anyway."

He grinned, clearly enjoying the compliment.

"And about the travel and everything…Don't worry, you will see it all. You will have one hell of an interesting life, trust me. You will get the girl, you will get everything you are dreaming of now. And you know why?" I leaned forward, watching him hanging on for the answer.

"Because you are *you*. As simple as that", I said truthfully.

He looked almost disappointed at the lack of revelation.

"But why? How? I really don't know what you mean", he shrugged, a little annoyed, "but then again you have always been a bit of a mystery to me. And at the same time I have seen that you, too, get to where you want to be. Maybe down a different path and not the way I would have done it, but you do. And that is what counts." His confident smile now almost had a sense of melancholy.

"You really think my life is going to be all that?" he asked again, taking another sip from his apple wine.

"I think so", I said reassuringly. "Maybe not all of it. Definitely some really good stuff. I'm just not sure about the end. The end is not often the way we expect it to be. Could get rough." I tried not to scare him.

"Ach Robert, we'll manage it. We always have. Together!" he again placed his hand on my shoulder the way he had always done when emphasizing this one consistent message.

"You can rely on that", I replied raising my glass.

We toasted, took another sip and then he looked at his watch.

"Oh, I need to pick her up from work. I never want to be late for her", he nearly jumped up from the bench.

"Wouldn't that be nice", I returned with a smirk, knowing that he had always easily lost track of time once he got focused on something else.

"I'm sorry. Are you sure you don't want to come along to the rowing club? It's a beautiful day for it and the others would love to meet you. *She* would love to meet you." He pulled up the collar of his jacket and straightened it, getting ready to leave. "Is my hair Ok? I want to look my best for her" he winked.

"Neat as always" I quipped and have him a thumbs-up, "Thanks for the invitation, but it's Ok. Just let me sit here for a while and reminisce. You go get the girl and live that great life of yours. I'll be waiting for you when you get there."

"*We* will get there. Together!" His smile as broad as they come, making his cheeks dance, and his eyes sparkle again mischievously.

"Yes dad. *Together*", I replied. But he was already out the door.

After months of emptiness, the dreams about dad had finally come. I now see him often. We get to spend some time together, his voice and mind as clear as they have ever been. In those peaceful hours where the mind is unencumbered, we can now continue our conversations; even the ones we were never able to have.

-------------

*"All the tragedies which we can imagine*

*return in the end to the one and only tragedy; the passage of time"*

*- Simone Weil*

In Loving Memory - Norbert Landeck

Made in the USA
Middletown, DE
24 August 2017